Data Visualization for Oracle Business Intelligence 11g

About the Authors

Dan Vlamis has been developing business intelligence and OLAP applications since 1986 when he graduated from Brown University with a Bachelor's degree in Computer Science. After graduating, he joined Information Resources Inc. (IRI) where he led the back-end team that wrote Oracle Sales Analyzer in Express. In 1992 he left IRI and moved to the Kansas City area where he founded Vlamis Software Solutions Inc., an Oracle Gold Partner, which has led more than 200 BI and OLAP implementations with some of the world's leading corporations and organizations.

Dan has been a popular speaker at major Oracle conferences such as Oracle OpenWorld, Collaborate, and ODTUG Kscope for two decades and is known for his live demos of Oracle software. As an Oracle Business Intelligence Warehousing and Analytics SIG (BIWA) board member of the IOUG, he chaired BIWA Summit 2014 and BIWA Summit 2015.

Recognized by Oracle as an Oracle ACE Director and on the editorial board of Oracle Magazine, he consults with Oracle Product Management regularly. Dan covers Oracle BI and related products through his popular blog at www.vlamis.com /blog. Dan was a co-author on the Oracle Press book *Oracle Essbase and Oracle OLAP: The Guide to Oracle's Multidimensional Solution*.

Tim Vlamis is an expert in the visualization of data and the design of business intelligence dashboards. Tim combines a strong background in the application of business intelligence (BI), analytics, and data mining with extensive experience in business modeling and valuation analysis, new product forecasting, and new business development scenario analyses. Tim is an instructor for Oracle University's Oracle Data Mining and Oracle R Enterprise courses and teaches in Benedictine College's Traditional and Executive MBA programs as an Adjunct Professor of Business.

Tim earned his Professional Certified Marketer (PCM) designation from the American Marketing Association and is an active speaker on BI and data visualization topics as well as marketing and business development. In addition to his life-long study of business processes, systems, and theories, Tim is a passionate student of complexity theory, the history of mathematics, and the principles of design. Tim earned an MBA from Northwestern University's Kellogg School of Management and a BA in Economics from Yale University.

Oracle Press™

Data Visualization for Oracle Business Intelligence 11g

Dan Vlamis
Tim Vlamis

New York   Chicago   San Francisco
Athens   London   Madrid   Mexico City
Milan   New Delhi   Singapore   Sydney   Toronto

Cataloging-in-Publication Data is on file with the Library of Congress

Data Visualization for Oracle Business Intelligence 11g

1234567890 DOC DOC 1098765

ISBN 978-0-07-183726-2
MHID 0-07-183726-4

Sponsoring Editor	**Technical Editor**	**Production Supervisor**
Paul Carlstroem	Brian Macdonald	George Anderson
Editorial Supervisor	**Copy Editor**	**Composition**
Patty Mon	Bart Reed	Cenveo® Publishing Services
Project Editor	**Proofreader**	**Illustration**
Howie Severson	Richard Camp	Cenveo Publishing Services
Acquisitions Coordinator	**Indexer**	**Art Director, Cover**
Amanda Russell	Jack Lewis	Jeff Weeks

Contents at a Glance

Contents

Preface

Creating data visualizations and dashboards is often an iterative, involved process. Reviewing and discussing the concepts, techniques, systems, and interfaces involved is not linear, but is rather, a layered, interconnected path. We've tried to create a logical structure, but invariably, some topics might be "out of order," so you should expect a fair degree of skipping around the chapters of the book to learn more about various topics. Additionally, the field of business intelligence generally and data visualization specifically covers an enormous amount of ground, far more than we can discuss in detail between the front and back cover of this book. What we have tried to provide then, is an overview of the capabilities of Oracle Business Intelligence 11*g* from a data visualization perspective along with some hard earned insights from a wide variety of implementations, workshops, and training sessions at client sites.

Throughout this book we've tried to emphasize the "why" rather than only address the "how." There are often many ways to do things and several approaches that make sense. A major objective of this book is to convince readers to consider alternatives rather than simply accepting default settings.

Oracle Business Intelligence 11*g* is comprised of an extensive set of middleware systems that are interrelated and interdependent. We do not address the architecture, structure, or component parts of the full OBIEE family. In fact, throughout the book we limit ourselves to addressing only the data visualization aspects. Data selection, processing, calculated metrics, and data modeling all have enormous implications for how data is presented visually. We are not unaware of the complexities and the importance of these topics to a successful OBIEE implementation; rather, we had to limit the scope of this book. Indeed, there are several areas that we wish we could have discussed in more detail, but space limitations restricted us.

Those familiar with data visualization best practices will find that we are largely in concert with the "visual cognition"–based approach to data visualization rather than the "engagement/entertainment"–based approach. We don't believe that data needs to be "dressed up" with visuals to get people to pay attention to it. Visualizations should not be pressed into the role of compensating for uninteresting data. With that being said, we have a high degree of respect and enthusiasm for the field of data visualization and recognize its evolving role and wide range of skilled professionals. Many, many valuable contributions are being made every day as this field matures and expands.

We encourage readers to visit the website www.vlamis.com/DVforOBI, where all visualizations can be viewed in color and at different zoom levels. Because the printed book is only in grayscale, many of the insights and points are best viewed by seeing the original screenshots in color electronically. As we are discussing electronic dashboards and reports throughout the book, it seems particularly appropriate that example figures and screenshots be viewed via an electronic interface. Sophisticated readers will notice that some color palettes were altered slightly to reflect different grayscale values so that figures in the printed book could be interpreted. Additionally, some screenshots required tradeoffs between showing fine details and presenting an overall view of the computer interface. We ask for your forgiveness and understanding for our shortcomings and humbly suggest that you "do what we say," and not what we do.

Much of the first three chapters set the foundation for the rest of the book. We generally recommend that readers start by reading the first three chapters in order and then find their way to different topics as their needs and interests dictate.

Chapter 1 is a general introduction to data visualization in Oracle Business Intelligence 11*g*. In it we try to provide an overview of best practices and establish a summary of the topic. We offer the insight that "exploration" and "explanation" interfaces often suggest differing sets of compromises and resultant data visualizations. We establish the perspective that human cognition and "best practices" should guide choices for data visualizations rather than taste and opinion.

Chapter 2 is an overview of table design best practices. Unfortunately, few tables are well organized and promote fast scanning and interpretation by viewers. Elimination of grid lines, proper alignment and spacing, and judicious use of conditional formatting all contribute to superior table design. A preference for small tables versus large tables is explained and supported.

Chapter 3 is an overview of graph design best practices. The major styles of graphs are explained along with their business use cases. Color choice strategies are introduced. We explain best practices for representing additional dimensions in several types of graphs. We also explain why "3-D" effects should be avoided.

Chapter 4 is an introduction to map views in OBIEE. Maps are perhaps the densest and most intuitive interface for any data set that includes a location component such as address. We review the different visualizations that are available in map layers and offer a brief overview of the technical architecture and function of Oracle MapViewer.

Chapter 5 covers several different topics loosely grouped into the term "advanced visualizations." By this we mean "not often used" or "require additional effort or understanding." The chapter addresses trellis charts, gauges and dials (which we generally recommend against), configured visualizations, ADF visualizations, R visualizations, and D3 and other JavaScript extensions of OBIEE.

Chapter 6 is a brief introduction to BI Publisher. We cover the typical use cases for BI Publisher as an integrated component of an overall OBIEE implementation (not the use of BI Publisher as a standalone product). We show the basic web Layout Editor for BI Publisher and how to configure basic visualizations. We address the use of dual-Y axis charts and explain when to utilize them.

Chapter 7 is an overview of dashboard design and layout. We cover how to "think through" dashboards and design them with a specific audience in mind. We cover the Dashboard Builder layout interface and how to use it. We also address how to best use columns and sections and guide users through their formatting and positioning.

Chapter 8 covers user interaction with dashboards and analyses. We talk about how to visually reflect dependencies and relationships between different interface components and how to help drive user involvement and understanding. We address Master Detail Linking, dashboard prompts, and navigation links.

Chapter 9 offers a brief overview of Oracle Scorecard and Strategy Management. We describe KPIs, Initiatives, and Objectives and show the Scorecard Editor. We also briefly cover the additional visualizations used in OSSM and their typical use cases.

Chapter 10 attempts to cover the rapidly changing and evolving topic Mobile OBI and how the use of mobile devices has important implications for data visualizations. We cover different platforms such as Oracle BI HD and BI Mobile App Designer. We address different screen resolutions, "dark" background styles, and factors that influence the design of dashboards and visualizations intended for a mobile device audience.

Chapter 11 includes several different topics. We address the principles of design and how they apply to data visualization. We also cover theory and three important web-based tools that we use extensively: colorbrewer2.org, iWantHue, and W3schools' HTML color picker. We offer a brief overview of OBIEE skins, styles, and messages. We also cover filters, selection steps, and dealing with "real world" data distributions.

Chapter 12 summarizes the content from the book and offers general advice on development, organization, and strategies for developing data visualization standards. We include insight on presenting and developing a stronger appreciation for data visualization. We conclude with advice on potential approaches for data visualization assessments, workshops, and training sessions.

Our major goal for this book is help readers develop a finer sense of awareness for the importance and power of data visualization. We know that there are never any "perfect" data visualizations and that OBIEE 11*g* is not a "perfect" BI tool, but we are also passionate promoters of OBIEE and believe that it is unmatched for presenting data in compelling and insightful ways for very large audiences.

Acknowledgments

We owe many thanks to many people for making this book possible. OBIEE has a strong community of practitioners and consultants who have generously shared their knowledge, talent, and skills. We are deeply grateful to have worked with you, learned from you, and to call you colleagues and friends. This book would not have been possible without the direct support and help from many in Oracle Corporation. Thank you to Jayant Sharma and the entire Oracle MapViewer and Spatial team. Thank you to Philippe Lions and the SampleApp team! Your hard work and genius, not to mention your continual support and assistance, mean that we had a powerful demo platform and an almost inexhaustible supply of fantastic examples of great data visualization work. We cannot overstate the importance of your work producing SampleApp and the influence it has had on our consulting practice and business. Thank you to Jack Berkowitz, Paul Rodwick, and so many other Oracle executives who encouraged us to pursue this topic and continually act as sponsors and supporters of data visualization. Thank you to everyone on the OBIEE product management team for the years of help and support that we have received.

Thank you to Amanda Russell, Bettina Faltermeier, and especially Paul Carlstroem of Oracle Press/McGraw-Hill Education. We appreciate your endless supplies of guidance, encouragement, and patience.

An enormous thank you to Brian D. Macdonald for being our technical editor and sharing his powerful insights on business intelligence and data visualization. Your guidance, support, encouragement, and constant positive contributions kept us going! Thank you to our staff at Vlamis Software Solutions, Inc. for filling in for us, contributing to the content of the book, and (as usual) keeping the practice rolling.

Thank you to our clients for constantly challenging and pushing us. We have the best clients in the world.

Finally, thank you to our parents Ted and Betty Vlamis. In business and in life, you've shown us the path. Thank you to our wives and families for their unending love and support. Lauren, Sally, Chris, and Katherine, you make this all worthwhile.

Dan Vlamis

Tim Vlamis

CHAPTER
1

Introduction

"I see what you mean." We understand and interpret the world through our sense of vision. If we hope to share understanding in large organizations, we have to find ways to communicate a consistent, coherent message to hundreds or even thousands of individuals across large distances, time zones, and even cultures. The fastest and most effective way to do this is through the presentation of data-driven insights displayed as graphs, tables, maps, simple statements, and patterned visuals. Business intelligence dashboards and reports are exactly this—attempts at visual communication. If we are to communicate effectively, however, we must pay close attention to the visuals we present to each other.

About Oracle Business Intelligence 11*g*

Oracle Business Intelligence 11*g* is one of the most capable and comprehensive business intelligence platforms in the marketplace. The average user size for an OBI 11*g* implementation is more than 2,000 users. These are very large, very complex implementations. Building an OBIEE implementation is much like constructing a 40-story office building for several thousand employees. Many of the tools, techniques, and data structures are necessarily geared to a very large scale. In contrast, many smaller business intelligence systems operate at a decidedly smaller scale. This is particularly important to the discussion of data visualization, or, if you prefer, design. The approach one takes to designing a functional modern skyscraper and making it "beautiful" is somewhat different in terms of the materials, tools, and techniques that are used when contrasted with designing a modern house and making it beautiful. Much of the "beauty" that lies in a modern office building exists in the functional environment of moving people physically through the structure and providing them expected services (such as plumbing, heat, air, light, and so on). There is a fundamental difference between designing something practical that is expected to be used simultaneously by thousands of people and designing something customized for a single family.

Business Intelligence System Goals

One of the most important attributes of a large enterprise business intelligence system is its ability to drive a common understanding of an organization's business situation. This situation can be characterized differently. We often organize analysis in three ways:

- **Position analysis** looks at the "state" of the organization at a point in time. You can think of it as a "snapshot." That snapshot can use a "wide-angle" lens and capture a very broad landscape from great distances or heights, or it can be highly focused and extremely detailed.

- **Performance analysis** characterizes what has happened over a period time, with specific attention paid to the end position. This typically involves summaries and "slices and dices" of categorized information.

- **Flow analysis** evaluates a particular type of data or account and how additions and subtractions to it change over a period of time. Although most people are familiar with (or have heard of) cash flow, there are several other types of flow, such as inventory flow, customer flow, data flow, and so on.

There are almost always multiple ways to visualize data, just as there are multiple ways to characterize analysis. There is not a "defined hierarchy" of value in which we can say "this is better than that, which is better than the other." There are always multiple perspectives and methodologies, and they all have both advantages and disadvantages.

NOTE
We will stay focused on the topic of data visualization and not address the inner workings of OBIEE software and the complexities of its environment. For instruction on how the software works, several excellent titles on Oracle Business Intelligence are available—in particular the Oracle Press book Oracle Business Intelligence 11g Developers Guide by Mark Rittman.

Understanding visual perception and the representation of quantitative information is a life-long study, and far more content has been collected on these subjects than can be presented in this book. Reports, dashboards, and interactive BI displays all share the same issues of the most optimal way to present information so that it informs users and supports decision making. The need has never been greater to translate vast amounts of data into information that provides evidence for choices between alternative actions and promotes a shared understanding of business situations and situational dynamics.

This brief overview highlights three key concepts:

- BI reports and dashboards should be viewed primarily as communication devices, and both the principles of human cognition and the needs of the individual user should help guide their proper use.

- BI reports and dashboards are used either in the exploration of data or in the explanation of data.

- It's much easier to misuse BI tools than to use them well.

Humans Evolved to Sense the World, Not to "Do Numbers"

Computers are very powerful tools for manipulating large sets of data and performing all kinds of mathematical operations, including aggregation, division, correlation, regression, K-means attribute clustering, and Markov Logic Network construction. However, it turns out that as human beings, we're not terribly good at seeing objects and translating them into numbers. Indeed, once there are more than about seven of something, we have a hard time counting exactly how many there are at a glance, and we settle for knowing that there are "a whole bunch."

We're even worse at visualizing basic mathematical operations such as addition, multiplication, and division. Visualizing complex mathematics takes a tremendous amount of time and practice, and like juggling while riding a unicycle, the average person can't do it easily. We humans are good, however, at other things, such as finding patterns in raw visual data and constructing three-dimensional schemas; we dynamically interpret colors and light levels and the size and angle relationship of lines. We're good at understanding moving objects and motion in general; we're good at navigating landscapes; we're superb at recognizing patterns. In fact, we're so good at recognizing patterns that we insist on seeing them even when they're not there, and we often refuse to acknowledge a new pattern that violates an existing pattern. Our brains are optimized for helping us survive in the wild, but not for deciphering BI dashboards and reports.

We all know that BI systems provide value to organizations only when they are used. Calvin Mooers coined his famous Mooers' Law and its corollary in 1959:

> *An information retrieval system will tend not to be used whenever it is more painful and troublesome for a customer to have information than for him not to have it.*

> *Where an information retrieval system tends not to be used, a more capable information retrieval system may tend to be used even less.*

This reminds us that there may be a natural resistance to using BI systems in many situations. BI systems may point out situations that managers don't want to address. Compounding this, when BI systems poorly present or distort data, they ultimately lead to misuse, mistrust, or abandonment of the system. Proper visualizations and data presentation lead to business insights and build trust in the system. As executives and managers begin to rely on them, they improve their decision-making abilities. Effective BI interfaces also build a more coherent and consistent view of the business and its operational environment.

Basic Principles of BI Dashboards

The effective implementation of BI systems requires both knowing the basic principles of data communication and thinking critically about who is using a BI system, how they are using it, and what their needs and goals are. In his seminal work, *The Visual Display of Quantitative Information,* Edward Tufte emphasizes five key principles:

- Above all else, show the data.

- Maximize the data-ink ratio.

- Erase non-data-ink.

- Erase redundant data-ink.

- Revise and edit.

If Tufte's advice is to be followed, only information that is absolutely necessary for the contextual understanding of the data will be depicted. The general rule for BI displays is "less is more." Eliminate as much visual clutter as possible and let the data present itself as simply as possible. Drop shadows, 3-D effects, and extra graphic elements should be avoided because they draw attention away from the data. The purpose of business intelligence systems is to relate a clear message about data that is easily understood and interpreted consistently across the highest percentage of users. It is not about entertainment or visual interest for the sake of decoration. Designers of business intelligence reports, graphs, and dashboards should approach data visualization the way Strunk and White approached writing in *The Elements of Style,* by stating their case with "cleanliness, accuracy, and brevity."

Many of the built-in data-visualization tools such as graphs suffered as computers became more powerful and additional "visual effects" were added—not for the sake of communicating a message more effectively, but rather for the sake of "eye candy" or simply because the effects had become possible. Software designers forget that data visualization is a representation or a visual metaphor, and the emphasis should be on making it as easy as possible for people to interpret and understand the information consistently and accurately. Instead, they get sidetracked by trying to represent physical objects, by replicating cockpits and physical dashboards designed for very different purposes, such as flying a plane, and by adding unnecessary design elements unrelated to analytic communication needs. The best example of this is the use of three-dimensional renderings of pie charts, bar graphs, and line graphs. Three-dimensional renderings do not add any quantitative content that is not present in two-dimensional renderings, and they misrepresent and distort values in order to add the illusion of depth. Software designers contribute to this problem by showcasing new features in a product that implementers then copy in an attempt to appear "fresh" or "cool."

Two books in particular offer clear and accessible information on human cognition and visual processing: *Visual Intelligence: How We Create What We See,* by Donald Hoffman, and Information *Visualization: Perception for Design,* by Colin Ware. These works provide the scientific justification for the summary statements in this book.

Every schoolchild is exposed to optical illusions and understands that magicians trick us. However, adults (particularly in large organizations) sometime forget that the presentation of information must be designed carefully according to the way it is perceived. This involvement in and active guidance of the visualization process is sometimes less than ideal. Too many people will simply accept the system defaults set at the time of installation, but these are seldom reflective of fundamental data visualization best practices. Of course, this does beg the question of whether an organization should set system defaults and establish an organizational style guide so that those who are less inclined to edit and improve the presentation or who are simply in a hurry do not produce poor results. This important topic is addressed more fully in Chapter 12.

BI Systems Need Training

BI implementations typically require tremendous time and money, but also offer the potential for significant returns in comparison with the investment in developing and deploying the system. Just as most developers benefit tremendously from training, not only in the functional aspects of software systems ("this button does that") but also in basic system architecture strategy and data flows, users become far more effective in reading and understanding a BI system when they are shown both the basics of "how" and "why."

Most executives and managers have not had training in visualizing data, and many may also have not had training in analysis techniques and are therefore unlikely to do either properly by chance. The most successful BI implementations "finish the project" by including a training budget that is not spent within a compressed amount of time at the end of implementation when everyone is exhausted. Rather, a relatively modest portion of the total project budget should be allocated to training and workshops and should be spread over the first year of implementation. A series of classes on visualization and data analysis with executive users in combination with follow-up sessions (often one-on-one with highly placed executives) reinforce the information and ensure that the BI system is fully leveraged by the organization. What people can learn in initial training is limited because they can absorb only so much information at a time, so these follow-up sessions allow those who will rely on the BI system to expand their use of it more completely. As they gain experience, they are able to learn more and leverage the tools in a more sophisticated and complete manner.

Dashboard Best Practices

What is the most important part of your dashboard? If you want to draw attention to certain areas of your dashboard, you need to know what draws the eye. The three most powerful ways to draw attention are motion, color, and alignment/position.

Motion Demands Attention and Cannot Be Ignored

Motion draws the human eye more effectively than size, shape, color, pattern, or any other visual characteristic. It is now possible in many dashboard systems to embed scrolling messages and incorporate moving displays of data. These displays will command attention, and if the user requires constant monitoring of changing data, such displays can be extremely effective. However, these displays can also be extremely annoying. Using motion can be distracting and often calls attention away from other important features of the dashboard interface. Make certain that motion is used sparingly so that the dashboard doesn't become distracting and annoying to the user community.

Color Is Powerful

Color is a powerful visual clue and should be used consciously and sparingly. Colors will stand out immediately against a plain background but can easily be missed when bright and overly garish colors dominate the screen. The overreliance on bright colors is a major drawback of many BI dashboards and reports. Bright colors should only be used in exceptional situations to call attention to unusual circumstances.

Keep in mind that approximately 10 percent of men and 1 to 2 percent of women have some form of color blindness. Red/green is the most common form of color blindness. Therefore, designs requiring the distinction between red and green are best avoided for general use. Also, the more color is used, the less effective it is. Soft, muted colors are recommended for the vast majority of visualizations. The online tool ColorBrewer 2.0 (colorbrewer2.org) offers several selections of color palettes that are professionally designed. Although ColorBrewer was designed with map interfaces in mind, its color palettes are also good for most dashboard designs. See Chapter 11 for more information about color choices.

Alignment and Position

Humans are relatively good at comparing and seeing alignment (or lack thereof), which is why we're so quick to understand and interpret basic bar graphs. People can immediately see fine distinctions between adjacent bars and whether they're higher or lower. We tend to form patterns so that we see "wholes" before we see "parts." Most people using business dashboards read from left to right and from top to bottom, so choosing where you place things and how you organize your overall layout is very important.

As good as we are at seeing alignment, we're actually not so good at judging relative sizes. If you want people to see that something is bigger than something else, it has to be significantly bigger. Size can indicate importance on dashboards, but only in the sense that "this is excessively, unusually large so that you'll look at it."

A Little Bit about Tables

When precise values are required, it's generally better to show numbers in text rather than as a graph or some other complex visualization. Eliminate grid lines in tables or render them in a light gray. Basic tables are best used for data lookup, not for data comparison. Other visualizations, including charts and graphs, are useful in comparisons and pattern recognition.

Most tables can be immediately improved through the removal of unnecessary gridlines. When tables were hand-drawn, gridlines enabled people to keep their columns and rows straight. If tables are properly designed, gridlines are generally unnecessary. Place related information in close proximity and provide space between unrelated data. This will help the user understand the layout of tables more than trying to separate information through the use of lines. It can also be effective to use highly contrasted display styles with different tables to help differentiate between various data sets. One of the real strengths of OBIEE is its ability to combine data from different sources for simultaneous presentation. One of the most basic methods for communicating "hey, we want you to see these data sets at the same time, but you should be aware that they are different" is to use different formatting and styles for them. Of course, this only works if you are otherwise consistent in your use of formatting and styles. Differences should always be a conscious choice to communicate to the audience, not a result of haphazard development or design.

Although massive tables can be displayed, requiring users to scroll excessively should be avoided. If scrolling is unavoidable, make sure the titles and headers are locked so that users can immediately see what an entry is associated with. Many tables suffer from the display of too much detail. Particularly for budgets and forecasts, where future values are estimates, excessive detail not only clutters the interface, it implies a level of precision that does not exist.

Conditional formatting asks the system to apply a format such as a background color to a table cell based on the results. This can vastly improve the user's ability to recognize a significant value because color draws the eye very effectively. However, a screen of blaring colors does little to impart meaning. The sparing use of soft colors can more easily attract attention to a particular value than can a screen of bright colors. Conditional formatting is especially powerful for data exploration when users are looking for anomalies or for patterns in the data. Regular reports can often be improved by removing colors that do not highlight extraordinary information or are not communicating a pattern directly (as they are in "heat map" styled tables). It is best to avoid putting any text in color because colored text is more difficult to read.

We often sees dashboards with a large selection of prompts where users can assemble very large tables containing dozens if not hundreds of columns. Although the desire for some executives and managers to "have everything" available for inclusion on a dashboard is understandable, organizations should not encourage these "one table to rule them all" strategies. Every element (table, graph, text, icon, and so on) that is placed on a business intelligence dashboard should have a primary purpose and then be designed to best accomplish that purpose. Broadly speaking, dashboard prompts and selection mechanisms should not function as unlimited query design tools. Users who want to perform ad hoc analysis on large, complex data sets should generally use OBIEE's "Analyses" interface (also known as "Answers") and learn how to appropriately filter and form their queries. Of course, exceptions can typically be made for highly placed executives who lack an interest in learning how to create and edit their own analyses but still possess a strong desire to define large tables of numbers.

Chapter 2 covers these points in greater depth and gives other tips specifically on using tables.

Background Thoughts on Graphs

When we design a graph, we have to carefully think about what it is we want to convey. Thoughtful consideration of choices between alternatives is the key to designing effective graphs. All graphs have a primary message or purpose. Sometimes that message is determined in advance, and the graph is designed to communicate that primary message to a broad audience. Sometimes graphs do not have a predetermined message, but rather are designed to uncover or reveal patterns and relationships in data there were previously unknown. It should be noted that data analysis and perception are individual activities, like reading a book, and are not a shared experience such as attending a concert. Although some may argue that the search for new insights is the primary purpose of business intelligence systems, for many large organizations the primary value of business intelligence systems lies in the creation of a shared understanding of business situations and dynamics and fostering a sense of strategic coherence often is difficult if not impossible without a shared foundational view of organizational data. These shared and common presentations of business information should be designed to present an objective, agnostic view of business situations.

Organizational Dashboards Typically Feature Explanation Views, Whereas Individual or Departmental Dashboards Typically Feature Exploration Views

Exploration involves individuals or small teams discovering new, previously unknown or unrecognized insights. Think of exploration as a process of "finding." Newly found insights can often inform a decision that is taken by the discoverer, but often these findings must be shared with others in the organization who are also involved in making decisions and would benefit from the newly discovered information. Explanation is communicating a common message to a group or organization. This ability to accurately convey information or evidence to a large, diverse group of people in an organization helps build coherence in decision making. Think of explanation as a process of "communicating." Insights discovered during exploration need to be shared in a consistent, effective manner. Dashboards designed for exploration are often necessarily different than dashboards designed for explanation.

A carefully designed visual presentation of a major point does not mean the view is distorted or biased. To the contrary, visualizations have to be designed carefully in order to avoid bias, distortion, and confusion arising from inconsistent interpretations. Indeed, the worst kinds of distortions are those unintentional or unconscious ones that arise because of a lack of care in the design process. Just as someone needs skill and practice to prepare excellent-quality meals, conscious decisions regarding details are necessary to prepare excellent data visualizations. Although it's possible to get lucky and fix something tasty for a big crowd without much prep, making carefully considered decisions each step of the way greatly increases the chance for success.

Data Visualization Graph Views

There are four common data visualization graph views:

- ■ **Line graphs**   Line graphs are best used to depict a pattern over a continuous range (such as time). Unlike bar graphs, line graphs can be valued within a range to highlight more granular detail without distorting the meaning of the chart. Any time a different data range is used, it should clearly marked. Line graphs should maintain a rectangular shape (roughly according to the Golden Proportion, or approximately 5:8). If the graph is excessively tall and narrow, the data will show an excessive amount of change. If the graph is short and wide, the change will be minimized.

- **Bar graphs** Bar graphs depict the value of nominal data. Bar graphs should start with zero and use a clear scale. Bar graphs are often used for comparison of the value of data items in a group with one another. Bars should be depicted as two-dimensional objects.

- **Pie graphs** Pie graphs are used for the comparison of the size of individual data items in a set with the size of the whole set (most typically as percentages totaling 100 percent). Pie graphs are not effective when too many items are included (more than seven or eight) and are best used for approximate relationships. Data visualization guru Stephen Few recommends avoiding the use of pie charts altogether. Pie graphs should never be depicted as three-dimensional objects, because the relative size of the pieces of a pie are distorted to achieve the illusion of perspective.

- **Scatter plots** Scatter plots depict combinations of two measurements— one on the x-axis and one on the y-axis. They are most useful for visually displaying the relationship between those two measurements. Scatter plots can represent hundreds of individual data points and are useful for seeing overall patterns in the comparison of two variables.

Chapter 3 covers these points in greater depth and gives other tips specifically on using graphs.

Map Views Communicate Effectively

The new inclusion of map views as a native view type in OBI 11*g* adds greater value than almost any other addition. People intuitively recognize and know how to navigate landscapes and easily make the abstraction to geographical representations of location. Spatial representations of data make sense to most people and provide an extremely dense visualization. The interactive capabilities of maps further promote the involvement of users and offer an ideal interface for master detail linking and other interaction effects.

Chapter 4 covers these points in greater depth and gives other tips specifically on using maps.

Dashboard Design Examples

Let's now look at some of those general principles in a sample dashboard. Think of this as a "sneak preview" of what lies ahead in other chapters.

Oracle's OBIEE SampleApp

Throughout this book we will be using Oracle's OBI SampleApp Virtual Machine as a source for information and inspiration. Most of the examples are pulled from SampleApp V406. You can download the SampleApp virtual machine at the SampleApp home page at:

> http://www.oracle.com/technetwork/middleware/bi-foundation/obiee-samples-167534.html

The OBIEE SampleApp is a standalone VirtualBox VM for creating a comprehensive collection of examples and integrations designed to demonstrate Oracle BI capabilities and product integrations.

The Sample Dashboard Is a Good Start

Let's look at the 11.10 Flights Delay overview dashboard page, pictured in Figure 1-1, from Oracle's SampleApp V406. This dashboard has several attributes that make it a

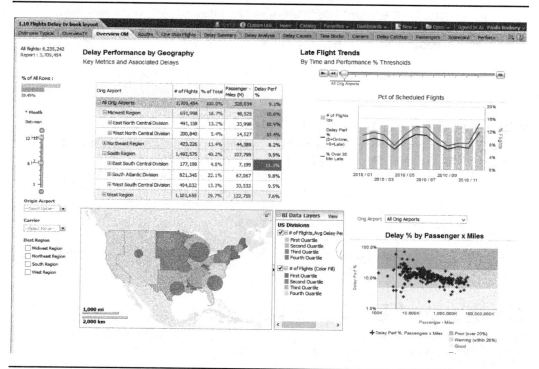

FIGURE 1-1. *The Flights Delay overview dashboard from Oracle's SampleApp V406*

significant improvement over the typical dashboard of large tables seen every day in large corporations and government agencies. After we review some of the key features of this dashboard, we'll look at some suggested improvements and a slightly different version that should set the stage for the rest of the book.

The Flights Delay dashboard summarizes and presents publically available information regarding flight departure and arrival information for several years. Information regarding delays and their causes is also included.

The Flights Delay overview dashboard has more visuals than tables. Typically, a minimum of 60 percent of the dashboard should be composed of graph views rather than table views. The ratio of three graphs to one table is about right. The prompts are organized on the leftmost column. Placing the prompts in that position or along the top of the dashboard provides a consistent location for users to easily find them, and they do not move depending on the content presented in the dashboard (OBIEE dynamically adjusts the position of content based on the data returned).

At the top-left corner, you can see a small two-cell table and a small summary bar chart underneath it, as shown in Figure 1-2. This "contextual" information regarding the current data selections and what is being represented in the table and graph views is valuable to users. The raw numbers tell the user that out of the 6,235,242 flights in the data set, only 3,709,454 are being reported. This table is actually created via a narrative view. Small tables are typically more useful than large tables. One of the most common data visualization "mistakes" is an overreliance on big tables. The meaning and purpose of this table is clear, and it's extremely effective. The small bar chart presents the same information, but allows the user to perceive at a glance how many of the flights are being represented by the current data selection. The bar chart and the table are repeated on several pages of the dashboard and offer consistent contextual information about more detailed and involved views.

All flights: 6,235,242
Report : 3,709,454

% of All Rows :

59.49%

FIGURE 1-2. *Small tables and graphs are big communicators.*

All four featured views are strong visualizations. The pivot table features yellow and red conditionally formatted cells calling attention to the results. The Line and Bar Combo graph utilizes an indexed measure, ensuring a normalized presentation of the number of flights for a hierarchy of airports (displayed as a slider prompt with animation). Map views are always a preferred methodology for displaying data that has a geographical component. Scatter plots (particularly when they employ background data range bars, as this one does) can show the relationship for hundreds or even thousands of individual data points across two dimensions.

Improving a Dashboard from SampleApp

Although we are in deep admiration of the Flights Delay overview dashboard, a few visualization "tweaks" can be made that can strengthen it even more (see Figure 1-3). This discussion will preview some of the topics we delve into later in this book.

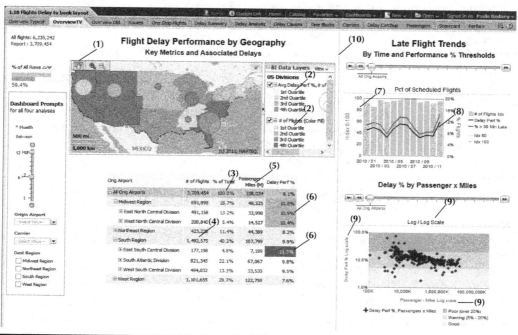

FIGURE 1-3. *The revised Flights Delay overview dashboard*

Several changes are immediately apparent. The first is the placement of the map in the upper-left quadrant (1). Maps communicate data faster and more intuitively than any other visualization method. In the revised dashboard, the map is placed in the most visually dominant space on the dashboard and the pivot table is moved below it. Placing maps in the upper-left position and tables toward the bottom (and right) of dashboards is a preferred arrangement for the following reasons:

- Tables are ideal for looking up precise values and act in support of overall conclusions, which are more succinctly communicated in maps and graphs.

- Graph views show patterns and typically have a main point. Graphs better summarize a major insight than do tables and deserve a more prominent placement.

- Tables and pivot tables can often be expanded both horizontally and vertically in OBIEE dashboards and affect other views below and to the left of the table.

Specifically in the map, notice that the color ramps have been changed in the revised dashboard (2). In the original, the color-fill for the region started with a dark blue for the fewest number of flights and progressed to a light blue for the highest number of flights. However, it is more intuitive to use the light blue to reflect fewer flights and the dark blue to reflect more flights. Additionally, the color ramp progression for the variable-shaped circles is changed to a "sequential" color scheme that more accurately reflects progression. (Throughout the book, Dr. Cynthia Brewer's Colorbrewer2.org website is used to specify preferred color schemes for data visualization.)

The grid lines in the pivot table have been changed to a less intrusive white color (3). (Note that grid lines can often be eliminated completely.) Also, spaces or "padding" was added to the columns (4) to help organize the data and make the table more readable. In addition, the column headers were aligned to the right for numeric columns and to the left for text columns (5). Note that the yellow and red conditional formatting (6) for cells exceeding the threshold value has been retained because the information is important and deserves to be so visually prominent. Indeed, it could be argued that the conditional formatting is more pronounced in the revised dashboard than in the original, despite the less prominent placement, simply because there is less saturated color in the revised dashboard and therefore the yellow and red cells stand out more.

The scale of the Line Bar Combo graph was changed to be exactly 100 points for the indexed value, and the scale is shown (7). Also, a scale marker was added at an index value of 50% for context purposes (8).

Explanatory text was added to the Scatter Plot graph to indicate that a Log/Log scale has been used (9). Although the relationship between the variables is more perceptible with the Log/Log scale, its use should generally be avoided for dashboards intended for a broad, general audience, and it should always be labeled specifically when it is used.

The column structure in the dashboard layout has been changed from two columns (one for prompts and one for visualizations) to three columns (10). The visualizations are organized into Flight Delay Performance by Geography and Late Flight Trends. Aligning the visualizations and separating the columns with a light rule better organizes the dashboard and makes it easier to see the relationships between the visualizations. There are other slight "tweaks" that have been made, and there is no doubt that plenty of reasonable edits remain.

Tradeoffs are always involved in making choices when you're designing visualizations and dashboards. One of the key decisions that must be made is to determine how much time will be invested in editing and tweaking visualizations and dashboards. The cost in terms of time must be balanced against the return of better understanding and improved consistency in interpretation. This is covered in more depth in Chapter 7. However, many organizations are often too quick to accept the default settings and therefore suffer from having less optimal visualizations for years.

Where the World of Business Intelligence Data Visualization Is Headed

Many of the latest trends for data visualization overall, and for Oracle specifically, mirror the discussion in the earlier part of this chapter. Two trends in particular are the use of a cleaner look and the adaption of a common "grammar of graphics" methodology.

There is a strong movement toward a "cleaner" interface with fewer visual gimmicks and extraneous graphics. As of the writing of this chapter, Oracle's latest "skin" release is called Skyros (named after the Greek island). Here is a quote from the Skyros release document:

> "Skyros…embodies a fresh, lighter weight and cleaner appearance…. Specific design changes includes a focus on current UI visual design trends, such as a flatter, cleaner display. It uses light and/or white color themes, with a few touches of well-placed color. In addition reduced use of gradients and borders replaces background images, enhancing the lighter weight feel."

This fits extremely well with a strategy of deemphasizing the use of gradients, 3-D effects, and bright colors in data visualization graphs. The sparing use of color will make its placement more important and more effective in drawing the eye and highlighting important evidence and database insights. Even Apple Computers, long held in high esteem for their sense of design, is abandoning their preference for the graphic representation of real-life items (called "skeuomorphism") in favor of a flatter, cleaner look. This is likely a long-term trend that will continue to see the emphasis placed on the accurate visual representation of data along with a de-emphasis on visual decoration and embellishment. One might say that as business intelligence systems have grown in size and scale, we are moving toward a "Miesian" aesthetic, where less is more and clean lines and balance are more treasured than garish flourishes and screams for attention. You can see this Skyros style reflected in Figure 1-4.

The second major trend is movement toward a "grammar of graphics" approach to data visualization. We are already seeing some fantastic extensions of OBIEE with JavaScript, D3, R (ggplot2 package), and other "open" scripting languages. The primary paradigm is to define objects and attach attributes to them, which includes

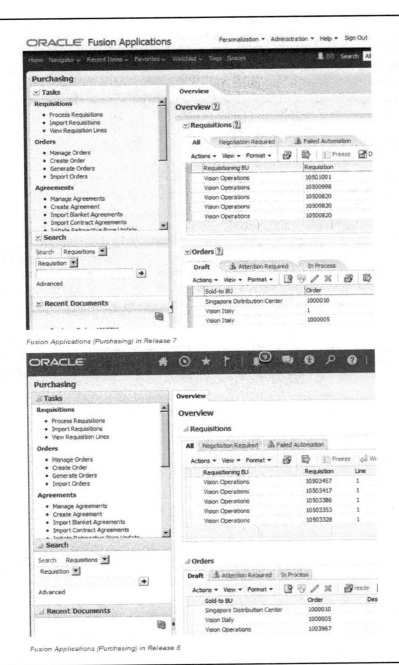

FIGURE 1-4. *Screenshot from Oracle's press release announcing their new "Skyros" CSS, which has a cleaner look than the older "FusionFX" style*

the maturation of web interfaces toward HTML5 and away from Flash. This approach deals with graphics more as combinations of components (and structures). You can think of this as "data poetry," where structure and syntax (in short, "composition") all become essential elements of a thoughtful communication. Just as the patterns and "rules" of grammar guide how we formulate sentences and combine and organize them to form larger works, the patterns and rules of graphics guide the formulation of graphs and visualizations. This is addressed more in Chapter 5. A finer integration of "grammar of graphics" style methods can be anticipated in future releases of OBIEE.

Summary

Editing and improving business intelligence visualizations and dashboards takes a certain amount of time and effort. We should be guided not by "taste" or opinion, but rather by understanding the fundamentals of human visual perception and cognition. Our job is to present data accurately and clearly. We must understand that visualizations, which are presented as communications to broad audiences to explain certain business situations, are different from exploratory dashboards, which are designed to reveal previously unknown results to an individual. There is a great emphasis in many data visualization circles on "discovery," and several parts of this book are dedicated to this subject. However, there is also a need to leverage the power of business intelligence systems and dashboards to communicate a shared, coherent understanding of business information across large organizations—that is, to explain organizational position and performance. Much of this book deals with the strong need to understand the implications of design choices for queries, views, and dashboards as they relate to communicating to a large, diverse audience.

CHAPTER
2

Tables

Tables are everywhere on business intelligence dashboards and form the foundation of most BI systems. Because they are the most common and pervasive visualization, it's critically important to design them properly. Formatting, spacing, data selection, table size, table type (standard or pivot), interactivity, and more contribute to the ability for tables to function effectively. In other words, there is a lot that goes into effective table design.

Understanding Table Design

Understanding table design is fundamental to dashboard design and the visual presentation of data. Tables show data organized for the lookup of specific or precise values. They are organized in rows and columns. There is good reason why the default view of data in most business intelligence systems (including OBIEE) is a table. Fundamentally, visualizations are about understanding data. The raw data presented as readable values is the simplest presentation of data possible. A table does not tell a story, depicting a relationship between data and a perspective on it; a table is not the visual presentation of a relationship between data elements; nor is a table a singular interpretation or insight regarding the data. A table does, however, commonly present data from a particular perspective so that readers can look up specific, precise values and understand a data point within a particular context or frame. An example of a table is shown later in this chapter in Figure 2-1.

Tables are all about presenting data points, not interpreting them. Tables are simultaneously the simplest and the densest presentation of individual data values possible. Because they can mix data of many different data types and because there is no limit to the scale range of data presented within a row or column, they do not suffer from many of the design considerations and limitations that other data visualization techniques must necessarily include.

Tables can also function as effective interfaces for sorting, drilling, and navigating to other presentations of data. OBIEE facilitates a great deal of interaction with tables and offers the opportunity for the tables to be a navigation vehicle for data sets, not just the end presentation of them.

Given this power and flexibility, it is important to first know the primary purpose of a table when placing it on a dashboard. The placement of columns and rows and their physical adjacencies and interactive relationships, such as drill paths, sorts, and the like, are important to how they are "read." People "read" tables, and their skill, experience, biases, and expectations all play an important role in how tables are designed.

Because there are so many examples of the "all-inclusive table" that attempts to include all information within a data set, executives should be asked to rank the most important columns for others in an organization to read in a large table. If the answer is "it depends," you should try to ascertain what the various use cases are. This may lead you to replacing an all-inclusive table with several simpler tables that are more appropriately designed for a single use case. For example, finding out whether it's more important to compare Year to Date sales with Last Year to Date or with Sales Forecast or with an industry growth index for a particular table can be extremely helpful in making sure that the organization is seeing and understanding data points in a consistent way. Significant tradeoffs exist for including everything in a single large table. Think of large, "all-inclusive" tables as data exploration tools rather than data communication tools.

Considerations for Designing a Table

- How easy is it to scan this table visually?
- Is there a compelling reason to include gridlines?
- How should data values be formatted?
- How much precision is required for the data?
- What column names and row names should be used?
- How wide should column names and row names be?
- How should additional information be included as annotations to the table? Where should they appear? To the side, above, or below? Should rollovers be used?
- Is conditional formatting needed and, if so, what insights are being communicated?
- Should the table be part of a master detail plan for a dashboard?
- What filters were used in determining which data is being shown? How should that data selection/filtering information be presented?
- What selections of data are included in drill down? (Use selection steps to exclude particular drill path elements.)

Executives are generally better able to recommend an importance ranking for others than they are for themselves. Making this shift away from "what helps me" to "what helps the organization" can be an effective way to guide the discussion of large table design and inclusion on dashboards.

Large tables contain more information, but they also take up more screen real estate. Generally, between 25 to 50 rows of data can be effectively shown at the same time. If part of the key value of a table is the ability to sort through data quickly and reorient the data shown, then a case can be made for the inclusion of tables with more rows of data. However, most tables are far too big rather than too small. In fact, very small tables can be extremely effective in presenting data insights in a small amount of space. (One can think of a "performance tile" view as a single row, single column table.) We'll talk about filters and selection steps a little later in the chapter. Filters and selection steps should be used to help shape the presentation of numbers in tables.

Many people get used to overlooking the "noise" on tables when they've used a particular table for a long period of time. This can be called the "my house" phenomenon. People (particularly executives) often want a table to be exactly the same as it was before, even though it may be inefficient or misleading to other people. This is similar to the way that people get used to quirks or inefficiencies in their homes. Even multimillion-dollar manufacturing plants are subject to this phenomenon. People get used to certain workflows, even though they might be highly inefficient. Someone with "fresh eyes" might properly ask, "Why are these two sequential operations on different sides of the plant?" The only answer is, "Because they've always been there." Change can be awkward, but most people adjust relatively quickly to finding the information they are looking for in well-organized and well-designed table views. Newer, preferred table views should be placed toward the top of a dashboard page and the older table views of the same data placed underneath (when executives insist). Soon most people become used to the new, cleaner presentation and end up preferring it in the end.

Tables can be effective data exploration tools because they are so data dense and include automatic data treatment capabilities, including sorting, conditional formatting, drilling, and pivot table cross tab capabilities. Tables should be seen as an interactive presentation of data, not just a static presentation.

Keep in mind the following characteristics of tables:

- Tables can present data at drastically different scales.

- Tables can present very different data types simultaneously.

- Tables can repeat and include multiple sets of the same data values.

■ Tables are extraordinarily dense and include numerous data relationships without direct distortion of the data itself.

■ Tables can present "federated" data from different sources in a single simultaneous view.

NOTE
Tables show data organized for the lookup of specific or precise values.

Table Views vs. Pivot Table Views

The two main types of tables in OBIEE are table views and pivot table views. Both have specific advantages and disadvantages.

Tables are basic collections of columns and can usually be read or "scanned" faster than pivot tables, which always require an "intersection" of columns and rows to be interpreted. Tables are the default view chosen for analyses that include attribute columns and/or measure columns. A basic table has two parts: the column headers and the data cells. Headers and data cells are formatted separately. Tables are used for displaying transactions and allow for duplicate data. For example, a table may show multiple orders for a given customer, time period, and product. Figure 2-1 shows an example of a table.

Order Type	No of Orders	Sales	Billed Quantity	Actual Unit Price
Express	13,980	$14,027,034	1,117,199	$12.56
Secure	29,347	$28,513,745	2,326,540	$12.26
Standard	27,673	$27,459,221	2,213,482	$12.41
Grand Total	**71,000**	**$70,000,000**	**5,657,221**	**$12.37**

FIGURE 2-1. *Simple table*

Pivot tables are powerful and flexible, but they can be somewhat more complex to read and understand. Pivot tables have a "measures" section that shows a unique value in each cell in relation to specific row and column labels in a crosstab format. The organization of these row and column labels can be "stacked or layered" and moved and reoriented to reveal different insights. Pivot tables are particularly well suited to representing and analyzing multidimensional (or "cube") data. The ability to analyze this data by various dimensions is often called "OLAP" (On-Line Analytic Processing). Figure 2-2 shows an example of a pivot table.

| Order Type | Genmind Corp | | Stockplus Inc. | | Tescare Ltd. | |
	Sales	Billed Quantity	Sales	Billed Quantity	Sales	Billed Quantity
Express	$3,599,937	283,819	$5,393,563	434,016	$5,033,534	399,364
Secure	$7,425,344	601,575	$11,075,456	901,005	$10,012,945	823,960
Standard	$7,256,507	575,768	$10,601,466	864,509	$9,601,248	773,205

FIGURE 2-2. *Simple pivot table*

Stating a "Need" Sentence

It's possible to compare the use of tables and pivot tables by thinking out the "need" statement (or sentence) they address. It can be helpful to think about the specific needs or benefits that a data visualization provides by summarizing with a simple statement. The need statement (or sentence) for a table would be, "I want to look at the following columns." These columns can contain attributes, measures, or hierarchies. The need statement for a pivot table would be, "I want to look at this specific measure by this attribute across this other attribute." Pivot tables typically contain at least one measure as well as attributes (or hierarchical columns) along both rows and columns. Oftentimes, these attributes are nested and may be drillable. We'll discuss pivot tables in more depth later in the chapter.

Table Views

In most situations, smaller tables are preferred over large tables. Smaller tables are faster for the eye to scan, focus the business problem to a primary issue, and avoid the problem of providing detailed information that is not needed. They are also easier to place onto dashboards and can provide excellent navigation possibilities to detailed views when additional information is required. Smaller tables are also much easier to structure and organize than larger tables. Later on, we will discuss how the judicious use of conditional formatting can make large tables more meaningful and easier to view.

Giving tables meaningful names through the use of Title Views helps users understand their primary purpose and points to the value they are designed to provide. This is especially true for tables that incorporate sections, prompts, and selectors and allow users to make parameter choices. If you find yourself having a hard time naming a table, it may be because you are asking it to do too much and the focus of its purpose needs to be further refined.

The Criteria Tab Sets the Basic Properties

The Criteria tab is used to specify which columns will be used for an analysis as well as how the data will be filtered. Filters will be addressed later and in Chapter 11. When specifying a column, you can choose a sort order, override the formula for a column, and specify formatting for the column. It is possible to select a column or hierarchy more than once in an analysis and to make different choices and modifications regarding its use and appearance within a single analysis. For example, you might want to show decimal points for sales in one view where specifics are important, whereas another view would use a rounded value. The two different instances of the sales column would each have its own formatting. Although the data is pulled from the data source only once, individual choices regarding each included instance of a column or hierarchy allows a wide degree of flexibility in designing analyses and views. Figure 2-3 shows an analysis with P4 Brand and 1-Revenue each repeated two times.

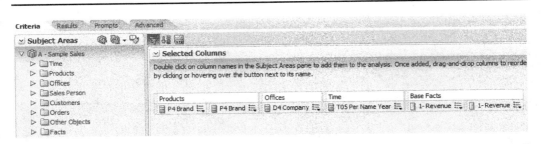

FIGURE 2-3. *The Criteria tab with repeated columns*

The Column Properties Dialog

Click the drop-down list next to the column name and select Column Properties to make choices regarding the appearance of a single column in analyses and views. The Column Properties dialog shown in Figure 2-4 is shared with multiple view types. It contains several important tabs for specifying the appearance of content for a column. Modifications made in the Column Properties dialog generally override OBIEE's style sheets and the system defaults.

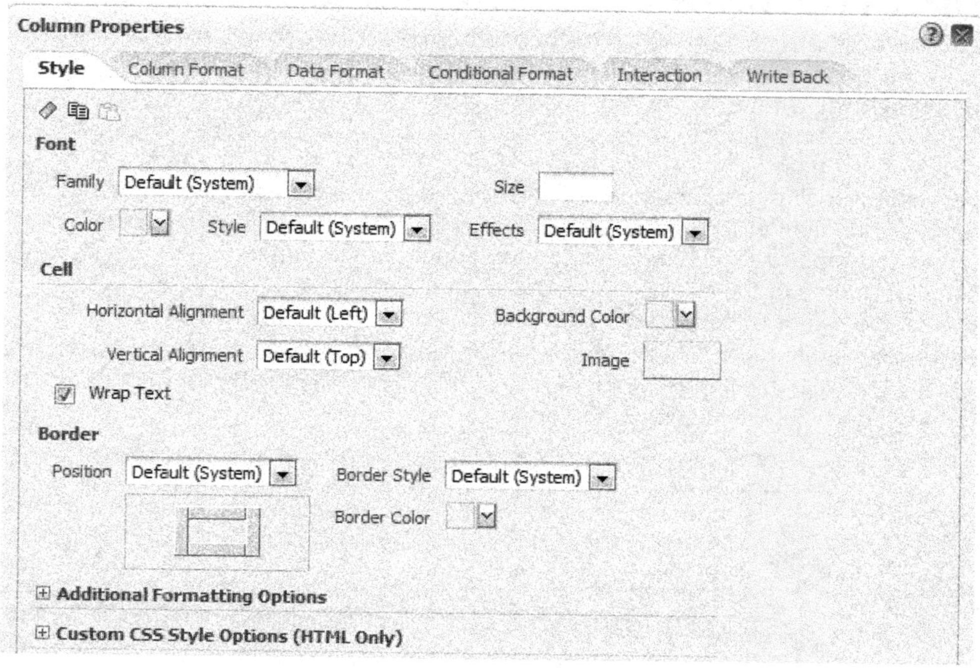

FIGURE 2-4. *The Column Properties dialog's Style tab*

The Style Tab

The Style tab specifies how you want each cell and its contents displayed in the analysis. Font choices modify the content of data in the cells, but not the header. The same is true for all choices made on the Style tab.

Notice the eraser icon and the double-page copy icon at the top of the tab sheet. The eraser allows you to reset to the default settings, and the copy icon allows you to copy all the settings so that you can paste them onto another column without having to replicate all the settings. This is a huge timesaver when you have common settings for many columns. When you have a cell format copied onto your system clipboard, the paste icon will appear on the Style tab page.

The font section is fairly straightforward. Use this to make font, size, color, style (bold, italic), and effect (underline, strikethrough) choices. If you require the ability to further customize the display of data in the cell, use Custom CSS Style Options to make HTML display choices. Figure 2-5 shows how checking the CSS box on the

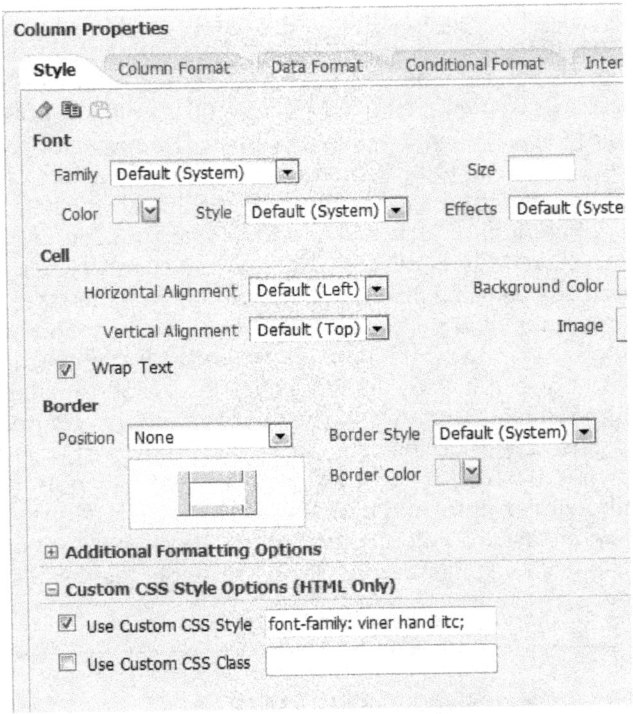

FIGURE 2-5. *Using the CSS style options to change fonts*

Style tab enables you to enter CSS code directly. Figure 2-6 shows our simple table with the Company field changed to the Viner Hand ITC font. CSS style sheets can also be saved in OBIEE and called by name (see your OBIEE administrator).

The cell section specifies both horizontal and vertical alignment. Cells that display text or attribute information should generally be left justified (for both data

Company	No of Orders	Sales	Billed Quantity	Actual Unit Price
Genmind Corp	18,472	$18,281,788	1,461,162	$12.51
Stockplus Inc.	27,496	$27,070,485	2,199,530	$12.31
Tescare Ltd.	25,032	$24,647,727	1,996,529	$12.35
Grand Total	**71,000**	**$70,000,000**	**5,657,221**	**$12.37**

FIGURE 2-6. *Basic table with company names in Viner Hand ITC font*

and column heading values), whereas numeric data should be right justified (for both data and column heading values). The Wrap Text check box causes the data in the cell to wrap to more than one line when the width of the cell is smaller than the data. This is particularly useful for time/date stamps and other information that can otherwise be lengthy. Vertical Alignment can be set to Top, Center, or Bottom; this is useful if a value applies to more than one line (because of wrapping or repeated values) of a table. Remember that OBIEE dynamically adjusts the width of tables, pivot tables, and dashboard sections and columns depending on the data selection.

The background color interface allows you to designate a fill color for a cell, which can be useful to make it stand out in a table. A little later on we'll look at how to do this dynamically by using the conditional formatting interface. If you do use a color fill, make sure that it has a compelling purpose because too much color can make analyses too busy and actually detract from their central message and destroy value rather than add to it. You can either choose a color from the selector or enter a hex color code directly in the field showing #CC99FF in Figure 2-7. There are many places to get hex codes on the Web, such as the previously mentioned online tool ColorBrewer 2.0 (colorbrewer2.org), i want hue (http://tools.medialab .sciences-pc.fr/iwanthue/index.php), and the HTML color picker at the W3Schools site (www.w3schools.com/tags/ref_colorpicker.asp). We'll talk more about picking colors in Chapter 11, but above all else, don't limit yourself to the default selections.

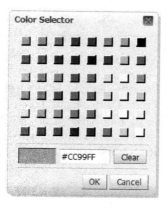

FIGURE 2-7. *The color selector interface. Click a color or enter a hex code.*

Clicking the box next to Image allows you to choose a graphic element to be displayed to the right or left of the data or in place of data. You can either select a standard image or manually enter a path to a custom image either using a URL or the fmap syntax for custom images that are stored locally in the OBIEE environment, as shown in Figure 2-8.

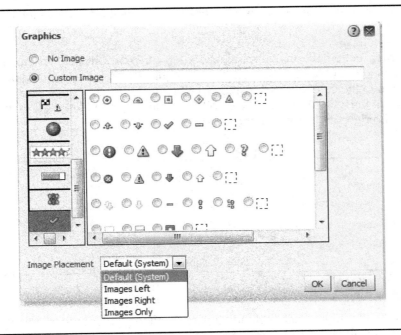

FIGURE 2-8. *The Graphics image selection interface*

Figure 2-9 shows an example of inserting graphic elements into a table view and "sparkline" line graphs using JavaScript from SampleApp (this shows a section of a table of results from a predictive analytics Decision Tree classification algorithm running in the database that predicts the Life Time Value, or LTV, of customers according to human-understandable rules). Table views can incorporate not only

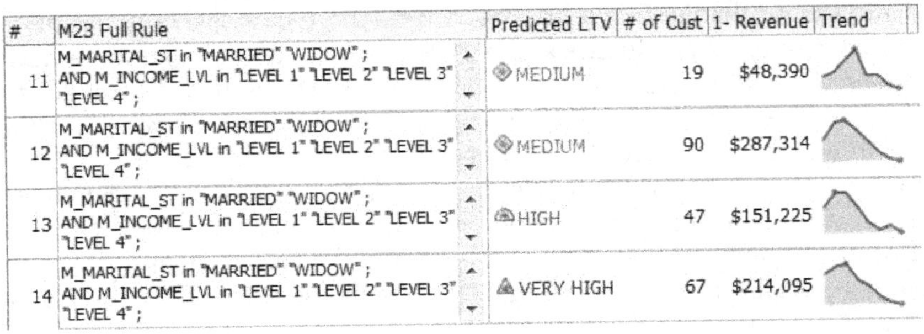

#	M23 Full Rule	Predicted LTV	# of Cust	1- Revenue	Trend
11	M_MARITAL_ST in "MARRIED" "WIDOW" ; AND M_INCOME_LVL in "LEVEL 1" "LEVEL 2" "LEVEL 3" "LEVEL 4" ;	MEDIUM	19	$48,390	
12	M_MARITAL_ST in "MARRIED" "WIDOW" ; AND M_INCOME_LVL in "LEVEL 1" "LEVEL 2" "LEVEL 3" "LEVEL 4" ;	MEDIUM	90	$287,314	
13	M_MARITAL_ST in "MARRIED" "WIDOW" ; AND M_INCOME_LVL in "LEVEL 1" "LEVEL 2" "LEVEL 3" "LEVEL 4" ;	HIGH	47	$151,225	
14	M_MARITAL_ST in "MARRIED" "WIDOW" ; AND M_INCOME_LVL in "LEVEL 1" "LEVEL 2" "LEVEL 3" "LEVEL 4" ;	VERY HIGH	67	$214,095	

FIGURE 2-9. *Graphics included in a table view*

numbers, but other graphic elements as well. JavaScript methods such as the one used to display the sparkline graph will be addressed further in Chapter 5 on advanced visualizations.

The Border section allows you to select borders for cells. Click any of the four sides of the box to add borders. The side bars will turn black, indicating that borders will be added to the cell for those positions. Light gray indicates no borders. The settings shown in Figure 2-10 will place borders on the right and left sides of the cell, but no borders on the top and the bottom.

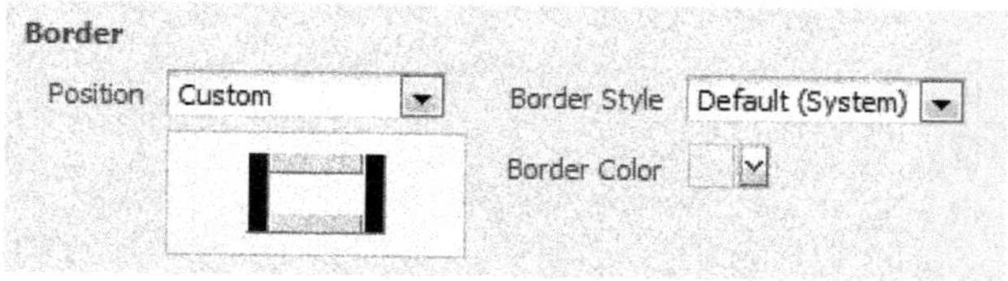

FIGURE 2-10. *Border selection interface*

OBIEE default settings often include borders for all four sides of each cell. You should eliminate all unnecessary gridlines and borders in tables and pivot tables. To do so, select None for Position. Gridlines typically add unnecessary visual "noise" to tables. Use the logical structure of the data to help organize information into "groupings" of rows or columns when possible. If you must use gridlines, use a very light gray, or even white when a background color is employed.

Additional Formatting Options allows you to specify pixel count settings for both Width and Height for each cell. Padding settings specify indentation spaces on the top, bottom, left, and right of the cell. Adding a padding to cells and headings allows data to have its own space and to be more easily seen and perceived. Adding "white space" between elements of a table can be as important to table design as configuring the data elements themselves. White space is often better at organizing data cells into groups than gridlines are. If you have more than five columns and/or more than five rows, you should break down the presentation of data more finely into some type of grouping (see Figures 2-28 and 2-29, later in this chapter, for a good example of this). If you are thinking of using gridlines, first ask yourself, "Can I accomplish this better with padding or formatting?"

The Save as Default drop-down in Figure 2-11 allows you to set the default for that particular column for the entire system or for all columns for that data type. This is a very powerful feature and is particularly useful in the earliest phases of development for OBIEE 11*g* systems. Organizations should establish standards for

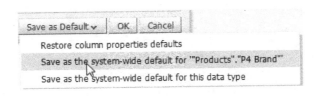

FIGURE 2-11. *Save as Default is used for system-wide settings.*

visualizations and employ a change process for implementing modifications to their standards.

CAUTION
If you change the default settings for a column, it will modify all existing analyses, views, and dashboards in which that column appears. If you modify the system-wide default for a data type, it will modify all columns of that data type and their analyses, views, and dashboards. Experiment with changing default settings in a development area that can be restored from a backup in case you do not like the result from changing the defaults.

The Column Format Tab

The Column Format tab, shown in Figure 2-12, enables you to modify the appearance of column headings as they appear in tables and pivot tables and folder headings as they appear in analyses editing and design interfaces, such as the Criteria tab, and in interfaces for editing views. Folder headings are used to organize columns and measures. By default, the folder heading and column heading names are pulled from the Presentation layer of the repository file. Click the Custom Headings check box to override this default and provide a custom column heading or folder heading for the specific analysis. The Hide check box will remove the appearance of a column that is necessary for an analysis, but does not add value to views. This is useful, for example, if a column is included because it is required for a sort definition, but its appearance is not required in any views.

Click the edit format button to edit the appearance of the Folder Heading and Column Heading text. Developers often forget that names are a critically important component of a table design and must be written and edited with the primary

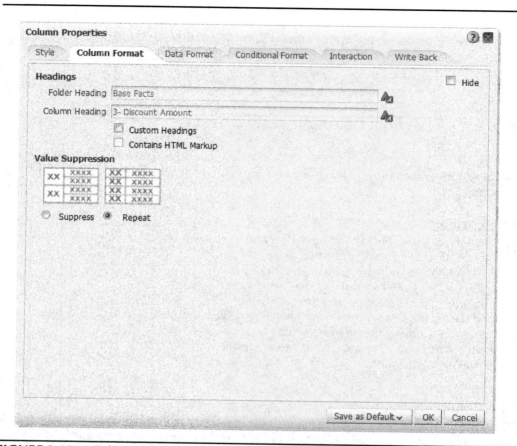

FIGURE 2-12. *Column Format tab for the Column Properties interface*

audience in mind. The Edit Format interface is the same as the interface for the Style tab and features the same options to edit Font, Cell, Border, Additional Formatting Options, and Custom CSS Style Options. These options modify the appearance of the column heading in the table rather than the appearance of the data in the cell.

One of the most powerful features in this interface is the ability to use HTML code to modify the appearance of the column headings. When the Contains HTML Markup box is selected, HTML code syntax may be used. In Figure 2-13, a line break (<br>) has been added between the terms "Actual" and "Unit Price." This will force the name of the column heading to two lines with a break in the designated place.

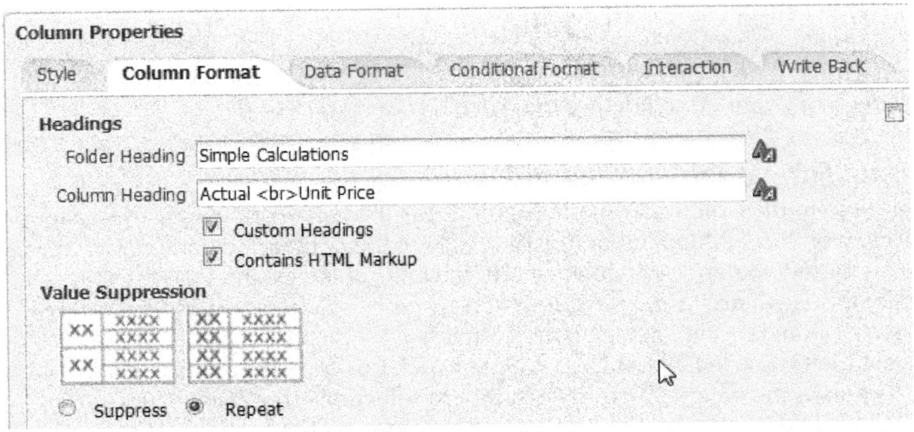

FIGURE 2-13. *Column Format tab containing HTML tags*

In Figure 2-14, a hover text field has been added by using the "span" HTML tag. Here is the exact string:

```
<span title="DateTime order placed in customer's time zone">Order <br>
Date-Time</span>
```

When the cursor is placed over the Order Date-Time column heading, the additional data is shown in a small window. This is a relatively easy method for placing additional metadata for columns when space for column headings is at a premium. A slightly different font color or other format choice can help indicate visually that a hover-over message is available to users.

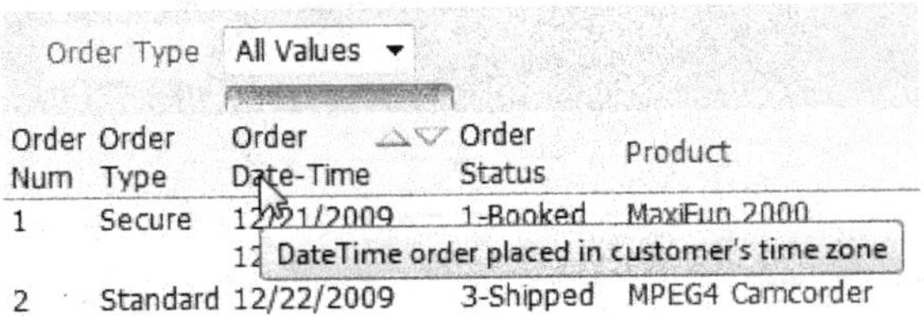

FIGURE 2-14. *HTML hover-over text example with the cursor placed on Order Date-Time*

OBIEE has the option to repeat values or to suppress repetition for cells. In general, repeated values should be suppressed because having less ink in a table is preferred to having more. When tables have many columns and many rows, it may be necessary to repeat values so that context is maintained, especially if values will be offscreen or exported to another tool such as Microsoft Excel.

The Data Format Tab

The third tab in the Column Properties interface is the Data Format tab. The options that display on this tab depend on the data type of the column (text, numeric, or date) and modify the appearance of data in the cells of tables and views. For example, this is where it is possible to add a currency symbol for those measures that have a financial value associated with them.

Select the Override Default Data Format check box to make modifications to the format of the data. Text columns have the selections shown in Figure 2-15. The Custom Text Format box will display the proper syntax for each of the selections. To edit the string, select Custom Text Format after making your initial choice. In the following example, we have selected the Override Default Data Format box and then selected HyperText link. We then selected Custom Text Format in Figure 2-16. OBIEE inserts the HTML string that can then be edited. When this column is used in a table, the cell value will appear as an underlined hypertext link and will enable the user to navigate to the URL entered into the Custom Text

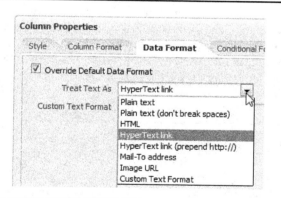

FIGURE 2-15. *The Data Format tab*

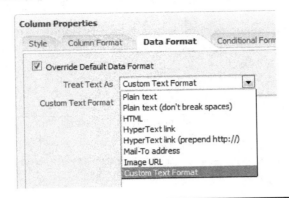

FIGURE 2-16. *Select the custom text format*

Format field in Figure 2-17. This may be useful to add links to navigate quickly to other content. For example, imagine that a table used for financial analysis included changes in stock prices for a firm and its competitors. It might be useful to provide a direct link to a finance website for each firm listed.

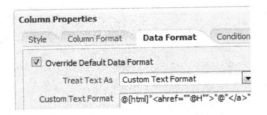

FIGURE 2-17. *Edit the custom text*

CAUTION
Hard-coded hyperlinks such as these can be difficult to maintain and should be used only when they provide significant benefit from a navigation perspective and are likely not to change. There are few things more frustrating in a browser-based interface than broken links. There are few jobs more challenging than maintaining a large number of buried, hard-coded hyperlinks.

Columns with numeric values have a different set of selections on the Data Format tab.

When numbers are treated as currency, as shown in Figure 2-18, you can select a specific currency symbol from the list of currencies defined by the system administrator as shown in Figure 2-19, or you can select the "user's preferred currency," as defined by the individual user.

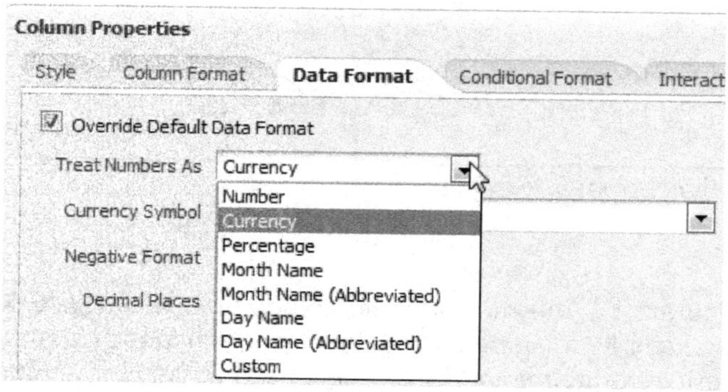

FIGURE 2-18. *Choosing Currency as the data format*

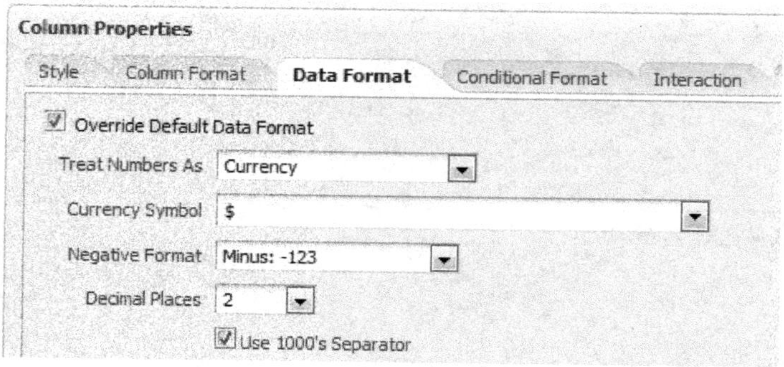

FIGURE 2-19. *Selecting the currency symbol and the number of decimal places*

When the custom number format selection is chosen, you can specify how you want numbers to appear and add verbatim text. Date and Time columns have their own set of options, as shown in Figure 2-20 and Figure 2-21. Additionally Date and Time columns have a large number of preconfigured formats—more than 50 in all.

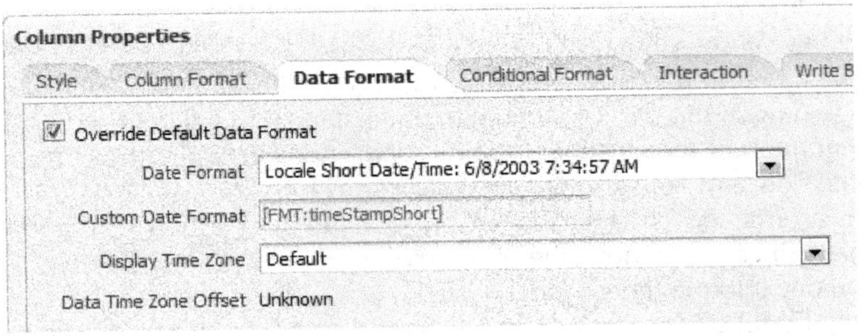

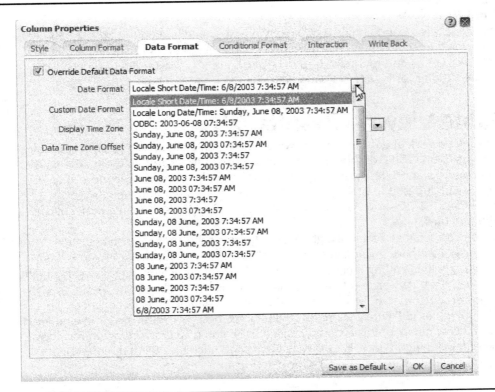

FIGURE 2-20. *Choosing a date/time format*

FIGURE 2-21. *Available date/time format list*

The Custom Format Strings option allows you to further configure the presentation columns that contain time stamps, date information, and time information if the preset settings do not fit your needs.

One of the more useful custom format strings offers the ability to convert time since the beginning of the day into a human understandable time of day. [FMT:time] converts the number of seconds that have elapsed since the beginning of the day into a hh:mm:ss display. For example, the value 60 is formatted as 12:01:00 AM, a value of 126 is formatted as 12:02:06 AM, and a value of 43200 as 12:00:00 PM. Similar format strings can convert the number of minutes or hours since the beginning the day into the time of day.

Leveraging OBIEE's native power with time and date formatting, formulas, and data presentation is one of the most underdeveloped opportunities in most OBIEE implementations. If an Oracle database is used as a primary data source for OBIEE, the opportunities to do time series analysis and other date/time-related functions is even greater.

The Other Tabs

The tab labeled Conditional Formatting will be covered later in this chapter. The tab labeled Interaction will be covered in Chapter 8. Sort order parameters can be set for columns and hierarchies in several different places and will be used later in this chapter for Figure 2-37 and addressed in Chapter 11.

Table Views—Results Tab

Let's take a look at editing table views on the Results tab and preparing our tables to be used on OBIEE dashboards. Remember that the default view for an analysis that contains attribute columns and/or measure columns is a table view. If an analysis includes at least one hierarchical column, the default view is a pivot table. Figure 2-22 shows two tables that we will use to develop the concepts of editing tables.

We can see that a total of eight different views have already been created. Notice that we have given names to four of the tables so that we can refer to them more easily than calling them "Table (2)" and "Table (3)." To rename views, highlight a view in the Views pane (Order Summary Table is highlighted in the Views pane in the lower-left corner of Figure 2-22) and click the Rename View button.

Both tables in Figure 2-22 reflect many of the best practices listed in the bulleted list in the summary of this chapter. By aligning column values with column names and eliminating grid lines, we are able to present much cleaner and more visually appealing tables that are easier for the eye to scan.

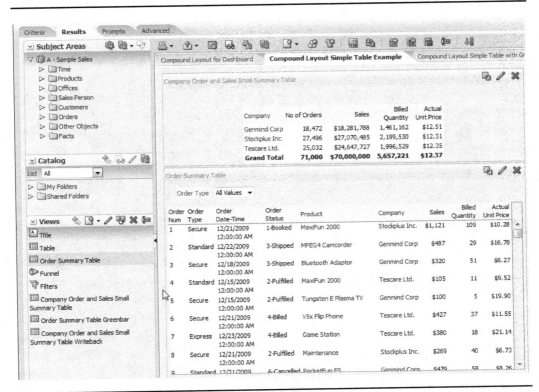

FIGURE 2-22. *The Results tab with simple tables*

Editing Table Views

To edit a table view, click the pencil icon either on the view in the layout or in the Views pane. Let's edit the Company Order and Sales Small Summary Table, as shown in Figure 2-23.

The Layout pane shows the primary editing interface, while the results pane immediately above it shows the appearance of the view. Let's first look at the outlined box called "Columns and Measures" in the center of the Layout pane. All of the columns chosen for an analysis do not need to be visible in each view. Columns, measures, and hierarchies can be dragged between the Column and Measures box and the Excluded box. In our example, more columns have been excluded than included in our small table. Columns can similarly be dragged and

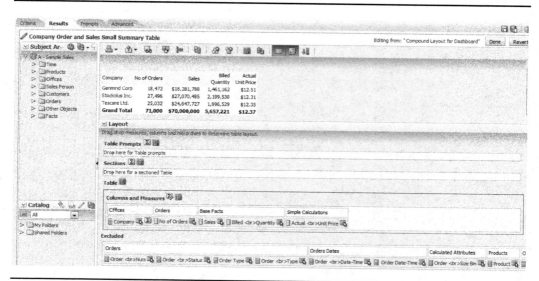

FIGURE 2-23. *Editing a table view*

dropped to be reordered. A thin blue line will appear to indicate when a new "drop target" placement has been identified. Additionally, formatting interfaces for both column headers and data values can be accessed from the "other options" icon (arrow on a lined box) for each column. The choices made here override the choices made on the Criteria tab and allow for separate formatting for different views.

There are four primary ways of visually organizing columns in a simple table to indicate that a relationship exists between the columns or to group similar columns that stand together as a group:

- Empty space in the form of padding can be added between dissimilar columns so that the columns are presented in groups (most preferred method).

- Different font formats can be used in adjacent columns to signal similarity and difference (for example, italics could be added).

- A light background color can be added to adjacent columns using the color fill interface.

- A line can be added the left and right sides of columns on the edges of groups (least preferred method).

Adding Totals to Table Views

The sum (Sigma) icon enables totals to be added either before (above) or after (below) a group of rows. You can also format the appearance of the totals and labels. Tables cannot be sorted on these automatically generated "sum" columns and rows. To enable sorting for totals, create a new "sort" column in your analysis (see Heat Map view in Figure 2-37 later in this chapter for an example of this). Using bolded "sums" in tables along with the appropriate use of space can help organize a table and make it much easier to scan visually. Remember, we tend to see groups before we see individual parts. If you have more than six or seven cells that are "grouped" together with no visual guide or organization, you will have a table that is hard to read.

Adding Prompts to Table Views

Figure 2-24 shows an example of a second "Order Type" column being placed into the Table Prompts section. This creates a drop-down list immediately above the table. This does not act as filter parameterization of the query results, but is a selector that limits the display of information (conceptually similar to Selection Steps). In the example, Order Type "Secure" is selected and Order Number 2 is not

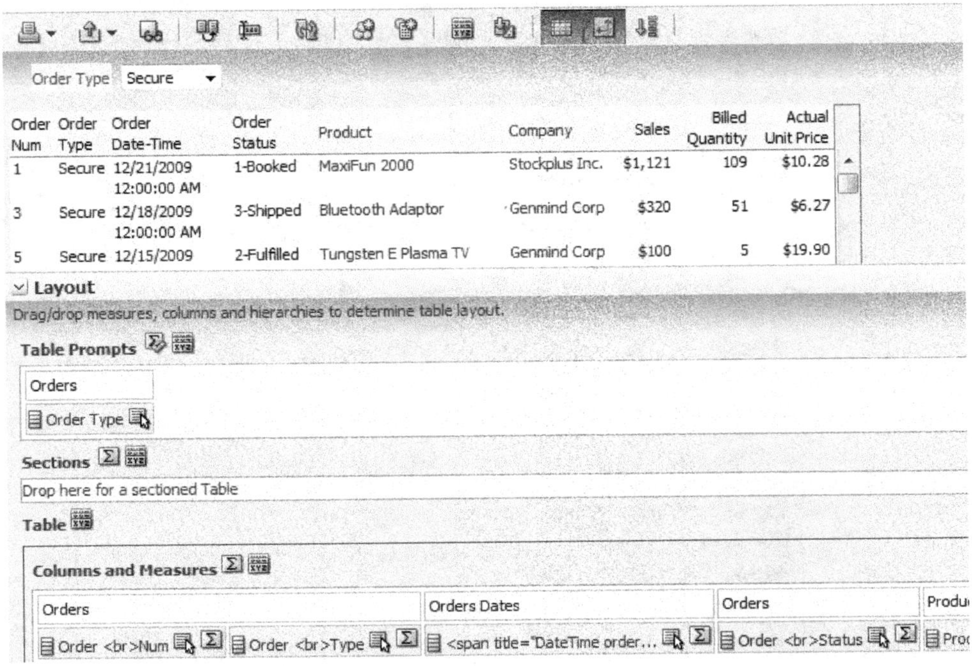

FIGURE 2-24. *Table prompts*

displayed because Order Number 2 is not of Order Type "Secure." Table prompts promote user interactivity with tables (a good thing) and allow users to focus on specific data selections. Caution must be used, however, to avoid confusion with the interaction of other views and analyses on dashboards. Table prompts only control the table to which they are connected (the table may control other views through Master Detail linking, which is addressed in Chapter 8.)

Adding Sections to Table Views

When a column is dropped into the Sections field, multiple separate "mini" tables are created, one for each value of the column. Figure 2-25 shows three mini tables, one for each order type. Sectioned tables require more space, but clearly show all of the values at the same time.

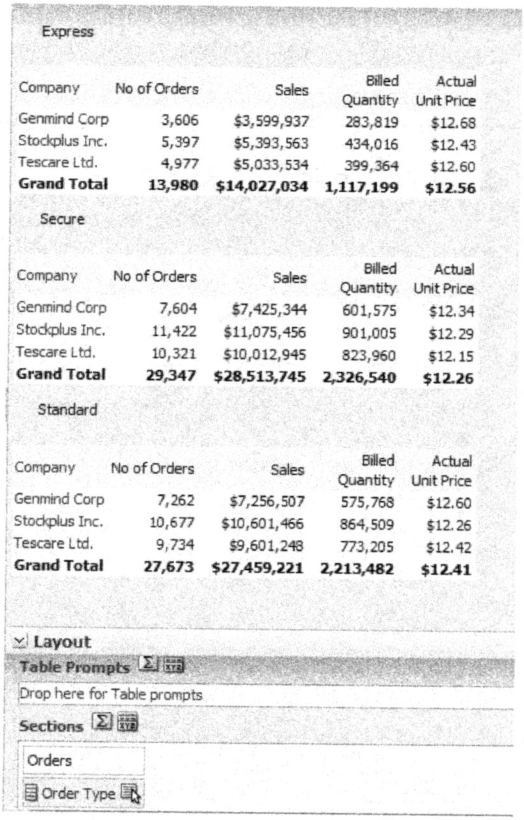

Express

Company	No of Orders	Sales	Billed Quantity	Actual Unit Price
Genmind Corp	3,606	$3,599,937	283,819	$12.68
Stockplus Inc.	5,397	$5,393,563	434,016	$12.43
Tescare Ltd.	4,977	$5,033,534	399,364	$12.60
Grand Total	**13,980**	**$14,027,034**	**1,117,199**	**$12.56**

Secure

Company	No of Orders	Sales	Billed Quantity	Actual Unit Price
Genmind Corp	7,604	$7,425,344	601,575	$12.34
Stockplus Inc.	11,422	$11,075,456	901,005	$12.29
Tescare Ltd.	10,321	$10,012,945	823,960	$12.15
Grand Total	**29,347**	**$28,513,745**	**2,326,540**	**$12.26**

Standard

Company	No of Orders	Sales	Billed Quantity	Actual Unit Price
Genmind Corp	7,262	$7,256,507	575,768	$12.60
Stockplus Inc.	10,677	$10,601,466	864,509	$12.26
Tescare Ltd.	9,734	$9,601,248	773,205	$12.42
Grand Total	**27,673**	**$27,459,221**	**2,213,482**	**$12.41**

⌄ Layout

Table Prompts Σ ▦

Drop here for Table prompts

Sections Σ ▦

Orders

▤ Order Type ▣

FIGURE 2-25. *Sectioned table*

Adding Green Bar Formatting to Table Views

A common request for large tables is to add "green bar" formatting, where a color fill (typically light green) is added to alternating rows. This was originally done to facilitate scanning of wide dot-matrix-style printouts in the early days of computing when formatting options were extremely limited in comparison to modern printers and screens. Although there are exceptions to every rule, you should typically use alternative methods for formatting tables to facilitate row scanning and generally avoid recommending green-bar-formatted tables.

Figure 2-26 shows a modified version of the Order Summary Table Greenbar, demonstrating the recommended methods for use when a client or an executive insists on a table using green bar formatting. (Use alignment and padding space to organize columns, not grid lines.)

Order Summary Table Greenbar

Order Type All Values ▾

Order Num	Order Type	Order Date-Time	Order Status	Product	Company	Sales	Billed Quantity	Actual Unit Price
1	Secure	12/21/2009 12:00:00 AM	1-Booked	MaxiFun 2000	Stockplus Inc.	$1,121	109	$10.28
2	Standard	12/22/2009 12:00:00 AM	3-Shipped	MPEG4 Camcorder	Genmind Corp	$487	29	$16.78
3	Secure	12/18/2009 12:00:00 AM	3-Shipped	Bluetooth Adaptor	Genmind Corp	$320	51	$6.27
4	Standard	12/15/2009 12:00:00 AM	2-Fulfilled	MaxiFun 2000	Tescare Ltd.	$105	11	$9.52
5	Secure	12/15/2009 12:00:00 AM	2-Fulfilled	Tungsten E Plasma TV	Genmind Corp	$100	5	$19.90
6	Secure	12/21/2009 12:00:00 AM	4-Billed	V5x Flip Phone	Tescare Ltd.	$427	37	$11.55
7	Express	12/23/2009 12:00:00 AM	4-Billed	Game Station	Tescare Ltd.	$380	18	$21.14
8	Secure	12/21/2009 12:00:00 AM	2-Fulfilled	Maintenance	Stockplus Inc.	$269	40	$6.73
9	Standard	12/21/2009 12:00:00 AM	6-Cancelled	PocketFun ES	Genmind Corp	$479	58	$8.26
10	Express	12/20/2009 12:00:00 AM	5-Paid	Game Station	Stockplus Inc.	$340	18	$18.89
11	Secure	12/27/2009 12:00:00 AM	9-On Hold	LCD 36X Standard	Tescare Ltd.	$93	5	$18.65
12	Express	12/23/2009 12:00:00 AM	5-Paid	Touch-Screen T5	Stockplus Inc.	$381	26	$14.65
13	Standard	12/20/2009 12:00:00 AM	5-Paid	Plasma HD Television	Stockplus Inc.	$189	8	$23.65
14	Standard	12/26/2009 12:00:00 AM	5-Paid	Plasma HD Television	Stockplus Inc.	$189	8	$23.66
15	Standard	12/21/2009 12:00:00 AM	5-Paid	Touch-Screen T5	Stockplus Inc.	$390	29	$13.46
16	Standard	12/31/2009 12:00:00 AM	1-Booked	ComCell RX3	Genmind Corp	$66	6	$11.07

FIGURE 2-26. *Sample green bar table*

To add green bar formatting to a table, first click the Table View Properties icon in the top toolbar when in the "edit view" interface. Select the Row Styling check box and click the edit format button to edit font, background color, cell alignment, and cell border formatting options. Be sure to use a very light color for green bar styling. In this example, a custom value of #EBF6EB in hex color format is used. The exact color you choose may depend on the monitors in your organization, but you should pick a color no darker than is necessary to see a difference.

Adding Writeback to Table Views

OBIEE allows you to write back values to the physical source tables. Configuring a table for writeback involves the Table Properties tab in the front-end interface as well as the repository .rpd file, and is beyond the scope of this book. When writeback is enabled for columns in tables in OBIEE, you should employ a visual signal to users that writeback is employed. Although this can be accomplished through a variety of formatting methodologies, the use of a colored border and italics for the values that may be changed by users is encouraged. This combination of border color and italics can be established as a part of an official "style guide" and be reserved strictly for the use of writeback cells. We will discuss narrative views and the importance of adding instructional copy, timestamp information for actions and updates, and other contextual information that facilitates the use and understanding of business intelligence systems at a later point in the book.

Pivot Table Views—Results Tab

Pivot tables are the workhorses of business intelligence systems; they're flexible, powerful, and pervasive. In fact, pivot tables are so appealing to so many BI developers (especially those who grew up creating Excel spreadsheets) that they are almost overused. The secret to designing good pivot tables is to decide in advance for what primary objectives and use cases each pivot table is envisioned. Earlier in the chapter the idea of a need statement (sentence) was introduced. At least one or more prepositions are included in a typical need statement for a pivot table—for example, "I want to see Sales *by* Product Type *across* Year." The words "by" and "across" tip us off that we should consider the use of a pivot table so that we can show specific sales results for individual combinations of product types and years. Remember, pivot tables include a specific value in each interior cell that relates both to the horizontal row headings and the vertical column headings. Figure 2-27 shows a simple pivot table reflecting the preceding need statement and the relative positions for the columns in the edit pivot table interface.

Pivot tables are often used for more complex views of data. The order of presentation for categorical data in rows and columns defines the pivot table view and has a significant impact on the logical ordering of data cells in the table and their relation to one another. Different insights are highlighted by using different sort orders.

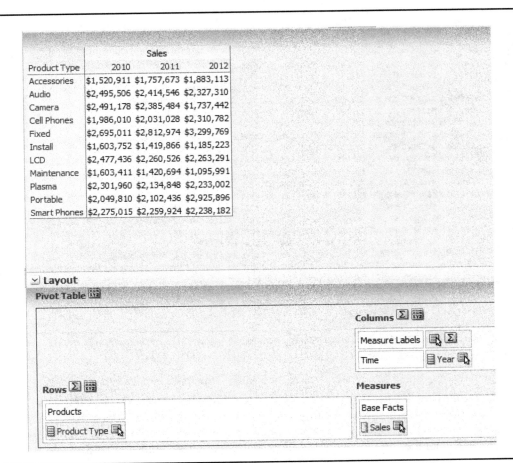

FIGURE 2-27. *Pivot table for "Sales by Product Type across Year"*

Need statements help users understand why they are organizing a pivot table in a particular way. For example, the pivot table for "I want to see Sales by Product Types and Company across Year and Customer Segment" is shown in Figure 2-28. This is a large table with a significant degree of complexity, but by stating what we want to see in an organized way, we know exactly how to design our pivot table quickly. These need statements are also excellent guides for reorienting pivot tables by dragging and dropping column headers into different positions on the pivot table.

Product Type	Company	2010 Active Singles	Baby Boomers	Others	Rural based	Seniors	Students	Urban based	Active Singles	Baby Boomers	Others	Rural based
Accessories	Genmind Corp	$95,916	$29,746	$23,710	$40,947	$60,397	$59,891	$77,722	$96,477	$35,327	$18,269	$51,309
	Stockplus Inc.	$128,470	$29,693	$38,455	$68,506	$100,349	$120,508	$111,572	$166,128	$42,287	$31,121	$98,712
	Tescare Ltd.	$104,461	$35,374	$27,900	$56,392	$96,501	$121,121	$93,280	$123,201	$51,116	$29,919	$66,659
Audio	Genmind Corp	$168,612	$50,236	$21,842	$74,952	$126,754	$133,788	$124,072	$145,912	$37,929	$20,932	$81,346
	Stockplus Inc.	$215,921	$42,336	$55,632	$124,469	$149,511	$169,330	$144,029	$210,808	$57,870	$34,136	$110,538
	Tescare Ltd.	$173,022	$61,713	$30,048	$102,717	$162,078	$202,451	$161,995	$174,856	$60,383	$38,731	$117,529
Camera	Genmind Corp	$154,930	$50,453	$23,935	$73,360	$129,189	$143,608	$136,459	$146,356	$47,582	$21,618	$87,780
	Stockplus Inc.	$189,520	$45,571	$57,449	$88,445	$154,237	$181,047	$162,000	$198,591	$44,463	$41,045	$122,031
	Tescare Ltd.	$182,757	$83,650	$45,512	$89,213	$140,187	$208,441	$151,215	$178,164	$56,695	$34,016	$102,932
Cell Phones	Genmind Corp	$120,376	$40,799	$24,293	$61,451	$82,200	$103,754	$97,480	$126,235	$33,530	$19,032	$71,188
	Stockplus Inc.	$161,238	$47,570	$37,670	$71,548	$129,511	$133,459	$144,812	$178,568	$50,864	$21,351	$101,297
	Tescare Ltd.	$157,717	$50,948	$30,873	$79,242	$130,167	$164,272	$116,630	$125,300	$69,426	$30,606	$93,300
Fixed	Genmind Corp	$144,814	$35,190	$20,000	$94,115	$128,411	$152,767	$138,280	$183,043	$55,049	$22,359	$82,690
	Stockplus Inc.	$234,518	$56,263	$53,554	$109,985	$160,065	$238,484	$180,872	$217,207	$73,673	$54,498	$158,362
	Tescare Ltd.	$197,073	$57,671	$50,893	$121,302	$170,018	$173,601	$177,137	$221,255	$94,856	$41,554	$103,079
Install	Genmind Corp	$84,523	$26,677	$12,529	$48,368	$75,119	$95,233	$55,935	$82,523	$18,074	$21,853	$52,331
	Stockplus Inc.	$145,809	$24,921	$28,766	$52,863	$138,259	$143,856	$111,937	$111,397	$33,913	$31,400	$85,942
	Tescare Ltd.	$139,065	$30,558	$30,859	$56,523	$75,289	$110,982	$115,682	$105,208	$20,191	$35,447	$74,477
LCD	Genmind Corp											
	Stockplus Inc.											

FIGURE 2-28. *Multidimensional pivot table example*

The following is a generalized need statement that you can use as a starting point for putting together your own need statements for different situations. Note that we start with the measure or fact and then define the rows followed by the columns. Remembering this order can help you in gathering requirements and designing pivot tables based on your notes.

I want to see fact/measure (specifies cell values) by dimension and dimension (defines rows) across dimension and dimension (defines columns).

Organizing Dimensions in Pivot Table Views

Large tables with many cells can be difficult to scan visually and understand. Therefore, these tables should be organized through their visual presentation. The primary purpose and insight for these tables, combined with the likely ways in which they may be reorganized by users, should guide the visualization formatting choices that are made. Here are three primary ways of organizing large pivot tables (combinations of these techniques can be also be used):

■ Use of blank space between rows or columns

■ Use of totals before/after groups of rows or columns

■ Use of color to group rows or columns

Figure 2-29 improves upon Figure 2-28 and shows how totals for the Product Type category have been added along with space after the totals (12 pixels of bottom padding were added to the Sums format values), thus separating each grouping of product type. Six pixels of right-side padding were also added to Sales format values to help prevent the bolded sums from running together visually.

Product Type	Company	Active Singles	Baby Boomers	Others	Rural based	Seniors	Students	2010 Urban based	Active Singles	Boo
Accessories	Genmind Corp	$95,916	$29,746	$23,710	$40,947	$60,397	$59,891	$77,722	$96,477	$3!
	Stockplus Inc.	$128,470	$29,693	$38,455	$68,506	$100,349	$120,508	$111,572	$166,128	$4;
	Tescare Ltd.	$104,461	$35,374	$27,900	$56,392	$96,501	$121,121	$93,280	$123,201	$5
Accessories Total		**$328,847**	**$94,813**	**$90,064**	**$165,845**	**$257,247**	**$301,520**	**$282,574**	**$385,807**	**$128**
Audio	Genmind Corp	$168,612	$50,236	$21,842	$74,952	$126,754	$133,788	$124,072	$145,912	$3;
	Stockplus Inc.	$215,921	$42,336	$55,632	$124,469	$149,511	$169,330	$144,029	$210,808	$5;
	Tescare Ltd.	$173,022	$61,713	$30,048	$102,717	$162,078	$202,451	$161,995	$174,856	$6(
Audio Total		**$557,555**	**$154,285**	**$107,522**	**$302,137**	**$438,343**	**$505,569**	**$430,096**	**$531,576**	**$156**
Camera	Genmind Corp	$154,930	$50,453	$23,935	$73,360	$129,189	$143,608	$136,459	$146,356	$4;
	Stockplus Inc.	$189,520	$45,571	$57,449	$88,445	$154,237	$181,047	$162,000	$198,591	$4
	Tescare Ltd.	$182,757	$83,650	$45,512	$89,213	$140,187	$208,441	$151,215	$178,164	$5(
Camera Total		**$527,207**	**$179,675**	**$126,895**	**$251,019**	**$423,613**	**$533,096**	**$449,674**	**$523,111**	**$148**
Cell Phones	Genmind Corp	$120,376	$40,799	$24,293	$61,451	$82,200	$103,754	$97,480	$126,235	$3;
	Stockplus Inc.	$161,238	$47,570	$37,670	$71,548	$129,511	$133,459	$144,812	$178,568	$5(
	Tescare Ltd.	$157,717	$50,948	$30,873	$79,242	$130,167	$164,272	$116,630	$125,300	$6!
Cell Phones Total		**$439,331**	**$139,317**	**$92,837**	**$212,241**	**$341,879**	**$401,484**	**$358,921**	**$430,103**	**$153**
Fixed	Genmind Corp									

FIGURE 2-29. *Basic formatting makes this pivot table easier to read.*

To edit the formatting for the sums, click on the large sigma (sum sign) and select Format Values as show in Figure 2-30. Also note that "After" was selected and shows a green check mark next to it. Sums can appear above or below each section or only at the very top or bottom.

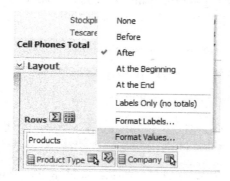

FIGURE 2-30. *Editing the format for the Sums in the layout*

Conditional Formatting

Now that you have seen how to edit table and pivot table views, we can talk about the Conditional Format tab within the Criteria tab. Although we will discuss their specific use for pivot table views, many of the concepts are the same for table views.

Pivot tables are the default view for hierarchical columns. Whereas drilling on a standard column adds additional columns with more granular detail, hierarchical columns show as an expandable and collapsible outline. Hierarchies add a tremendous amount of interactivity and flexibility to tables and pivot tables. One of the challenges of using hierarchies involves the use of visual cues to organize large pivot tables as they are expanded so that users can quickly consume and understand their details. OBIEE can display hierarchies with children after parents or before parents. Note that in the following examples, parents are shown below the children of a hierarchy. Figure 2-31 shows how powerful color can be in directing the eye. In this example, the level of the product hierarchy determines the color of the row. The three brands, HomeView, FunPod, and BizTech, share a common color, whereas the second level, Communication and Electronics (part of BizTech) and Digital and Games (part of FunPod), share a different color. The third level of the hierarchy, represented by Accessories and Audio and Fixed and Portable, also share a color.

Figure 2-32 shows the same table, but with color assignments made by product brand rather than hierarchy level. It's important to recognize that neither of these color strategies is right or wrong, but rather that they emphasize and group different elements within a hierarchy. The business use case would determine which view is preferred on a dashboard. Note how the lighter, more subtle versions of the colors in Figure 2-32, along with bolded totals and thin, white border lines for Years on the Time hierarchy, help organize the data and improve its presentation.

For both pivot tables, the color assignments are made through the use of conditional formatting. Conditional formatting is a powerful technique for bringing

	◁ 2010	◁ 2011	◁ 2012 Q1	◁ 2012 Q2	◁ 2012 Q3	◁ 2012 Q4	▽ 2012	▽ **Total Time**
▷ Communication	4,261,025	4,290,952	692,816	1,239,957	1,741,109	875,081	4,548,963	13,100,940
▷ Accessories	1,520,911	1,757,673	303,959	533,432	645,621	400,102	1,883,113	5,161,698
▷ Audio	2,495,506	2,414,546	349,357	723,386	795,165	459,402	2,327,310	7,237,362
△ Electronics	4,016,417	4,172,220	653,316	1,256,818	1,440,786	859,504	4,210,423	12,399,060
△ BizTech	8,277,442	8,463,172	1,346,132	2,496,774	3,181,895	1,734,585	8,759,386	25,500,000
▷ Digital	2,491,178	2,385,484	319,214	506,429	533,419	378,381	1,737,442	6,614,105
▷ Fixed	2,695,011	2,812,974	617,151	815,655	1,037,949	829,014	3,299,769	8,807,753
▷ Portable	2,049,810	2,102,436	602,042	704,171	836,930	782,754	2,925,896	7,078,142
△ Games	4,744,821	4,915,410	1,219,192	1,519,826	1,874,878	1,611,769	6,225,665	15,885,895
△ FunPod	7,235,999	7,300,894	1,538,407	2,026,254	2,408,297	1,990,149	7,963,107	22,500,000
▷ Services	3,207,163	2,840,560	308,138	616,070	954,317	402,689	2,281,214	8,328,938
▷ TV	4,779,396	4,395,374	595,737	1,121,429	1,972,781	806,346	4,496,292	13,671,062
△ HomeView	7,986,559	7,235,934	903,875	1,737,498	2,927,098	1,209,035	6,777,507	22,000,000
△ **Total Value**	23,500,000	23,000,000	3,788,413	6,260,527	8,517,290	4,933,770	23,500,000	70,000,000

FIGURE 2-31. *Pivot table with color by level*

	◁ 2010	◁ 2011	◁ 2012 Q1	◁ 2012 Q2	◁ 2012 Q3	◁ 2012 Q4	▽ 2012	▽ **Total Time**
▷ Communication	4,261,025	4,290,952	692,816	1,239,957	1,741,109	875,081	4,548,963	13,100,940
▷ Accessories	1,520,911	1,757,673	303,959	533,432	645,621	400,102	1,883,113	5,161,698
▷ Audio	2,495,506	2,414,546	349,357	723,386	795,165	459,402	2,327,310	7,237,362
△ Electronics	4,016,417	4,172,220	653,316	1,256,818	1,440,786	859,504	4,210,423	12,399,060
△ BizTech	**8,277,442**	**8,463,172**	**1,346,132**	**2,496,774**	**3,181,895**	**1,734,585**	**8,759,386**	**25,500,000**
▷ Digital	2,491,178	2,385,484	319,214	506,429	533,419	378,381	1,737,442	6,614,105
▷ Fixed	2,695,011	2,812,974	617,151	815,655	1,037,949	829,014	3,299,769	8,807,753
▷ Portable	2,049,810	2,102,436	602,042	704,171	836,930	782,754	2,925,896	7,078,142
△ Games	4,744,821	4,915,410	1,219,192	1,519,826	1,874,878	1,611,769	6,225,665	15,885,895
△ FunPod	**7,235,999**	**7,300,894**	**1,538,407**	**2,026,254**	**2,408,297**	**1,990,149**	**7,963,107**	**22,500,000**
▷ Services	3,207,163	2,840,560	308,138	616,070	954,317	402,689	2,281,214	8,328,938
▷ TV	4,779,396	4,395,374	595,737	1,121,429	1,972,781	806,346	4,496,292	13,671,062
△ HomeView	**7,986,559**	**7,235,934**	**903,875**	**1,737,498**	**2,927,098**	**1,209,035**	**6,777,507**	**22,000,000**
△ **Total Value**	**23,500,000**	**23,000,000**	**3,788,413**	**6,260,527**	**8,517,290**	**4,933,770**	**23,500,000**	**70,000,000**

FIGURE 2-32. *Pivot table with color by brand*

insight and clarity to both table and pivot table views of data. Conditional formatting allows table designers to assign formatting for data cells based on a wide range of results, states, values, and rules. Let's take a look at the interface for configuring conditional formatting.

There are three typical use cases for conditional formatting:

■ Organize information by creating groupings among and distinctions between different data sets, as shown earlier with pivot tables. This "organizational" formatting helps users understand what data elements logically belong together.

■ Create visual prominence or call attention to data that is exceptional. This is done by writing rules that OBIEE can use to first identify exceptional data points or situations and then to format them differently than other information on the same screen. Threshold levels can be set for different data along with different responses for when those thresholds are exceeded (or missed). These can be thought of as "alerts." That is, attention is being brought to a certain condition or state.

■ Create or reveal a pattern between or among large sets of data elements to communicate an overall insight or understanding. Heat maps are the classic example where hundreds or even thousands of cells are color coded to reveal relationships between adjacent (or nearly adjacent) data elements and other clusters or sets of data elements.

You can think of these three major uses as prescriptive organization, alert presentation, and pattern discovery. Let's take a look at the interface for configuring conditional formatting. Each column in an OBIEE analysis definition can be configured to include a conditional format by using the Column Properties interface on the Criteria tab. Click the Conditional Format tab and then the Add Condition button and select a column from the analysis, as shown in Figure 2-33.

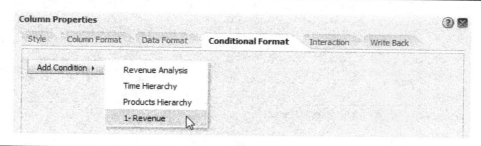

FIGURE 2-33. *The Conditional Format tab. Select a column for the conditional formatting formula.*

All attribute, hierarchical, and measure columns are included. Note that the format or appearance of a column can be based on the results or state of another column. That is, you can add a conditional format for the Sales column cells in a table based on the values or results of Year or Office, or anything else. Indeed, it is possible to string together these conditions and design quite complex rules and outcomes. In the case of a conflict when trying to merge multiple formats and conditions, the condition that is last verified as true by the system determines the format that is displayed. Once a column is chosen as the determiner of the condition, an operator (is equal to / is in, is less than, and so on) is chosen and a value (or values) is chosen. Additionally, presentation variables can be included to offer users the ability to set conditional rules dynamically. The standard Edit Format interface with a Style tab, shown earlier in Figure 2-4, and a Data Format tab, shown earlier in Figure 2-15, is used for enabling font differences, background colors, borders, cell alignment, padding, and CSS style sheets to modify the presentation of data.

Figures 2-33, 2-34, and 2-35 show the process of building a conditional format to call attention to Product Type, Company, Year, Customer Segment sales combination values that are greater than the threshold value of $200,000 by highlighting them in a light green color, as shown in Figure 2-36. This conditional formatting example shows how quickly the eye can scan our sample pivot table and spot exceptional combinations. One of the keys to successful use of conditional formatting for calling attention to exceptional results is to use conditional formatting very sparingly for this purpose. Exceptional results cannot stand out visually if the

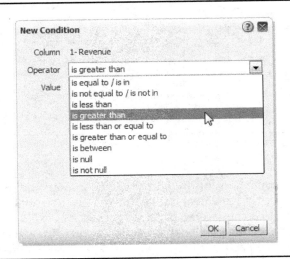

FIGURE 2-34. *Choosing an operator and formula for the conditional format*

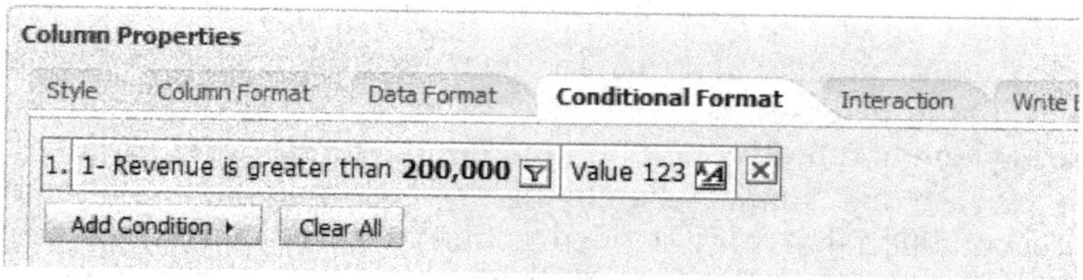

FIGURE 2-35. *Adding results to conditional formats*

pivot table example with conditional formatting

Product Type	Company	Sales								
		2010			2011			2012		
		Active Singles	Baby Boomers	Students	Active Singles	Baby Boomers	Students	Active Singles	Baby Boomers	Students
Accessories	Genmind Corp	$95,916	$29,746	$59,891	$96,477	$35,327	$85,730	$102,837	$30,257	$102,557
	Stockplus Inc.	$128,470	$29,693	$120,508	$166,128	$42,287	$125,064	$164,919	$46,298	$153,358
	Tescare Ltd.	$104,461	$35,374	$121,121	$123,201	$51,116	$124,715	$132,745	$44,773	$137,055
Accessories Total		**$328,847**	**$94,813**	**$301,520**	**$385,807**	**$128,730**	**$335,508**	**$400,500**	**$121,328**	**$392,970**
Audio	Genmind Corp	$168,612	$50,236	$133,788	$145,912	$37,929	$103,982	$152,424	$52,368	$105,074
	Stockplus Inc.	$215,921	$42,336	$169,330	$210,808	$57,870	$178,434	$208,513	$52,097	$137,207
	Tescare Ltd.	$173,022	$61,713	$202,451	$174,856	$60,383	$218,892	$175,146	$73,561	$150,112
Audio Total		**$557,555**	**$154,285**	**$505,569**	**$531,576**	**$156,183**	**$501,308**	**$536,083**	**$178,025**	**$392,393**
Camera	Genmind Corp	$154,930	$50,453	$143,608	$146,356	$47,582	$114,448	$118,700	$27,103	$104,021
	Stockplus Inc.	$189,520	$45,571	$181,047	$198,591	$44,463	$176,452	$148,755	$30,071	$127,373
	Tescare Ltd.	$182,757	$83,650	$208,441	$178,164	$56,695	$184,949	$144,254	$37,842	$130,634
Camera Total		**$527,207**	**$179,675**	**$533,096**	**$523,111**	**$148,740**	**$475,850**	**$411,709**	**$95,017**	**$362,028**
Cell Phones	Genmind Corp	$120,376	$40,799	$103,754	$126,235	$33,530	$114,026	$143,555	$31,372	$101,993
	Stockplus Inc.	$161,238	$47,570	$133,459	$178,568	$50,864	$154,975	$202,613	$38,343	$156,765
	Tescare Ltd.	$157,717	$50,948	$164,272	$125,300	$69,426	$158,507	$168,318	$60,207	$182,772
Cell Phones Total		**$439,331**	**$139,317**	**$401,484**	**$430,103**	**$153,820**	**$427,507**	**$514,487**	**$129,922**	**$441,529**
Fixed	Genmind Corp	$144,814	$35,190	$152,767	$183,043	$55,049	$145,979	$218,694	$43,825	$147,809

FIGURE 2-36. *Pivot table showing conditional formatting results*

interface is too busy. Stoplight colors (red, yellow, green) should be used sparingly, in particular as indicators of individual results. The next section addresses the use of conditional formatting to create overall patterns of results.

The third common use of conditional formatting involves creating visual patterns in a series of table or pivot table cells to communicate an overall understanding or insight. When colors are used to create these patterns, they are often referred to as "heat maps." Heat maps have the advantage of being able to show very large numbers of individual data points, sometimes in the hundreds or even thousands on a single visualization. Despite their power and relative simplicity, heat maps are seldom well designed. The purpose of heat maps is to show the location and "state" of an individual data point and how it relates to others in the set of data. Because of this, the sort order of both columns and rows is critically important. The sort order determines the nearness or distance between individual data points. Sort order in heat maps should always be a conscious choice, not a "default" selection. The single biggest error with most maps is using alphabetical sorting of categorical and hierarchical columns. Although alphabetical sorting can be useful for users looking for a specific value, there is seldom a direct relationship between the relative positions of data elements in an alphabetical sorted list. For this reason, other fields should be used for sorting values. To sort the values of the pivot table in Figure 2-37 by total revenue and not alphabetically by office or by line of business, a Sort column was added that identifies the rank of each table cell and then Ascending Sort for that column on the Criteria tab was chosen. The resulting pattern reveals the

Pivot Table Heat Map Sorted by Totals

Revenue

	Total	Games	TV	Communication	Electronics	Services	Digital	
Figueroa Office	3,842,965	914,919	729,827	681,779	701,456	407,920	407,063	
Guadalupe Office	3,724,738	862,509	693,366	664,895	707,271	406,200	390,496	
Madison Office	3,716,987	825,543	779,601	739,156	611,711	446,598	314,378	
Spring Office	3,709,601	858,957	717,341	667,680	685,668	422,951	357,004	
Eiffel Office	3,686,867	823,021	728,796	676,905	682,543	405,856	369,746	
Morange Office	3,641,190	811,880	721,387	665,290	663,009	418,864	360,760	■ Top 10
Perry Office	3,619,594	855,657	683,563	644,817	665,727	409,440	360,390	
College Office	3,585,286	819,320	694,641	651,727	657,580	405,023	356,995	■ Top 20
Copper Office	3,580,742	839,249	687,280	646,662	635,787	410,720	361,046	
River Office	3,492,153	818,434	680,537	623,381	619,210	407,934	342,656	■ Top 30
Montgomery Office	3,408,846	759,058	682,715	645,204	577,288	448,329	296,251	▨ Top 40
Mills Office	3,403,256	781,354	642,268	626,036	605,521	404,171	343,906	
Sherman Office	3,403,022	755,788	664,182	657,178	600,829	418,831	306,213	□ Top 50
Blue Bell Office	3,380,918	736,522	663,799	674,691	586,770	417,274	301,861	
Casino Office	3,375,543	748,233	667,623	650,517	585,016	427,787	296,367	
Eden Office	3,339,510	736,813	647,644	675,784	559,951	424,380	294,938	
Foster Office	3,314,839	739,522	658,719	638,517	570,502	416,799	290,780	
Tellaro Office	3,295,579	739,662	664,369	632,993	558,082	409,520	290,953	
Merrimon Office	3,267,581	736,803	636,912	623,936	568,729	407,793	293,408	
Glenn Office	3,210,784	722,649	626,495	613,791	556,409	412,547	278,893	
Total	**70,000,000**	**15,885,895**	**13,671,062**	**13,100,940**	**12,399,060**	**8,328,938**	**6,614,105**	

FIGURE 2-37. *The sorted fields create a logical "heat map" pattern.*

relationship of table cells to each other for the top 50 values. Once the columns and rows are sorted by revenue, we can see outlier cells such as Madison-Communication more easily.

Table and Pivot Table Right-Click Interaction Menus

One of the newer features in OBIEE is the ability for users to have access to an extensive "right-click" menu, as shown in Figure 2-38. This offers a wide range of capabilities for users to narrow which data is included in a table view. Although OBIEE has long had the ability to "drill" and add columns with additional detail to tables, now it also has the ability to "keep only" and narrow the selection of data. This makes OBIEE a much stronger data exploration tool and allows users to sift through large amounts of data to find interesting insights. This is not a data visualization topic per se, but does affect how you design a table of data.

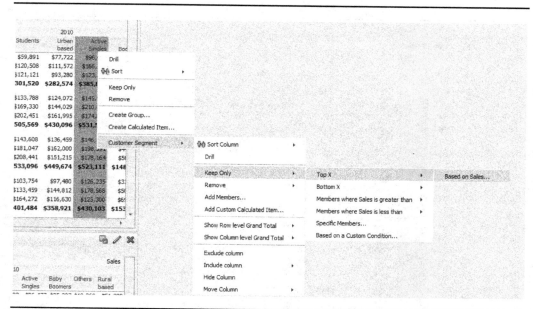

FIGURE 2-38. *Right-click menu for a pivot table view*

When tables and pivot tables are envisioned as data exploration tools, a narrative view can be added that briefly summarizes and explains the available and sensible selections that analysts might make. If users do not have a training class where they are shown how to manipulate tables or do not have specific directions encouraging them to interact with views, they are often reluctant to do so, and therefore many of the most powerful capabilities of the software go underutilized. We will explore the subject of interactions further in Chapter 11.

Performance Tiles

Performance tiles can be thought of as single-cell tables and are our most often recommended visualization type for several reasons. Performance tiles

- communicate summary information at a glance,

- require a small amount of screen real estate,

- can be used in combinations of tiles to communicate patterns,

- make excellent navigation buttons for master detail linked views,

- work exceptionally well on smartphones, tablets, and a wide variety of dashboards,

- and take well to conditional formatting to reflect new or updated information.

Figure 2-39 shows three performance tiles as they might appear at the top of a dashboard.

Discount Ratio	Avg Order Size	Act Unit Price
8.0%	**$986**	**$12.37**
Lower discount ratios desired	Higher order sizes are desirable	Higher actual unit price desired

FIGURE 2-39.   *Performance tiles*

Performance tiles show the title of a measure, the value of the measure, and a description field. There are several different styles to choose from. Perhaps the most effective is the simple, clean look, without text shading, drop shadows, or other effects. Additionally, conscious choices should be made about the fill colors for performance tiles. Although muted, soft colors are often preferred to allow truly exceptional colors to stand out, performance tiles are sometimes intended to be a visually dominant feature on dashboards, and it may make sense to utilize bright, visually strong color fills. Performance tiles are almost always conditionally formatted and carry meaning with their format. Not only are they capable of having color fills, but they can also incorporate colored borders.

Performance tiles are particularly good for executive dashboards and for common dashboards that are shared among large parts of the organization. For example, we the authors worked on a dashboard for a large organization with 14 different divisions. We arranged a single performance tile for each division in a field based on their sales versus forecast percentage. The executives could instantly tell how the overall organization was performing, and each division could immediately pick out how they were doing relative to everyone else. Clicking the performance tile would then bring a user to the division's summary dashboard. Performance tiles act both as a reporter of a specific value and as a comparative visualization.

We have also used performance tiles to report "TopN" performers. Another client had several hundred stores or locations. We had an executive dashboard that showed the top five in sales difference percentage versus last year for the previous week. We came up with different product line and performance metrics so that different locations were featured. This "find them doing something good" range of performance tiles was later promoted to a headquarters video board on a large wall that showed off the good news to a broad audience.

Performance tiles are one of the few visualizations that work equally well on dashboards, tablets, and smartphones. As more and more of the world uses mobile devices to stay in constant communication and expects to consume all kinds of data on their personal devices (including business intelligence data), it is more important to ensure a consistent presentation of results between different screens. You will find more information on mobile in Chapter 9, but performance tiles are considered to be an important element of every mobile dashboard and to be prominently featured on more executive dashboards.

Summary

Good design for table views and pivot table views is fundamental to every OBIEE implementation. They are, at the same time, the most visually dense form of presentation of information and the simplest form of presentation of information. Small formatting choices make big differences on the legibility of tables. Eliminate grid lines and use padding spacing to help organize columns and rows for easy scanning. Adding gridlines to a table is like drowning a salad in dressing or over cooking pasta. Even though it may be frequently done by amateurs, and a few people may say that they prefer mushy, soft pasta, it doesn't excuse the practice.

Prefer smaller tables over larger tables, especially for dashboards that are viewed by large, diverse audiences. Most dashboards are "explanation" dashboards. Tables with fewer columns and rows are easier to scan. More people realize a common set of insights and understanding from smaller tables. Be cautious of using very large tables with a large number of prompts on dashboards. They can be good for data exploration, but should not be overly relied on.

The sidebar shows a summary of recommended best practices for table design. It really comes down to making a few smart formatting decisions, knowing the differences between tables and pivot tables, and being extremely clear about what you want to communicate.

Best Practices for Table Design

- Prefer smaller tables.
- Words are important:
  - Enable rollovers for metadata for commonly used tables.
  - Write informative column head descriptions.
  - Write informative titles for tables.
- Make tables clean and easy to read:
  - Eliminate unnecessary gridlines.
  - Use space (padding) to create groups of data.
  - Left justify text cells.
  - Right justify numerical cells.
- Make numbers easy to read and understand:
  - Judiciously use conditional formatting.
  - Avoid putting text in color unnecessarily.
  - Use thousands separators.
  - Align the decimal point for numerical cells.
  - Denote scale and units of numbers when necessary (for example, thousands, millions of cases).
  - Use symbols to denote units of measure (%, $, and so on).
- Enable column and row sorting.
- Avoid scrolling (if possible).
- Be transparent about data selection.
- Use prompts and selectors to promote user interaction.

CHAPTER
3

Graphs

Graphs form the heart of any effective BI system. Whereas tables are optimized for the lookup of specific values, graphs convey a main idea about a data set. Graphs tell stories about data through the use of visual representations. They often highlight the relationship between different data sets and elements, compare results against predicted or anticipated values, reveal patterns and trends, or highlight a particular finding.

Choices abound with graph design, and default settings are seldom optimal. The decisions of which graph to use, how to specifically design a graph to convey a data insight in a consistent and accurate manner, and how to assess tradeoffs in graph design for different use cases must all be made from an informed, best-practices perspective.

Before we get into the specific graph types, be aware of the following related topics:

- Just as with tables, graphs should be clearly labeled, with axis descriptions (when not clear) and scaling units (K for thousands, M for millions, and so on).

- Graph interactions and master-detail linking are addressed in Chapter 8, where we discuss dashboard interaction.

- Interpretations of graphs are greatly affected by the selection of data (for example, too many bars!) and are addressed in Chapter 11.

- The "Best Visualization" and "Recommended Visualization For" features and color choices are also covered in Chapter 11.

Types of Graphs and When to Use Them

Oracle BI has an extensive range of a dozen or so graph view options. We'll review each one and discuss the best use cases, along with best-practice recommendations for formatting and presentation.

Line Graphs

Line charts are one of those "workhorse" graphs commonly used in reports, dashboards, and analysis systems. Line charts show a continuous measure across the horizontal x-axis with a dependent variable on the vertical y-axis. The y-axis value is said to be "graphed against" the x-axis variable (for example, sales against time). The shape of individual lines is the key message for line charts and should be emphasized in their design. This generally means eliminating prominent grid lines (you'll see later how to add contextual information regarding data ranges to line charts), consciously choosing the aspect ratio of width to height (which has a direct impact on the slope and the visual or intended message of lines), and carefully choosing formatting options such as color, thickness, pattern, and curved/stepped lines. Because they are so common, line charts are sometimes used inappropriately in situations where another type of visualization would be more effective. Never use line charts with categorical data on the horizontal x-axis such as product, office, customer, and sales channel—they are individually distinct classes and should not be represented as being continuous. This goes for line-bar combo graphs (more on those later in the chapter), plot graphs in which regression lines have been added, and other special graphs. Line charts can often be shrunk down to a small size and still convey information about a pattern or progression. They are often used in trellis charts (covered in Chapter 5).

Figure 3-1 shows a typical line chart with revenue graphed against time (at the Fiscal Week grain) for the years of 2010, 2011, and 2012. Two or three major insights are immediately apparent from looking at the graph. Revenue values have significant variance week by week, and there is a strong annual seasonal pattern to

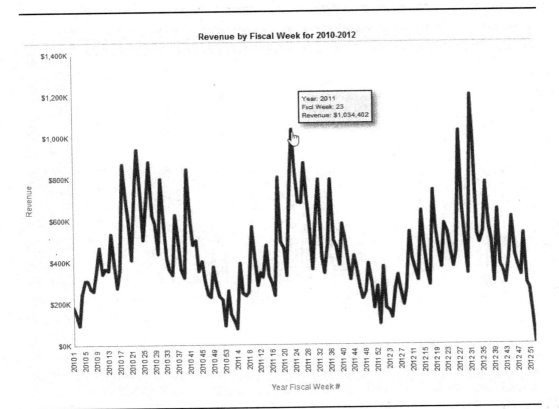

FIGURE 3-1. *A typical line chart*

revenue, as you can see from the three peaks and valleys. These patterns stand out partly because gridlines, data labels, and background graphics have been eliminated. You can enable mouse rollovers for graphs so that users who want details regarding individual points can get them, as shown in Figure 3-1.

One of the important factors to consider in line graph design is the pixel weight of the lines. The weight of the line in the Revenue by Fiscal Week for 2010–2012 graph shown in Figure 3-1 is three pixels, plenty wide enough to show up clearly, but not so wide that the detail of the different fiscal week values is lost. Let's say that we want to compare the revenue by brand for the same time period. We'd do this by showing separate lines for each of the three brands, but in order to avoid visual confusion, we can make the lines one pixel wide, as shown in Figure 3-2. This still shows the dramatic week-to-week shifts in revenue, but avoids an extensive amount of overlap of the lines.

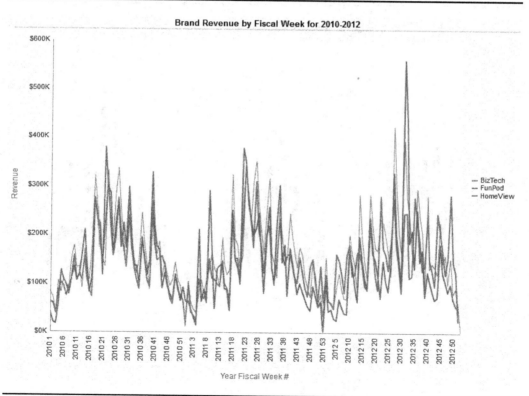

FIGURE 3-2. *Comparison of dimensioned-measures for the same period*

One of the very nice features in OBIEE 11*g* is the ability to enable the zoom and scroll functions for various graphs, including line graphs. This permits users to explore a graph at different zoom levels of detail without taking up a large amount of screen real estate on the dashboard. When Zoom and Scroll is enabled on the Graph Properties interface (General tab), a small magnifying glass will appear when a user scrolls over the axis line (both horizontal and vertical axes can be enabled). It works much like a zoom function on a map. Details that may not be clear on a larger scale become more visible when the interface is "zoomed" in to a deeper level. Figure 3-3 shows the zoom feature and the now revealed slider bar that "slips" the presentation of the graph over the larger, more detailed view (picture it as a window that slides over a larger version).

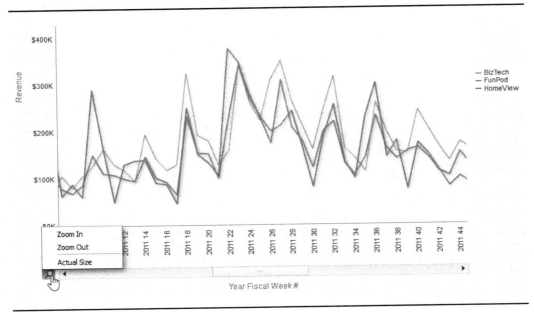

FIGURE 3-3. *Zoom feature*

There are three different options for Line Style for line graphs in OBIEE 11*g*:

- Standard Line
- Curved Line
- Stepped Line

For most situations, the Standard Line option shown in Figure 3-4 (the option that has been used in all the examples so far in this chapter) is the best option and should be chosen. Let's take a look at three identical graphs of brand revenue against fiscal quarter for the years 2010–2012.

As you can see, the curved line graph shown in Figure 3-5 smooths the line into its fundamental shape. If you wanted to make the point about the seasonality of revenue with high peaks and low valleys and the relative order of the three brands at the peaks, the curved line graph would serve well. The Stepped Line option

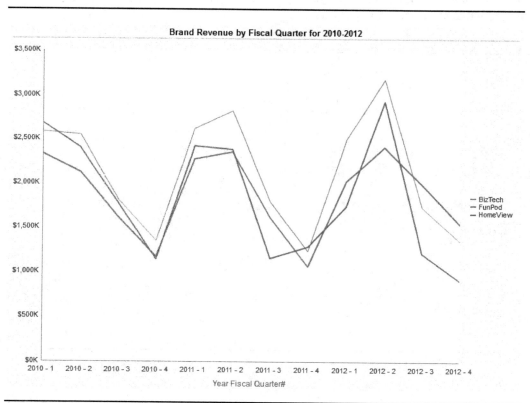

FIGURE 3-4. *Standard line graph format*

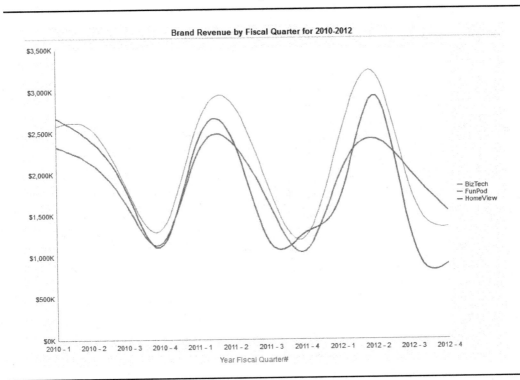

Brand Revenue by Fiscal Quarter for 2010-2012

FIGURE 3-5. *Curved line graph format*

shown in Figure 3-6 shows a single value for each brand for each fiscal quarter, but visually indicates continuity through the use of a vertical line connecting each adjacent value. Stepped line charts should be used when the data makes stepped changes over a continuous period, such as when prices are raised and held steady for a certain period of time until another change in price occurs. The series of stepped changes can be read as a progression or pattern in a similar way to a standard line chart. Stepped line charts can be very difficult to read when they contain multiple measures and are best used for single, relatively simple measures.

Graphic information that provides context for line chart results can add insight and meaning. Figure 3-7 shows revenue results as a percentage of the revenue target that was established (think of it as a forecast). A green background has been added for the range from 115 percent to 140 percent to indicate that results in this area are good, and a yellow background has been added to the range from 85 percent to

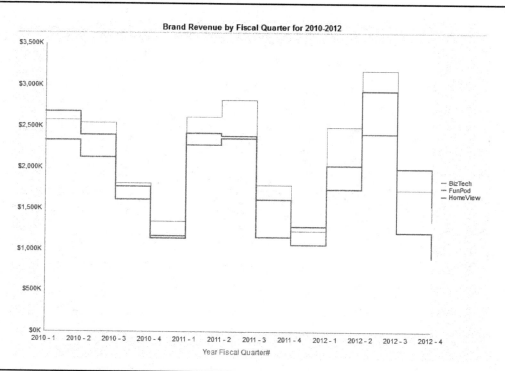

FIGURE 3-6. *Stepped line graph format*

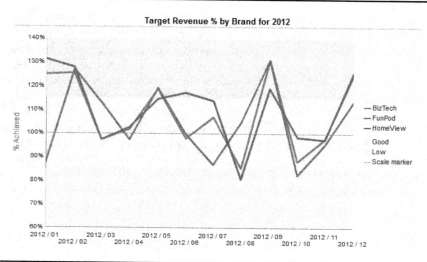

FIGURE 3-7. *Line graph with scale marker ranges*

60 percent to indicate that results in this range are low. The line added at the 100 percent mark indicates results that are above or below the forecasted target. (As mentioned in the Preface, some screenshots are clearer in color. See www.vlamis .com/DVforOBI to view screenshots in color.)

Scale markers can be set to a static value, to a variable (for example, for parameterization by dashboard selection), to a column name, or to a SQL query result. They are one of the most powerful and most often underutilized features of OBIEE visualizations. Because these results are on a normalized percentage basis, we can compare results for brands or products that may have far different data value ranges. This is a particularly good technique for "real-world" business situations where data values often have orders of magnitude differences in value.

To add the green and yellow backgrounds and the line at 100%, go to the Scale tab on the Graph Properties interface and add them as shown in Figure 3-8. Also, set Axis Limits to a specified range of 60 to 140 to match the top and bottom ranges of the scale range background colors. You can add thin, white-colored horizontal grid lines to the graph at 10 percent intervals. Although grid lines should generally be avoided, putting them in white, which matches the background color for the center of the chart, effectively limits their appearance to only the high and low ranges where the specific value comparisons might be of most value. Light green (hex #CCFFCC) and light yellow (hex #FFFF77) were chosen so that the background colors did not dominate the screen. Also, a mid-gray (hex #999999) was chosen so that the 100 percent line is visible but does not compete visually with the brand lines

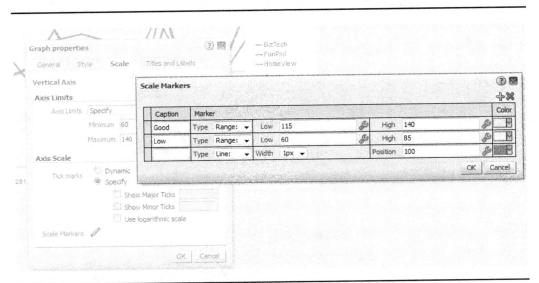

FIGURE 3-8. *Configuring scale marker ranges*

(the main point of the graph). It is generally a best practice to put "context" graphics in lighter or more receding color values than the main content of your graph.

Time Series Line Graphs

Time series line graphs have some nice advantages when you're working with real-world data sets. Oftentimes, there are missing data points for a given dimension of data within a series. When you want to show a break in the data, use a time series line graph. Figure 3-9 shows a custom period of time: the first 42 days of 2012, January 1 through February 10. In this graph, we are evaluating how much revenue customers of different tenure (three years, four years, and five years) generated during that time period. The challenge is that for some combinations of data and seniority, no revenue was generated. The time series line graph shows these breaks and still implies continuity on the x-axis. Note that there is no data for January 3, 4, 8, 9, 10, and so on. The time series line graph takes up space on the x-axis for these values, indicating a continuous time dimension. If a time value is represented by a row, but data is missing, the line is broken, as shown for January 19. Time series line graphs require a date or time stamp column for the "Group By" horizontal x-axis and do not support all other line graph options, such as drilling on the x-axis. The standard line, curved line, and stepped line formats are supported for time series line graphs.

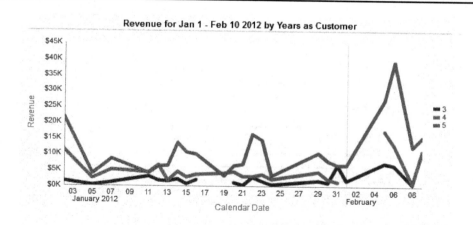

Years	1/2/2012	1/5/2012	1/7/2012	1/11/2012	1/12/2012	1/13/2012	1/14/2012	1/15/2012	1/16/2012	1/19/2012	1/20/2012
3	$1,526	$292	$1,133	$2,912	$1,830	$1,470	$2,108	$569	$1,842		$999
4	$11,181	$2,261	$5,167	$4,262	$6,553	$1,690	$4,516	$2,830	$3,669	$4,024	$4,549
5	$21,581	$3,738	$8,520	$4,104	$6,088	$6,296	$13,565	$10,639	$10,044	$3,271	$6,441

FIGURE 3-9. *Time series line graph*

Bar Graphs

Bar graphs are perhaps the most versatile and useful graph visualization. The human eye is able to quickly determine the relative heights or lengths of bars when they have a common base, and thus perceive information about numbers. Additionally, there is a high degree of consistency in how people interpret and understand bar graphs (however, differences can sometimes be significant, thus making visualizations a source of confusion rather than shared understanding). This ability to scan and make inferences and draw conclusions from bar graphs makes them ideal for many situations. There are six basic types of bar graphs in OBIEE:

- Vertical bar graph

- Horizontal bar graph

- Stacked vertical bar graph

- Stacked horizontal bar graph

- 100% stacked vertical bar graph (version 11.1.1.7 and above)

- 100% stacked horizontal bar graph (version 11.1.1.7 and above)

Figure 3-10 shows a traditional vertical bar graph for two different measures, revenue and costs, for product types for the year 2010. You can scan the graph and immediately see that revenue was greatest for the "fixed" product type and that costs for this type were significantly lower than revenue. You can also quickly scan the

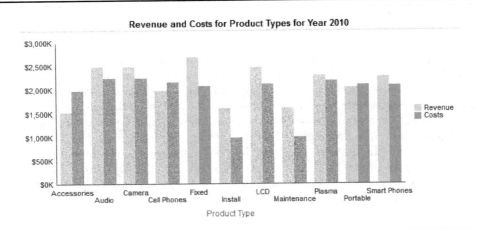

FIGURE 3-10. *Vertical bar graph*

graph and see that costs were highest for cameras, but that there were several other product types that had very similar costs. Although this particular graph shows product types organized alphabetically so that users can quickly find a particular product type without having to hunt for it, choosing a sort methodology would reveal a pattern and relationship between the individual product types. For example, Figure 3-11 shows the same graph with a sort field added for profit (the difference between revenue and costs) and reveals that, surprisingly, two of the three product types with the lowest revenue have the highest profit (install and maintenance) while the lowest revenue for a product type (accessories) has the lowest profit and appears the furthest to the right.

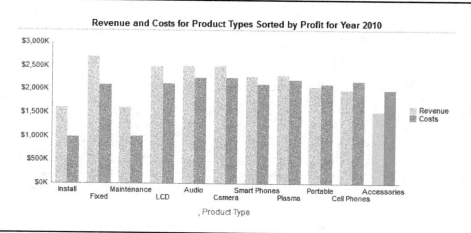

FIGURE 3-11. *A bar graph sorted by a value better reveals patterns in the data.*

This graph relates the relationship of the bar groups and their relative position from left to right, but sacrifices some of the ease of lookup for the individual product groups because a user would now have to "hunt" for a specific product type. Figure 3-12 adds a third measure revealed as a dark blue bar on the graph that directly shows the difference between revenue and cost as profit. This additional metric adds information and makes the profit amount more explicit, but that information necessarily detracts a bit from the core message of the first two bars. The dark blue color of the Profit bar is heavier visually than the light green and light orange of the Revenue and Costs bars and draws the eye, even though the bars are significantly shorter in height. We could reverse this effect and diminish

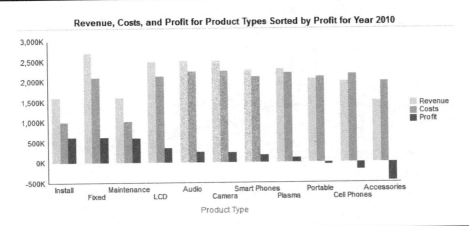

FIGURE 3-12. *Dark colors draw the eye and create emphasis.*

the impact of the Profit bars by choosing darker, heavier colors for Revenue and Costs and a lighter color for Profit. None of these three graphs is "right" or "wrong" or even necessarily better than another. Additionally, the more "dense" a graph is (that is, the more information it contains), the more care that must be taken in making choices reflecting its intended primary purpose. Note also that all grid lines have been eliminated from the bar charts. Detailed information regarding individual bars is best revealed in mouse rollover data markers, which are configured in the Graph Properties interface on the Titles and Labels tab.

Horizontal bar graphs are an alternative to vertical bar graphs that work particularly well in certain situations. Long data labels are the main reason to prefer horizontal bar graphs. Figure 3-13 shows our graph in a horizontal bar graph format. Notice even with a fairly square aspect ratio, the length of the lines seems to be longer in the horizontal format and that the right edge of the bars reads as a distinct pattern. It is a bit harder to visually perceive the individual bar differences reading up and down the rows than it is scanning across a series of vertical bars. Horizontal bars are fine for emphasizing end points and relative values on a single scale (there is often little difference between horizontal and vertical bar graphs for single value dependent variables); however, for grouped bars, as in our example, there typically is a preference for vertical unless there is a need for longer data labels.

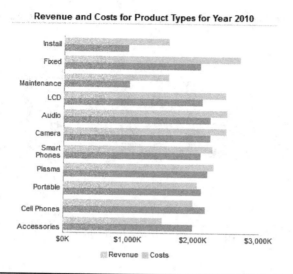

FIGURE 3-13. *Horizontal bar graph*

Both horizontal and vertical stacked bar graphs group data within a single bar to reveal an additional dimension of comparison. Stacked bar graphs look nice at first glance, and they are often used on dashboards, but differences between the relative heights of different pieces of bars are difficult to perceive without a great deal of care and study on the part of the user. Stacked bar graphs show the relative heights of the totals for each bar well. Figure 3-14 shows the contributions of three different brands to total revenue by fiscal quarter. It is fairly easy to scan the top of the bar charts and see the relative total sales figures for each fiscal quarter. The size of the pieces makes the most visual sense within a single bar. That is, we can see the contribution of each brand within each fiscal quarter. Stacked bar graphs may be used if the key insight of the visualization is the total, not the change in the size of the pieces between bars. In that case, either change should be graphed as a measure or another visualization should be chosen. In our example of evaluating brands across time, a line graph could indicate whether sales for a particular brand had increased or decreased between periods. Likewise, a grouped bar graph could show the relative size of the bars of the different brands for different fiscal quarters.

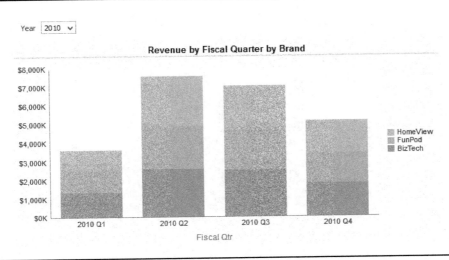

FIGURE 3-14. *Stacked bar graph with graph prompt selector*

Notice that our stacked bar graph visualization in Figure 3-14 also has a drop-down box labeled Year. This allows users to select each year individually and to focus on comparison between quarters for a given year. The presentation of 12 quarters side by side (all three years of 2010, 2011, and 2012) would emphasize progression and change over time. More data does not always mean more insight; it just changes the focus and primary message of the visualization. This can also be shown as a slider prompt that "plays" the changes between the years as the selection progresses (somewhat similar to a simple animation in Microsoft PowerPoint). These slider prompt animations work well when the data is relatively consistent for each selection and doesn't vary significantly in scale or member inclusion. The Graph Properties dialog (shown in Figure 3-15) allows axis limits to be set to specific range, to be dynamic (adjusts based on the data), or to "zoom to a data range," in which the system determines an appropriate zoom level given the range of data values included and their relative differences. If the Zoom to Data Range option is selected, visual indicators should be included in the design of the graph (such as different borders or backgrounds) and a narrative view should be included calling attention to the data range difference. In most cases, it is best to begin the data range scale at

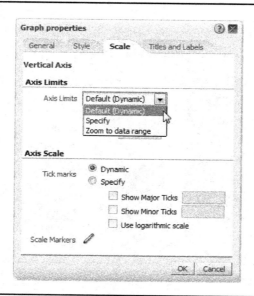

FIGURE 3-15. *Setting Axis Limits to Dynamic or Fixed*

zero. The "zoom" enhances differences in the results visually, which should not be done without notification to users. Scale markers can be included as a visual reference point for many OBIEE graphs that are dynamically scaled. This provides a reference point for users and promotes a stronger understanding of dynamically scaled results.

It is also possible to section the three years and to place them into three separate blocks, as seen in Figure 3-16.

This repetition is often quite effective both in enabling users to see graphs as total patterns and to perceive differences between certain sets of data (like years) and in emphasizing important data sets through multiple visual presentations. Selection prompts emphasize individual cases, slider prompts emphasize change between adjacent cases, and sections emphasize overall patterns and differences between cases.

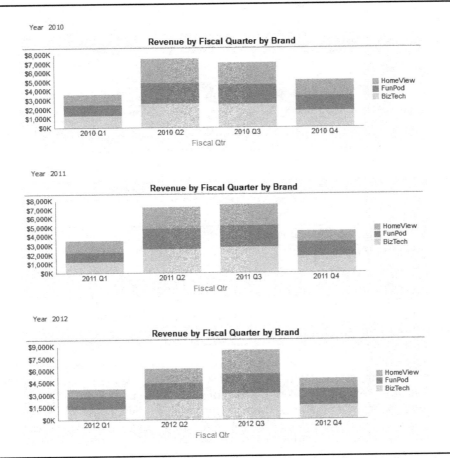

FIGURE 3-16. *Creating multiple graphs by using sections*

TIP
*You can change the color of a section of a stacked bar
graph to the same color as the graph background to
create an apparent separation between different data
groups. For example, the middle values are changed
to white to emphasize the distribution of the data
for the Top and Bottom values in the graph shown in
Figure 3-17. Light gray vertical grid lines were added
to help the eye focus up and down on the differences
between the top and bottom data distributions for
each period and not to scan horizontally across the
green and red elements themselves.*

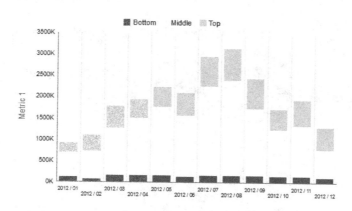

FIGURE 3-17. *The middle bar does not show up.*

100% stacked bar graphs show the distribution of a range of values on a normalized bar of standard height. In this way, it is much like a pie chart. It is best thought as showing the proportion of a single piece to the whole. Also like pie charts, this seemingly straightforward visualization can be deceivingly difficult for users to interpret on a consistent basis. People are best able to compare the relative lengths of the top and the bottom piece because they have a common edge and thus the eye can scan the length difference. Middle pieces are much harder to compare because they often will not have a consistent top and bottom edge. Whereas the proportion of the three brands (HomeView, FunPod, and BizTech) are shown by fiscal quarter in Figure 3-18, 100% stacked bar graphs with more than three pieces can be difficult to interpret unless there is an obvious interpretation—either that there is no discernable pattern or that one piece dominates the others. Sort order is easier to manipulate in stacked bar graph and 100% stacked bar graph views than in pie chart views. The lowest value appears on the top (in other words, if we sorted Brand by Sort Descending in the Criteria tab, the order of the brands in Figure 3-18 would be reversed and the sort order would be BizTech on top, FunPod in the middle, and HomeView on the bottom of the stack). Generally, more direct visualizations such as grouped bar charts are preferred over 100% stacked bar charts.

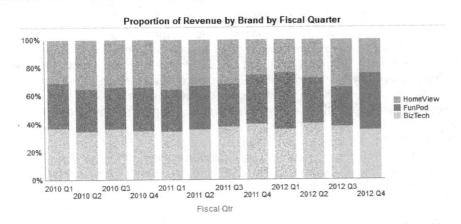

FIGURE 3-18. *100% stacked bar graph*

Line-Bar Combo Graphs

The line-bar combo graph has some natural advantages, but must be used carefully. It works like a normal bar chart with a measure on the left vertical axis, but adds a second measure that is displayed as either a line or a symbol on the right vertical axis. Figure 3-19 shows a histogram-style distribution of revenue and average number of orders by customer age in a line-bar combo graph. Because customer

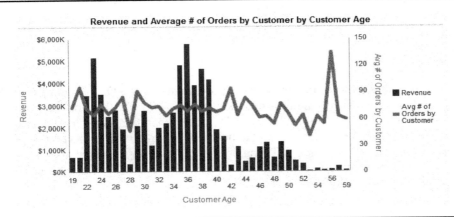

FIGURE 3-19. *Line-bar combo graph*

age is a "binned" continuous dimension, it is not objectionable to use a line for the second vertical axis. This visualization allows users to understand the relationship between two measures for a common dimension along the horizontal x-axis. We see that as the customer age increases beyond 40 years, revenue decreases, but that the highest average number of orders occurs at age 56. (We don't really know from this view if this is a result of a high average or an anomalous occurrence in the data that is skewing the average, but it is interesting and worthy of investigation.) We can tell immediately, however, that the average number of orders per customer does not vary negatively with age, as does revenue.

When the horizontal x-axis is not a continuous range, but rather contains nominal or discrete values, you should select a graphic element for the second vertical y-axis measure. In Figure 3-20, the line is replaced with round circles representing discrete data points.

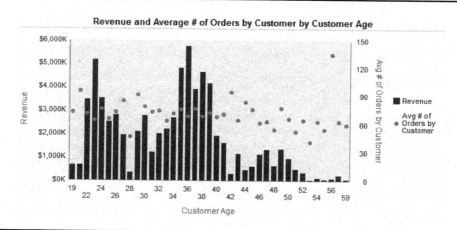

FIGURE 3-20. *Use graphic elements and not lines for noncontinuous x-axes*

To do this, you use the Graph Properties dialog. In the Graph Data section, select the Style and Conditional Formatting icon. Then set Line Width to 0px and select a symbol type and color, as shown in Figure 3-21. Notice that there is a very different visual impact for the graphic rather than the line. This is particularly important when the x-axis values are not continuous. Using lines implies that values exist at every point along the x-axis, including those between axis labels, and thus should be avoided when discrete values are being graphed.

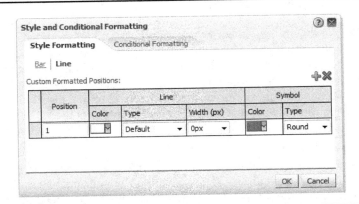

FIGURE 3-21. *How to change a line to a symbol in the line-bar combo graph*

The bar and line-bar combo graphs can also be used to create a traditional histogram series, as shown in Figure 3-22. In this case, we are viewing revenue for the different lines of business. The lines of business are broken down into age "buckets" of three to seven years with the firm. Notice the color distribution for the ages is along a continuous range from light to dark, indicating increased age. A slight background fill color for the plot area ensures that all five values stand out. To

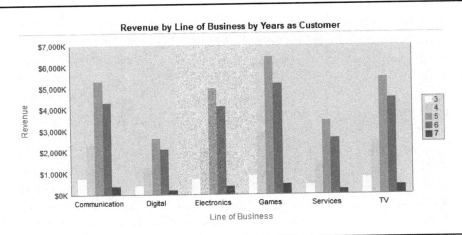

FIGURE 3-22. *Histogram example with contrasting background for sequential colors*

create this visualization, we add the Years as Customer column to the Vary Color by (Horizontal Axis) field in the Line-Bar Graph layout pane and then add custom colors in the Style and Conditional Formatting interface for the bar (similar to what we did for the line in the previous example). We leave the Lines (Vertical Axis 2) field empty and use a single measure, Revenue. It is also possible to create stacked line-bar combo graphs, where additional dimensions of data can be added. As stated before, the more complex graphics get, the more care that must be used in designing them, and the more time it takes for users to interpret them.

Waterfall Graphs

Waterfall graphs are special type of bar chart. Waterfall graphs show the relative positive and negative contribution for series of values on a cumulative basis. This shows the cumulative total contribution by changing where you start drawing each bar at each point along the horizontal x-axis. The larger the size of the bar, the greater the contribution is (either positively or negatively) to the total. Waterfall graphs are particularly good at visualizing "flow" measures over a period of time, such as profit/loss, cash flow, inventory flow, head count, and so on. Figure 3-23 shows gross profit contribution (an operating measure of profitability) for the year 2011 by month. A scale marker has been added at the $0 breakeven level to demonstrate for each month whether the company was below or above breakeven at the beginning and end of the period. A Total bar (shown at the far right in dark blue) is used to sum the cumulative impact for all months of the year. Showing this

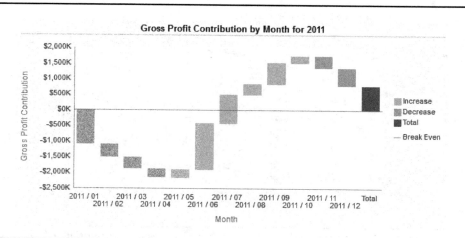

FIGURE 3-23. *Waterfall graph*

Total bar is optional. In some cases, the pattern will be clearer without the summation bar added at the end (the ending value can be seen by viewing the bottom of a negative bar or the top of a positive bar). Additionally, conditional formatting can be added for bars to create a multiscaled color range for increasing and decreasing values. When conditional formatting is used, a separate legend view should be added as well.

Pie Graphs

Pie charts are intended to show the relationship of a piece to the whole—that is, the size of an individual "piece of pie" to an entire circle. The pie chart is one of the most common and popular data visualizations. The only problem is that there are several challenges with pie charts from a human cognition and practical user perspective:

- The human visual perception system is notoriously bad at consistently perceiving both angles and size relationships.

- Pie charts typically require extensive legends and explanatory labels (which take up space and require cognitive processing).

- Pie charts are not particularly efficient with space utilization and often take up a significant amount of screen real estate in return for modest insights.

- Three-dimensional pie charts are notorious for distorting and misrepresenting data (they require that pieces in the "front of the pie" have more visual prominence than pieces in the back, thus distorting the underlying data).

In short, there are plenty of reasons to avoid using pie charts. However, the one major reason to use them is that everyone else does. If we return to our theorem that "every graph should have a main point," we can begin to understand the situations where a pie graph can be effectively used.

CAUTION
Avoid 3-D effects for all graphs, especially pie graphs, bar graphs, and line graphs. Adding the appearance of dimensional depth actually distorts the graphic representation of the data elements and can lead to misinterpretation and inconsistent interpretation between individuals. In other words, it does harm and offers no good in terms of additional insight or clarity.

Pie charts should be used when users are interested in comparing the size of various pieces to the total, not when users are mostly interested in comparing the relative size of various pieces to one another; when comparisons are most important, use bar charts so the relative height/length of different bars can be accurately and consistently judged at glance. When there are clear differences in the size of a small number of dimension values (pieces of pie), then a pie chart might be okay. When there is a large number of dimension values and the point of the graph is that no one piece is significant in size in comparison to the whole, then a pie chart can convey this insight (in this case, there is no need to clutter the chart with superfluous detail and callouts, just show the pie).

Figure 3-24 shows a series of three typical pie graphs representing the share of each brand to total revenue for 2010–2012.

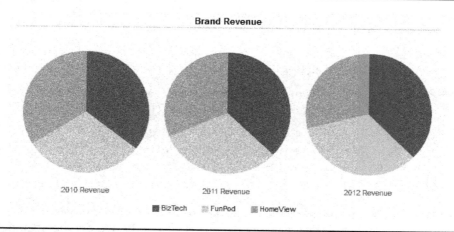

Brand Revenue

2010 Revenue   2011 Revenue   2012 Revenue

■ BizTech   ■ FunPod   ■ HomeView

FIGURE 3-24.   *Pie graphs show the relationship of the piece to the whole.*

The overall message that these pie graphs convey is that that revenue was split fairly evenly between the brands for the three years. It is very difficult for the viewer to perceive a difference between the pieces of pie for each brand or between the different pies for each year. Notice how much more easily bar graphs (clustered by year and by brand) show the differences between years and brands in Figure 3-25.

Bear in mind that in some limited circumstances, pie charts can effectively show a change in the share of a value. Just be sure to keep the number of pie slices down

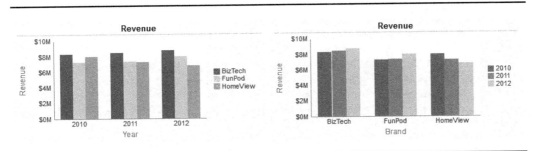

FIGURE 3-25. *Bar graphs often reveal differences better than pie graphs.*

to a reasonable number (consider grouping lower percentages into an "other" pie slice) and ensure that the data shows a difference. Again, sort order can make a big difference here. In Figure 3-26, we can see how the Maxifun 2000 product jumped from 5 percent to 11 percent in one year. In this case, because we want only the top five products shown, on the Criteria tab we can edit the column formula to bin all other products into an "Other" pie slice. The slices are ordered with the first slice occurring at the top of the pie (12 o'clock position) and subsequent pieces in the established sort order for the column appearing in a clockwise position.

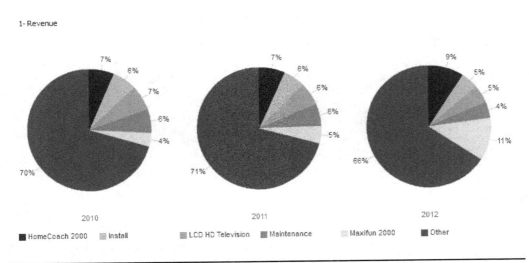

FIGURE 3-26. *Series of pies showing differences with all other*

Area Graphs

Area graphs combine many of the attributes of line graphs, pie charts, and stacked bar graphs. They are good for representing the value of a measure over a continuous dimension such as time. Area graphs are more visually dominant than line graphs (they typically have much higher color density). When areas for multiple dimension values are stacked on top of one another, comprehending differences in the areas become problematic, in the same ways that stacked bar graphs become problematic. When the eye is required to scan and perceive the relative distance difference between values and does not have a common base line, interpretation and understanding is compromised and is inconsistent among individuals. Figure 3-27 shows brand revenue for the fiscal quarters for the years 2010–2012 using the same measures and dimensions as shown in the line chart section in Figures 3-4, 3-5, and 3-6. As with stacked bar graphs, the easiest value to understand from area charts is the total of the three brands. The thickness of each area at any given Fiscal Quarter value on the x-axis is representative of the revenue for that brand. In other words, it is necessary to compare the thickness of each band to the others to understand which value is greatest (as you can see from the line chart in Figure 3-4, the rank order of the brands is different for the various fiscal quarters). The order of the stacking, the color choices, and the granularity of the x-axis dimension all play key roles in the interpretation of area graphs.

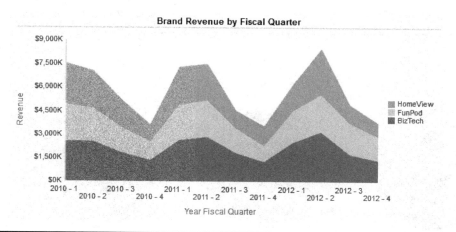

FIGURE 3-27.   *Stacked area graph*

A 100% area graph is similar to a 100% stacked bar graph. A 100% stacked bar graph can be used instead of a pie chart to represent the relative percentage contribution of a dimension value in comparison with a total, only over a continuous dimension such as Fiscal Quarter rather than discrete dimension values (see Figure 3-28). Once again, it is necessary for users to read the thickness of the band at a given value rather than the value of the band against the y-axis. In general, area graphs and 100% stacked area graphs are subject to misinterpretation by occasional business intelligence system users and executives and therefore should be implemented with caution. They are best employed for single- and double-valued measures and not for three values or more (the bottommost value is relatively easy to read). If the relative change for dimensional values over a continuous range in comparison with other dimension values is the objective of the visualization, it may be better to graph the relative change as its own measure (such as percent change in revenue from previous quarter) rather than asking users to interpret what can be a confusing chart.

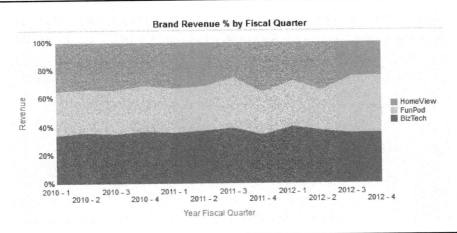

FIGURE 3-28. *100% stacked area graph*

Scatter Plot Graphs

Scatter plot graphs are a favorite graph type for data scientists and data visualization experts all over the world. Scatter plots have several advantages:

■ They reveal correlation patterns that can be hidden from calculated measures.

■ They can display hundreds if not thousands of individual data points.

■ They are extremely good at revealing outliers.

■ They require little training for users.

■ Interpretation tends to be consistent across diverse user groups.

Like all graph types, scatter plots require the graph designer to determine in advance what dimensions or measures to put on which axis. Two measures are required: one on the x-axis and the other on the y-axis. Typically, the dependent variable (the variable that responds) is put on the vertical y-axis and the independent variable (the variable that is responded to) is put on the horizontal x-axis. In Figure 3-29, we see a typical scatter plot graph showing the correlation of customer discount rate and total customer revenue for the years of 2010–2012. A slider prompt for the year enables us to "play" the scatter graph for each year, seeing how the points change. These types of simple "animations" are very compelling when played to a large audience and work well when presenting "stories about data."

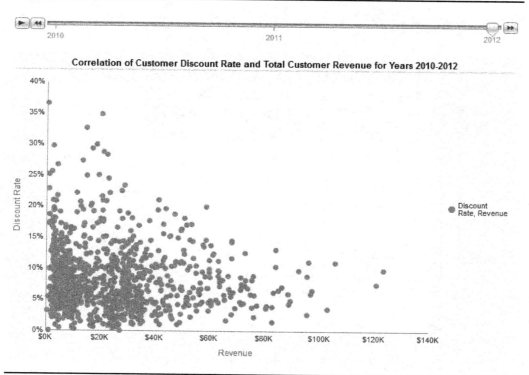

FIGURE 3-29. *Scatter plot graphs show correlations for many data elements.*

Although we might expect to see a distribution that generally is positively sloped, with larger customers receiving higher discounts, instead we see the opposite pattern: a more negatively sloped distribution, with some small customers receiving large discounts and some very large customers receiving relatively low discounts. Surprising! We can add dimensions to the analysis with a combination of color and shape choices to get a better understanding of the correlation. In Figure 3-30, customer type is added to the analysis and a variable marker is added to our scatter plot. Again, we are surprised to find an unexpected pattern that becomes immediately visible: nonmembers received the highest discounts, and referrals and platinum members are overrepresented in the customers with the largest revenue and lowest discounts. Data markers and data ranges can be easily added to scatter plots as well for further contextualization of the data results in a fashion similar to what was done in the line graph in Figure 3-7. Scatter plots are a very common visualization for data discovery, both because they can handle large numbers of data points and because they reveal patterns that may not otherwise be easy to find.

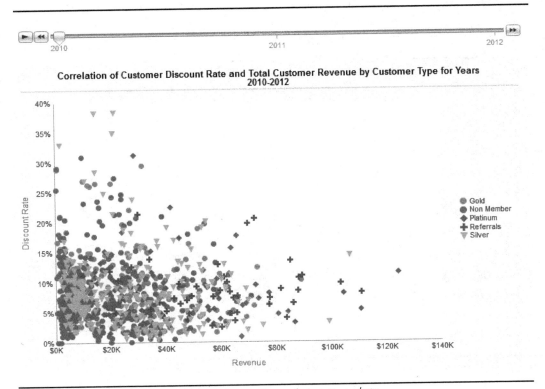

FIGURE 3-30. *Colors reveal grouping patterns in scatter plots.*

Bubble Graphs

Bubble graphs are a special type of scatter plot graph where a third measure is added to the visualization that is reflected by the size of the bubble. Because large bubbles take up more space than points, bubble graphs are more limited in the discrete number of points they can show in comparison with normal scatter plot graphs. In the example shown in Figure 3-31, Fixed Costs is added as a measure to our analysis. The size of each bubble is related to the amount of fixed costs allocated to that particular customer. Whereas variable costs would be nearly a linear function of revenue, the allocation of fixed costs could be quite different from customer to customer, depending on the allocation methodology. Adding this measure to the analysis can provide insight into the relationship between discount rate (an active pricing decision on the part of the business) and revenue (the size of the customer in terms of purchases) with the allocation of fixed costs (a decision on the part of the accounting/cost system) of the business. Thus, we get insight from a pricing strategy perspective as well as from a utilization of fixed costs perspective. In effect, the size of the bubbles indicates how much in fixed costs each customer type is costing the firm. Also, the two graph prompts allow users to make different selections of new dimensions. This promotes greater exploration of the data and also

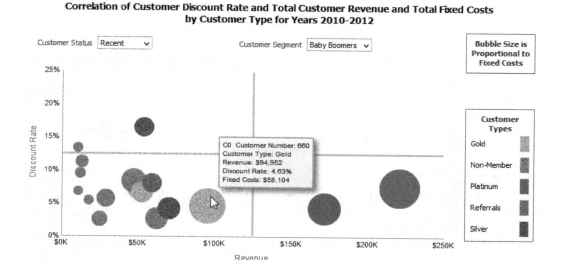

FIGURE 3-31. *Bubble graphs handle more dimensions of data.*

limits the number of customers shown on the bubble graph at any one time, resulting in an enormously rich data exploration interface.

We can see that customer number 660 (directly above $100,000 on the x-axis) has a relatively large Fixed Cost bubble size associate with it, particularly in comparison with the Platinum customer to the right. This allows us to further explore the data and discover new insights and patterns for further analysis in more precise interfaces such as pivot tables or for the development of new calculated measures. Although bubble graphs require additional time on the part of users, they can be an excellent tool for data analysts who invest significant time in data-discovery efforts.

Radar Graphs

A radar graph is a special type of graph in which measures are presented on a radial axis rather than a horizontal or vertical axis. You can think of a radar graph as being similar to a radial bar chart. It takes some practice getting used to reading the patterns in radar graphs, so they should generally be used more for analyst audiences who spend significant time with the featured data sets rather than with general business intelligence audiences. Radar graphs can form striking patterns in which strong separations and spikes have meaning. They are also often used for "indexed" measures of different origins, such as Key Performance Indicator (KPI) indexes, similar to the measures shown in Figure 3-32. In this example, average revenue per full-time equivalent employee, profit ratio, and average order process

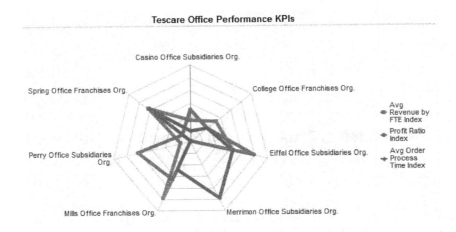

FIGURE 3-32.   *Radar graph*

time are all normalized to a common index and broken down by office to show which offices are performing particularly well or poorly versus other offices. From the radar graph, we can quickly see that the Eiffel office and the Mills office are the best performing offices on the three KPI indexes (most number of nodes on the outside), whereas the Casino and College offices are the worst performing offices (nodes closest to the center).

Pareto Graphs

A Pareto graph is a special type of bar chart that adds a cumulative line so that at any total cumulative percentage, the contributing members can be seen at a glance. An example is shown in Figure 3-33. Pareto graphs have the nice feature that the members on the horizontal axis are automatically placed in descending order from left to right. Conditional formatting can be used to highlight particular members so that they stand out from the others, and scale markers and ranges can be added to the left y-axis the same way they can be added for other bar graphs. Like radar graphs, Pareto graphs require some practice and familiarity in order to be effective. They should be reserved for use with more experienced data analysts and should not be featured on dashboards for general business intelligence audiences. Pareto graphs are commonly used to indicate a cumulative lift effect, such as the cumulative effect of sales as a result of a promotion of a product over a period of time.

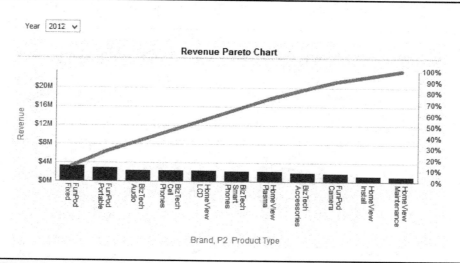

FIGURE 3-33. *A Pareto graph shows the accumulation of a metric.*

Summary

Graph design requires not only a tremendous amount of attention to detail, but also a finely tuned sensibility of the relative importance of making further modifications and edits. The "value equation" is often stated as Value = Benefits/Cost. To have a higher value, you can either increase the benefits or decrease the cost. Clearly in the case of designing graphs, the benefits include the accurate representation of data, the clarity of a major insight, and the consistency of interpretation among different users and groups. The costs are just the time that is put into editing and refining each graph. Always try to ask yourself the following questions:

- How important is the data in this graph and the decisions that are being based on it?

- How much time should I invest in editing and refining this graph?

- Is the story of the data as clear as it can be? Have all unnecessary graphic elements been eliminated?

- What style of graph is most appropriate for this data and for this key insight?

- What is the range of data that is likely to be represented on this graph?

- Is the data source understood? Is the data selection transparent (any filters or selections that are hidden from users)?

- Does the graph reflect the visual style guide reference standards for the organization?

- How much screen space does the graph require?

- Is the amount of screen space consistent with the importance of the information shown on the graph?

- Is the data properly formatted?

- Are the axes of the graph properly labeled?

- Does the scale of the data make sense for the graph?

- Do the color selections for graph objects follow best practices and are the color selections appropriate for the data they represent?

- Does the graph have a unique title that clearly explains the key point of the graph?

- Is any narrative text required to help users understand, interact with, and utilize the graph?

- Is there a clear and comprehensive legend that helps the graph be accurately interpreted and understood by all users?

Seven Steps to Better Graphs

1. Do not use 3-D effects.
2. Avoid the "stop light" color palette.
3. Prefer pastel color palettes and avoid bright colors.
4. Eliminate gridlines, drop shadows, and other graphics effects.
5. Enable interaction for "exploration" graphs.
6. Prioritize a single message for "explanation" graphs.
7. Above all else, show the data (advice from Edward Tufte).

CHAPTER
4

Maps

Maps communicate data faster and more intuitively than any other data visualization method. Most BI data sets already contain a geographic dimension such as store addresses, sales districts, or regions. Any time you have location information about where something exists or happens, you have a geographic dimension to your data and should at least strongly consider viewing that data on a map. Map views are a native view type in OBI 11*g*; once the initial configuration work involved in making them available is completed, users can create maps and show BI data on them without doing any coding work at all. This makes maps much easier to define than they used to be and a huge value addition when included in your dashboards.

Justification for Maps and When to Use Them

As stated in Chapter 1, because human beings evolved in landscape environments, knowing where things were located was a fundamental key to survival. Our ability to reason spatially and understand our world is guided by our understanding of location. A popular memory trick is to associate items with a particular location in a well-known place and thus have them instantly available for recollection. (More than 90 percent of the competitors in the World Memory Championships use a technique called "The Memory Palace" in which location associations are used. This mnemonic technique goes back more than 2,000 years to the ancient Greeks and Romans and is documented in various rhetoric sources.) We humans are better at visualizing, understanding, and remembering places than virtually any other kind of information, particularly numbers, names, and abstract descriptions (exactly the information that is included in most business intelligence systems).

Maps are also extremely effective because they have high information density. Figure 4-1 shows a typical business intelligence map view for a dashboard. This map shows revenue for European cities, and varies both the size and the intensity of the color of the circles marking the cities' locations. Big, dark circles show where revenue is highest; small, light circles show where revenue is lowest. Because this information is revealed on a map, we can instantly perceive the distance between the various cities and the relationships that exist between them. For each city's location, we get a distance relationship to all other cities shown on the map, both individually and collectively. Thus, we are literally shown thousands of relationships in one visualization with only a single data measure (the arrows represent these relationships). A table view would not only have to list all the cities and their revenue totals, but also all the distance relationships in kilometers or miles. The precision of these relationships is not nearly as important as their general pattern. All maps share the feature of allowing denser visualizations of data compared with other types of views.

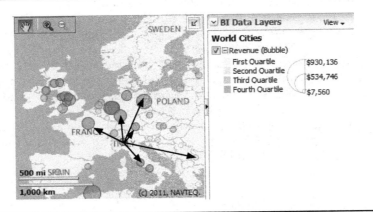

FIGURE 4-1. *A typical map view*

Maps are intuitively understood by the vast majority of the population and require little explanation of how to understand them. The concepts of distance and location are universal and fundamental to the human condition. As Waldo Tobler of the spatial academic community stated in his First Law of Geography, "Everything is related to everything else, but near things are more related than distant things." Compare maps to other visualization techniques and some of the graph types that serve as alternatives. Although views such as radar charts, waterfall graphs, and Pareto graphs might be able to convey data to experienced analysts who know how to read them, they are not fundamentally intuitive and should not be preferred on standard organizational dashboards. Much of this chapter will address how to utilize maps and build on their intuitive nature. Designers have a responsibility to reinforce this intuitive representation of data in maps precisely because most people will intuitively understand maps. The first responsibility for designers of BI dashboards and reports is to not misrepresent data (that is, to represent data as accurately as possible).

Maps' intuitive nature makes them easy to implement across disparate user groups in terms of language, function, level of organization responsibility, location, experience/age/generation, and more. Everyone recognizes a map outline of the United States or Europe, and when they don't recognize the geographical features of a particular map view, they know immediately that this is information about a place that they don't recognize.

Maps are visual representations of physical space and locations. The decision of what to show and what not to show in various map views in terms of geographical features, physical features, and place names should be taken into consideration. Maps made for hikers have contour lines showing elevation. Why? Because hikers want to know how steep or flat a particular location is and how the elevation varies. These lines, however, would likely add little value to a view of business information and should be omitted from background maps for BI systems. Although this may seem obvious relating to elevation, there are many other landscape features and names that can help users identify locations and add important "contextual" data that may help users understand the spatial pattern that exists. For example, large interstates and highways often serve as "attractors" for populations and businesses today, much as rivers did over the course of history. In fact, these large highway networks are likely more important than rivers in terms of their direct impact on business dynamics. Regardless, the decision of what to include or omit from background maps should be a conscious design choice. Include only those features and names that assist or add to the interpretation of the business data and are necessary for location recognition. Most BI background maps should be far simpler and less cluttered than other typical maps such as roadmaps.

Many patterns that are easy to perceive when rendered on a map are difficult to perceive with other types of visualizations. Most users are experienced in interacting with maps and intuitively understand how to pan, zoom, and drill.

TIP
In short, any time business intelligence information includes data elements that have a physical location, map views should not only be considered, but quite often should be preferred.

Maps, Layers, and Spatial Basics

Traditionally, maps were created by drawing basic outlines and features and then adding salient information on top of them. Base maps were created and traced over to create new maps. As transparencies became available, base maps were used with various layers of transparencies on top them. The order of the transparencies was important, as was the density of their content. It is often very useful to think of maps as being organized in literal layers of transparencies. Although we will not delve into all the technical detail of configuring maps in Oracle systems (a subject worthy of its own book), we will refer to the process of creating and thinking through map presentations of business data in OBIEE. As we will discuss later in this chapter, MapViewer, the component of Oracle Fusion Middleware that renders maps, organizes layers using "themes." These various layers are combined with additional layers of Oracle BI data (such as the points on the map in Figure 4-1) when rendering the final map view.

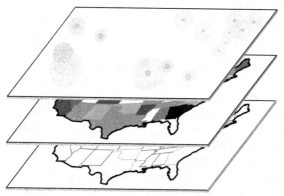

Here are the three major types of geospatial information in Oracle systems (refer to the Oracle documentation for information on the SDO_GEOMETRY object type):

- **Point**   A specific geospatial location that can be expressed as having a unique longitude and latitude (coordinates)

- **Line string**   The connection of two or more points in a linear, sequential order

- **Polygon**   An enclosed space that is defined by line segments

A point is a unique location on a map like an address. It has coordinates and can be described with two unique numbers: its latitude and longitude. Think of a house's address as being an example of a unique location or a point. Events or a series of events can be associated with this particular location (for example, purchases or purchases over a period of time).

A line string is the path between two or more points. Think of an airplane's route as being an example of a line segment. There is a departure airport and an arrival airport. The line encompasses both and can be visualized as the path between the two points. Again, an event or a series of events as expressed in measures can be associated with this line, such as total passenger miles (the number of passengers in the airplane multiplied by the distance).

A polygon is a defined geographical region where events occur. For example, a country or state is a legally defined region with specific boundary lines. Locations are either within the set boundaries or outside of them. Regions can also be defined independently by businesses or organizations such as sales territories, DMAs (Nielsen's Designated Market Areas in the United States), or Functional Urban Areas (European Union's OECD's definition). For example, the DMA for Kansas City includes about 2.34 million people who live in a total of 15 different counties across two different states (Missouri and Kansas). It is not unusual for sales territories to be constructed by logical definitions of what makes business sense in terms of travel and business patterns rather than by higher-order governmental defined regions such as states. Figure 4-2 shows three custom-defined regions of the world: Americas, EMEA (Europe, Middle East, Africa), and APAC (Asia-Pacific). The specific location addresses for all customers, business locations, suppliers, and other entities would be located in one of these regions. That is, a specific address is located in only one region or "polygon." This is typically determined by the longitude and latitude of the address.

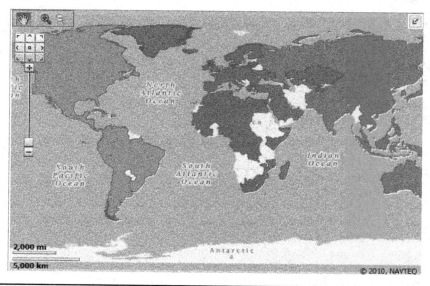

FIGURE 4-2. *Custom geographical regions*

Geocoding

Geocoding is the process of finding geographic coordinates for specific locations and areas. These are most typically defined in longitude and latitude. For example, you may know that a customer is at 1111 Main Street, Kansas City, Missouri, but in order to plot this on a map, that address has to be translated to the coordinates (-94.583239, 39.100747).

Longitude is the angular distance (measured in degrees) east or west from the prime meridian. *Latitude* is the angular distance (measured in degrees) north or south from the equator. If you have trouble remembering which is which, just remember that longitudes are just as "long" as each other (the distance from the North Pole to the South Pole is always the same). The order is important (obviously, switching around the numbers for a given longitude and latitude location would define a different, unique location), so remember that usually longitude comes before latitude in Oracle. You need to have geocoded data to use map views in OBIEE. The Oracle Spatial and Graph option for the Enterprise Edition of the Oracle Database manages geocoding. Also, many geocoding services are available that will append your addresses with longitude and latitude fields. Check with your OBI administrator for more on geocoding.

TIP
Be careful when specifying coordinates as pairs of numbers. Oracle uses them often in the order of (longitude, latitude), whereas other services often express these as (latitude, longitude).

MapViewer Basics

MapViewer is a component of Oracle Fusion Middleware and is included with every installation of OBIEE. MapViewer runs in WebLogic and other J2EE environments and manages the creation and rendering of maps in OBIEE. There are four types of metadata in MapViewer:

- **Styles** define the basic graphical attributes applied when MapViewer renders a geometry shape or point. The six main types of styles are COLOR, MARKER, LINE, AREA, TEXT, and ADVANCED. Just as you can define different fonts, effects such as bold and italic, and sizes, MapViewer styles define how to label and treat the various visual components and features of maps. These define attributes such as the weight or thickness of boundary lines and the color fill definitions of lakes and oceans.

- **Themes** specify logical organizations of data. Think of a theme as a layer or a transparency containing related geospatial information. For example, you might have a roadway layer that details what color styles, line styles, and such are used for different highways and interstates. These themes function in a similar way to layers in the Oracle BI map views.

- **Base maps** serve as a backdrop and are made up of an ordered collection of themes and map tile layers. Themes on a base map are typically associated with specific minimum and maximum scales in the tile layers. These scales are used at different zoom levels. For example, it might make sense to show interstates on a national map of the United States, but not on a global view of the entire world. The entire base map defines which background themes and elements are shown at different zoom levels.

- **Tile layers** provide the metadata regarding zoom levels, geographical coordinate system, and so on, for base maps.

MapViewer and OBIEE

OBIEE needs two sets of information. It needs base maps and it needs business data that is related to locations. MapViewer manages the "mashup" that joins the two. Base map information is either stored inside a database or is delivered to MapViewer via a web API call. The native data set for OBIEE is HERE (formerly known as NAVTEQ) data. All OBIEE implementations come with a set of tables from HERE that define fundamental information such as national boundaries. Additional data sets are available from HERE or other suppliers on a licensing basis. (Licensing is required for many map tile web services. Check with your OBI administrator.)

It's possible to configure OBIEE map views to use more than one base map for a single analysis. Base maps are the context in which business data is shown. Think of it this way: Perhaps you want to have users select between two different base maps—one that includes highway information but is more cluttered and one that does not include highway information and is more "clean." There is not one "right" way to view the data; rather, different insights are delivered and emphasized through the different views.

MapViewer Administration

Some administration and configuration work needs to happen in OBIEE in order for map views to work. Although we won't cover all the work that needs to occur, we will review conceptually what is happening in the front end of OBIEE. The Administration – Manage Map Data interface has three different tabs: Layers, Background Maps, and Images (see Figure 4-3).

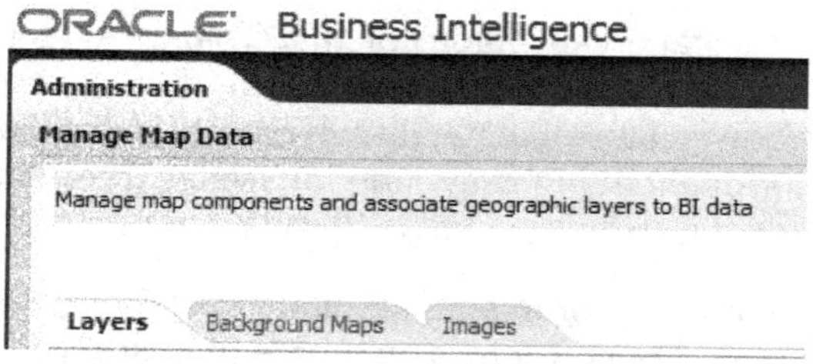

FIGURE 4-3. *The Manage Map Data administrative tabs*

In the Layers tab, keys are defined that join map layers with BI columns so that the rendering engine is able to place BI geospatial information on top of the base map information. Think of it like pegs for base maps and transparencies that make sure that all the lines are in sync. Both the base maps and the transparencies have their own point, line, and polygon definitions, but they have to be joined together in order for them to be able to be displayed together. When you add a new layer, you point to the source data and the BI column data (can be multiple columns) in a join interface. Ask your administrator for a list of BI columns that are joined with map data if you're uncertain which columns you can use in analyses and queries with map views.

The Background Maps tab defines the background maps that are available to the system and which interactive BI layers and feature layers are displayed at different zoom levels. Again, the ordering of the layers (just as the ordering of transparencies) is important in terms of which layers are "below" and which are "above" at different zoom levels.

The Images tab lists all the POI (point of interest) graphics available. If you want to add a company logo or other custom graphic so that you can display it as a marker of your organization's locations, this is where you would bring it into the system for display on map views.

Using Maps with OBIEE

Let's go back to the three fundamental kinds of geospatial information that can be shown on a map—points, lines, and polygons—and start evaluating different approaches to business intelligence visualizations using maps.

Creating Choropleth Maps

Polygons that are colored according to some measure or value are called "choropleth" thematic maps and are one of the most common types of map views. Figure 4-4 shows a simple map of the continental states of the United States of America, color-filled by their revenue in deciles (that is, 10 even "buckets"). Note that the arrow in the upper-right corner expands and collapses the legend for the map (see Figure 4-5).

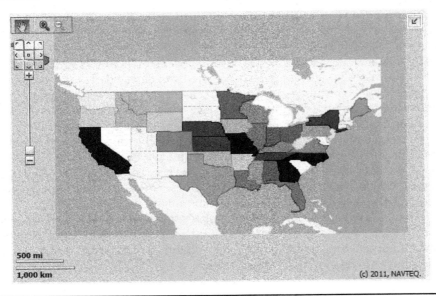

FIGURE 4-4. *A simple choropleth map of the United States*

FIGURE 4-5.   *Expandable and collapsible map legend*

In most dashboard implementations, we would write a comprehensive title for the map, include information about filters and data selections, show or explain how to view the map's legend, and add any other pertinent information regarding interactivity with the map. To create a choropleth, add a Color Fill BI Data Layer to your map. The color fill is set to percentile binning for the map view in Figure 4-5. This is a good strategy for creating "heat map"–style views where a similar proportion of each color is used on the map. In these situations, the visual emphasis is placed on the relative value of a given area compared to other areas.

Whereas percentile binning emphasizes comparative values, value binning emphasizes absolute value ranges (these values can be interactively set by users by clicking the Allow Dashboard Users to Edit Thresholds box in the Add/Edit Map Format interface). OBIEE will automatically construct an evenly divided scale based on the actual data range values, but these can be edited manually as well. In Figure 4-6. the values for the first three cells have been changed to 0 and 200,000 and 400,000, with the resulting map shown in Figure 4-7. You would normally continue changing the values to a more even and easily understood range (incrementing by 200,000). Typically, it is not recommended to use more than five buckets for value binning because the concept is to see the range of values in an absolute (individual) sense, and not necessarily in the context of the other values. Chapter 11 provides more information about color choices. Refer to that chapter to understand the difference between sequential color schemes, in which a progression occurs from the lowest to highest value in a color range, and nominal color schemes, in which color differences are not related and designed to appear different from one another. Nominal color schemes would not make sense for value binning (sequential color schemes are the smart choice), but they make sense if a particular threshold or thresholds were to be emphasized.

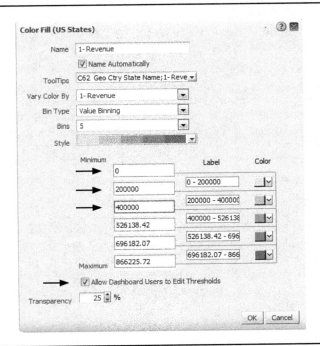

FIGURE 4-6. *Changing the bin colors for a choropleth*

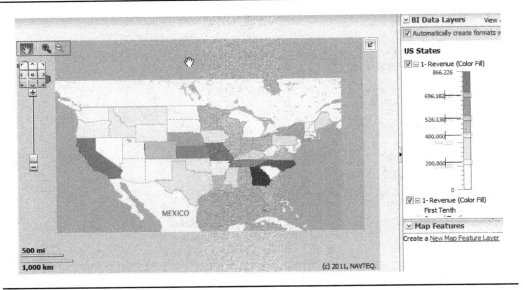

FIGURE 4-7. *Choropleth with colors changed*

Interacting with Maps

We will discuss interaction in depth in Chapter 8, but there are some interactions that apply especially to maps that we should discuss now.

Panning on Maps

Panning a map changes the portion of the map that is visible, like unfolding and refolding portions of a paper map. It slides the map underneath the visible window. To pan on a map, ensure that the Hand tool is selected (shown in the upper-left corner of Figure 4-7) and simply click and drag the map. The map slides within the display window.

Zooming on Maps

To zoom on a map, select the Zoom tool (the magnifying glass with a plus sign) and then click a portion of the map. Alternatively, you can click and drag the portion of the map you want displayed within the current window, or use the slider on the left side of the map. The map will "zoom in" to the area you select within the window and the zoom level of the map will increase. As you change the zoom level, more or less detail (such as city names, highways, streets, and parks) will be displayed, as configured in MapViewer.

Drilling on Maps

Maps are like other native view objects in OBIEE in that drilling and other typical user behavior can trigger automatic response from OBIEE. For example, Figure 4-8 shows the Criteria tab, and Figure 4-9 shows the default table view for the analysis of the simple choropleth map in Figure 4-4.

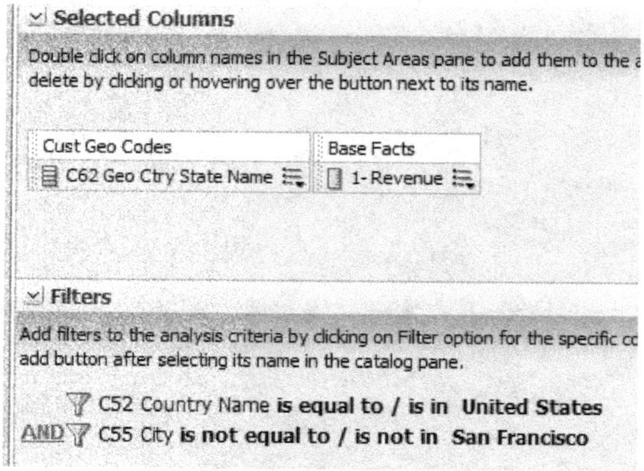

FIGURE 4-8. *Criteria tab for simple choropleth map*

Table

C62 Geo Ctry State Name	1-Revenue
USA_Alabama	294,818
USA_Alaska	228,638
USA_Arkansas	113,106
USA_California	524,597
USA_Colorado	206,414
USA_Florida	238,800
USA_Georgia	866,226
USA Hawaii	56 668

FIGURE 4-9. *Default table view for a simple choropleth map*

The analysis contains only two columns and two filters (the sample data set has a very large number of customers in the city of San Francisco, so we'll exclude them to have a more balanced result). When you hover over a particular state, you can see the revenue amount along with the column name and the specific state, as shown in Figure 4-10. Maps are a native OBIEE view and have the built-in behavior capabilities and response patterns that other views such as bar graphs and pie graphs have. When you drill on the column name, the next level down in the hierarchy (in this case, city) is automatically added to the analysis criteria and the map view visualization, as shown in Figure 4-11. We'll explore interactivity and drill paths in Chapter 8, but knowing that map views are native OBIEE views with tremendous built-in capabilities is fundamental to understanding why they are recommended so highly as featured visualizations in many OBIEE dashboards.

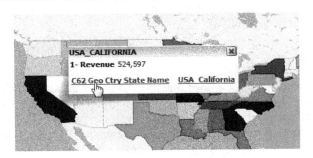

FIGURE 4-10. *Hover over a state and then drill into the column to add the next level down of the hierarchy.*

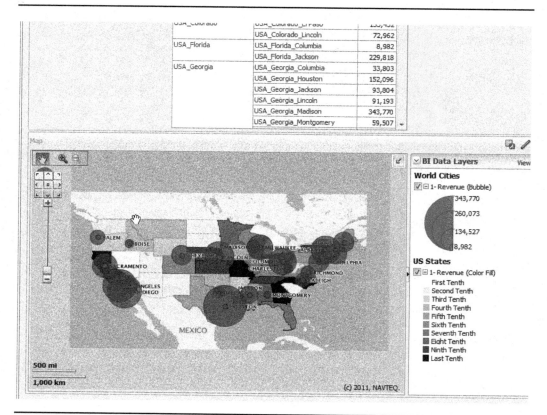

FIGURE 4-11. *OBIEE automatically responds to the drill by adding a new column and a new BI layer to the map view visualization.*

Map Color Choices

Color choice is extremely important for any map design, but particularly for business intelligence maps. Color can be used to highlight particular patterns in data sets as they relate to geographical location. The topics of how to choose different color schemes and strategies for effective map visualizations are addressed in Chapter 11. Your use of colors in background maps should be extremely limited. Reserve the predominant use of color to BI layers that communicate meaning regarding data and measures. Many background map systems are not optimized for use on business intelligence dashboards and include unnecessary color variation and features. Remember, the purpose of the background map is to give context to the business data, not to tell you how to drive from one city to another.

You can also use data markers to identify specific locations on maps. Figure 4-12 shows a map of San Francisco with the locations of customers shown as round circles. This allows the viewer to see where customer concentrations are highest and where they are sparse. The background map includes a fair amount of detail, including major highways, parks, railroads, and other geographical features that may have implications for the locations of customers.

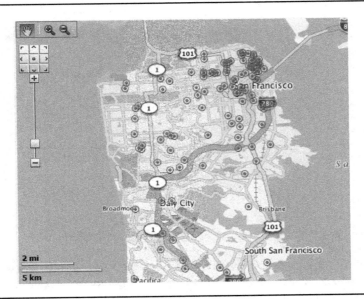

FIGURE 4-12. *San Francisco map with data markers showing customers*

In Figure 4-13, the map is zoomed further in to the Embarcadero neighborhood of downtown San Francisco (the dense cluster of customers in the northeast part of the map). Notice that where the customers were once overlapping each other, they now appear more spread out. There is more detail on the map. With the San Francisco base map, we have eight layers of detail (Level 0 through Level 8 at the most detailed view). In Figure 4-12, the map is zoomed to Level 1, whereas in Figure 4-13, the zoom slider on the far left side of the screen is about half way up to Level 4.

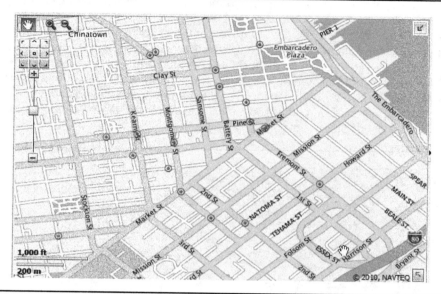

FIGURE 4-13. *San Francisco zoomed in to the Embarcadero neighborhood*

Bubbles and Variable Shapes on Maps

Bubbles and variable shapes are two other ways to mark specific locations on a map view in addition to an image. Both can be configured to communicate multidimensional information about a location.

Bubbles reveal most of their information through their size and they have a single color. Variable shapes reveal information through both their size (scaled and assigned by the system) and their color. The color can be set to percentile binning (even numbers of points in each bin) or value binning (specific thresholds can be set for each color). Figure 4-14 shows the interface for configuring variable shapes. Variable shapes can be circles, triangles, or diamonds. Typically, circles are used unless there is more than one variable shape layer, in which case you can assign a different shape to each layer so that patterns for different measures can be perceived more easily.

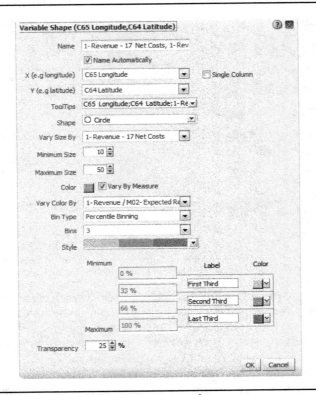

FIGURE 4-14.   *Variable Shape edit/configure interface*

TIP
Make certain your data selection in the query is relevant for your map view visuals. The auto-scaling feature in OBIEE will make the bubble size determinations according to the data included in the query definition. Adding an appropriate filter on the Criteria tab may be needed if you are getting a limited number of bubble levels. For example, a filter was added to include only customers in the city of San Francisco to ensure that the range of values for the rest of the customers was excluded and the automatic apportioning was done with only San Francisco data when Figure 4-15 was produced.

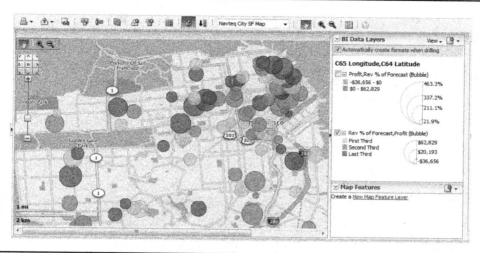

FIGURE 4-15. *San Francisco map with bubbles showing customers*

Variable shapes are placed on the map either by selecting a specific BI data layer that has been configured or by using longitude and latitude numbers to create a "custom point layer" on the fly. In essence, OBIEE is using the longitude and latitude as a key to tie the BI data point to the base map. Only images, bubbles, and variable shapes that are markers for specific points have this capability. All other map formats, including polygon fills and lines, must utilize a predefined BI layer.

Variable shapes can reveal striking patterns as well as communicate a tremendous amount of information about various locations via tool-tip rollovers. Figure 4-16 uses a circle for every customer location in downtown San Francisco. As you can see in the BI Data Layers pane, the color of the circles is used in percentile binning to show the highest, middle, and lowest thirds of the revenue performance versus forecast. Those circles that are dark gray have the highest sales compared to forecast, whereas those in light gray are in the lowest third of revenue versus forecast. The size of the circle varies based on the amount of profit that the customer earned for the firm, as defined by Revenue minus Cost. Large circles indicate high profit amounts, whereas small bubbles indicate low profit amounts. Initially, we don't see much of a geographical pattern to the distribution of the colors (light gray, gray, and dark gray) and the size of the circle. However, rolling over individual customers with the mouse reveals a tremendous amount of information. The large dark bubble in Figure 4-16 tips us off that the customer, Affinity Bank, has high profits (large size bubble) and was in the highest third of actual revenue versus forecast (dark color). We can roll over it to see the detail for Affinity Bank. The map tells us where it is located physically, and we can immediately see its relationship to other customers nearby.

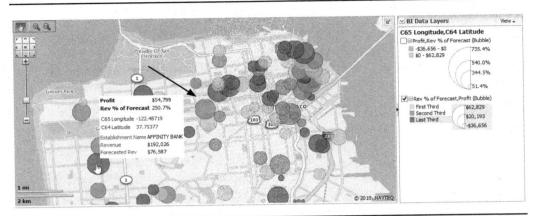

FIGURE 4-16. *San Francisco map showing a pop-up with detail on a customer*

As shown in Figure 4-17, rolling over a small light-gray bubble to the northeast shows that OReilly's Holy Grail was both under forecast and actually had negative profitability. The use of filters or selection steps in combination with visual effects can also yield different insights. For example, it would be relatively straightforward to apply filters to the query such that only customers who had negative revenue growth were included. In that case, a different set of visualization choices might make sense. Alternatively, the map can be set to respond to the powerful right-click options for a table view and Selection Steps through Master Detail linking, but we will cover those topics in Chapter 8.

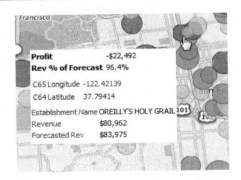

FIGURE 4-17. *Detail pop-up on OReilly's Holy Grail*

As mentioned before, color is a powerful visual tool, and great care must be taken in selecting the specific colors for markers and fills as well as in selecting the "break" points for the different colors of the bins and the number of bins. Although the system will assign default values for value binning, radically different insights will be revealed or different key points will be made depending on the settings. Let's take a look at our customers in San Francisco again, and this time assign a red color to those customers who had negative profitability (costs were higher than revenue) and a light green color to those customers with positive profitability (costs were lower than revenue). We'll also set the size of the circle to indicate the percent of revenue forecast. In Figure 4-18, we see a concerning cluster in the SOMA (south of Market) neighborhood with a higher proportion of unprofitable customers than might be expected. The large red circles, which indicate customers who are unprofitable (red) and who are over forecast with higher-than-predicted revenues (large), are especially worthy of further analysis and investigation. Although filtering, sorting, and conditional formatting might have revealed them on a table view, only a map can immediately reveal the location relationship. As mentioned in the Preface, some screenshots are clearer in color. See www.vlamis.com/DVforOBI to see this in color.

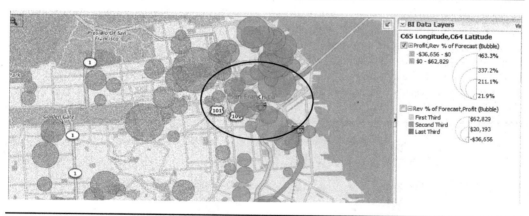

FIGURE 4-18. *Using a two-color scheme reveals an unprofitable customer cluster quickly.*

TIP
Unless there is a specific reason you do not want users to edit the thresholds of the visualization, you should always enable threshold edits because insights, results, and patterns can be strikingly different with different threshold settings.

Placing Graphs on Maps

A more advanced feature of map views in OBIEE is the ability to place bar graphs and pie graphs on top of regions in a BI data layer. Whereas users are accustomed to pie graphs being consistently scaled (the pieces of the pie represent the proportion of the unit to the whole) on a normalized 100 percent scale and can be compared one to the other, bar graphs are scaled independently and should always have an accompanying narrative that states "Bar graphs on maps are scaled independently and the height of the bars should not be compared across sets of bars."

Figure 4-19 shows a choropleth map of the United States with color fill by state, according to decile percentage binning. Also, a layer is added that shows the relative amount of revenue for each line of business by state. This is a very dense visualization with a lot of detail and should predominantly be used for analysts and those who aren't looking for a quick impression. As noted, each set of bars is individually scaled, and the height of bars should not be compared across sets. Users can turn on and off each layer individually in a dashboard setting by clicking the check boxes in the legend. This makes it possible to compare insights offered by different BI layers on map views quickly and efficiently.

CAUTION
Include only the layers that should be compared immediately or viewed simultaneously in a single map view. An excessive number of layers may slow performance and the loading of the dashboard page.

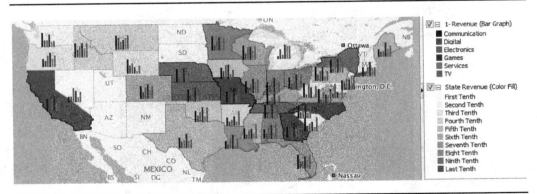

FIGURE 4-19. *Bar graphs on top of the map view*

Figure 4-20 shows the same bar graphs with the State Revenue Color Fill layer turned off. As stated before, the order of the layers is important for simultaneous viewing. If the color fill layer was on top of the bar chart layer, the bar charts would not be easily visible. It is possible to set the transparency of color fills from 0 percent (opaque) to 100 percent (completely transparent).

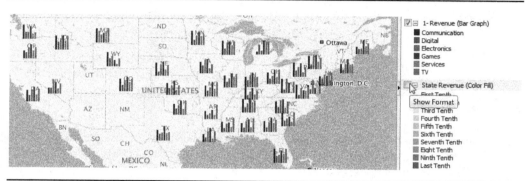

FIGURE 4-20. *The State Revenue Color Fill layer is turned off.*

Figure 4-21 shows a zoomed-in area of the Southern states of Louisiana, Mississippi, Alabama, Arkansas, and Tennessee. Opacity of the color fill has been increased to 100 percent but the sizes of the bars need to be increased.

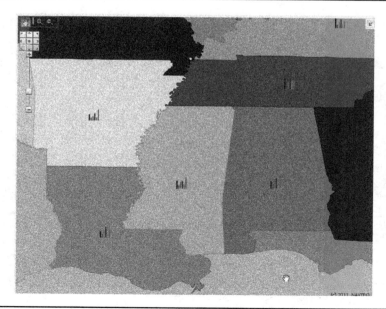

FIGURE 4-21. *States of the U.S. color-coded with bar graph*

Because the bars are independently scaled, both of these effects make them more visible and easy to understand. As is typical, rollovers give users detailed information and should be enabled, as shown in Figure 4-22.

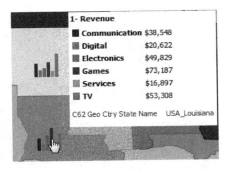

FIGURE 4-22. *Rollovers also work for bar and pie charts when added to map views.*

An alternative to placing graphs on top of maps is to use the map to control a graph in another view on the dashboard. We will cover this option more in Chapter 8 on dashboard interactions, specifically Master-Detail linking. Of course, this gives you much more control over the exact format of the graphs that display information associated with a map.

Placing Lines on Maps

Starting with release 11.1.1.7, OBIEE can configure line objects on map views to show BI data. Figure 4-23 shows the performance of airline flights originating in San Francisco and terminating in hundreds of airports around the United States. Each route has a "Flight Performance Index," which is a measure of its average lateness compared with its average in-air flight time and is pictured as a curved line between San Francisco and the destination airport. The line is colored according to the Flight Performance Index measure, and the line's thickness is weighted by the number of flights in the data set. This one map visualization is incredibly dense and aggregates tens of thousands of flights.

Immediately we can see that the Flight Performance Index is strongly correlated with distance. Longer routes tend to have greener lines, whereas shorter routes tend to be more red and darker. A zoomed-in view in Figure 4-24 shows us that each airport is marked by an airplane icon, and when the mouse is hovered over the airport, we get the airport code and number of flights. Lines can be set to be curved (as shown) or straight. Curved lines tend to visually signal a route (motion), whereas straight lines tend to visually signal a direct relationship or connection. Curved lines are used on most map views.

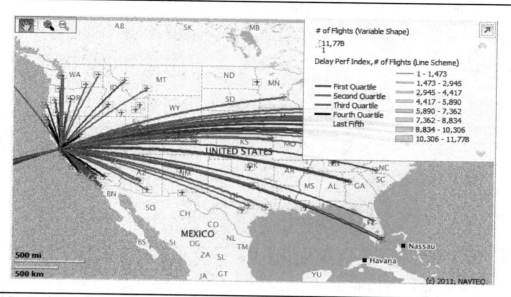

FIGURE 4-23. *Flight route performance lines on a map*

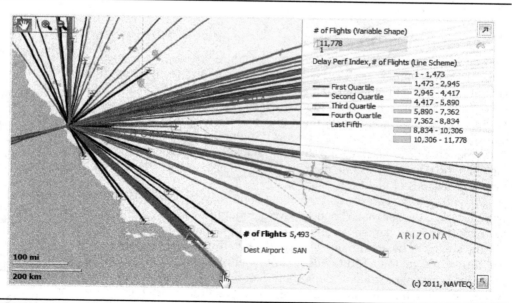

FIGURE 4-24. *Flight route performance detail zoomed in to San Francisco*

Combining Data Sets on Maps and Using Map Feature Layers

The power of maps truly becomes apparent when many of these insights and techniques are combined together. Demographic data enriches background maps and can provide important contextual information for BI layers. In addition, you can capitalize on the additional capabilities of MapViewer in creating background maps if features are not in OBIEE. Figure 4-25 and Figure 4-26 show two different Map Feature layers set up in MapViewer that can be turned on and off in a way similar to how BI layers are turned on and off. Figure 4-25 shows a U.S. counties heat map with a continuous color scheme.

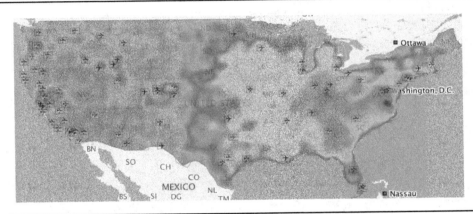

FIGURE 4-25. *County heat map with airports*

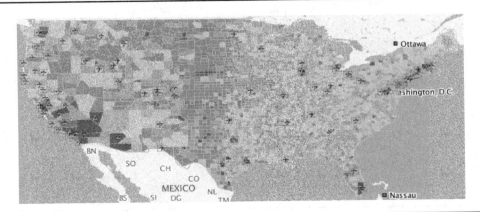

FIGURE 4-26. *U.S. population by county with airports*

Figure 4-26 shows a different Map Feature layer with the U.S. population by county. These are just background maps from MapViewer. The airport icons have been left on the map so that users can compare the airport locations with the background county information. This location information is known as POI information (or "point of interest" information). Literally millions of POI locations are now available from HERE and other data providers, which can be shown on OBIEE map views on background maps, on Map Feature layers, and on Map BI layers.

Figure 4-27 shows a geospatial query that evaluates U.S. census blocks within a configurable distance of different kinds of shops located in a specified ZIP code in downtown San Francisco. The shops are shown with a red circle to mark their location (red was chosen to stand out from all the color fill color ranges). The graphic also features a black border around the red circle to help it stand out against the background map. A total of 12 different shop types can be shown on the map. Additionally, dashboard users can select among four different Color Fill BI Data layers that reflect U.S. census data regarding target market customers: Females Aged 30 to 39 (in quintiles), Number of Households with Income Greater than $200,000 per Annum (user-selected ranges with slider prompts), Median Household Incomes (in deciles), and Total Population of Each Census Block (in quartiles). Additionally, a pivot table view lists the names and addresses of all marked shop locations within the specified range.

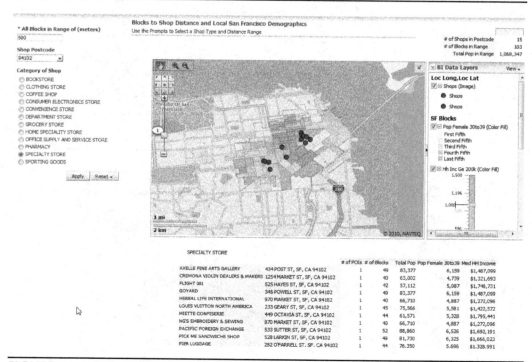

FIGURE 4-27. *Overall view of a dashboard for shops within block distance and demographics analysis*

Dashboards such as this one promote sophisticated analysis of current and potential shop locations for specific target markets and demonstrate the "mashup" power of OBIEE and its native map views. This dashboard would be ideal for evaluating not only direct competitors, but also "substitute" competitor stores that compete for the total market spend of the target audience.

The prompts on the dashboard shown in Figure 4-28 allow for a dynamic selection of blocks within a given distance of the shops in the postal code specified. Oracle BI then creates an SQL select statement that retrieves the correct blocks using the SDO_WITHIN_DISTANCE function.

* All Blocks in Range of (meters)

500

Shop Postcode

94102

Category of Shop
- BOOKSTORE
- CLOTHING STORE
- COFFEE SHOP
- CONSUMER ELECTRONICS STORE
- CONVENIENCE STORE
- DEPARTMENT STORE
- GROCERY STORE
- HOME SPECIALITY STORE
- OFFICE SUPPLY AND SERVICE STORE
- PHARMACY
- ● SPECIALTY STORE
- SPORTING GOODS

Apply   Reset ▾

FIGURE 4-28. *Dashboard prompts*

The integration of external data sources such as census data can lead to important insights when combined with internal organizational data. Map views offer an excellent interface for data mashups because of OBIEE's ability to easily turn on and off data layers. Figure 4-29 shows a zoomed-in view of the density of households with incomes greater than $200,000 per annum. The configurable slider prompt allows users to choose different data ranges in order to reveal different geographical patterns. As data gets more granular and more specific to certain use cases, the ability for users to configure color fill ranges dynamically becomes more important.

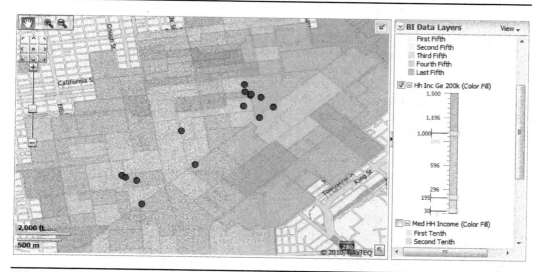

FIGURE 4-29. *Detailed view of households with incomes greater than $200,000 per annum and specialty stores*

Figure 4-30 shows the distribution of median household incomes split evenly into 10 "bins" (or "decile binning"). Median incomes are more appropriate for percentage binning because they are a "centered" distribution measure. Continuing

FIGURE 4-30. *Median household income in deciles*

our analysis by turning on the last BI layer, Population Blocks in Range, we would see that although the shops are surrounded by dense population blocks, they are not generally in the blocks with the highest incomes.

Custom Integration of Maps in OBIEE

So far in this chapter, all of our discussion has been about using the built-in map views in OBIEE. Bear in mind that only some of the capabilities of MapViewer are exposed in the built-in map views. By using Java Script and integrating HTML5-based MapViewer, you can do a lot more with maps, including creating true heat maps, using the lasso and individual selection of points for master-detail analysis, grouping densely packed points based on zoom level, and much more. These features are showcased in the SampleApp application from Oracle and may be available in the base product by the time you read this.

Summary

Maps are some of the most intuitive, powerful, and easily understood visualizations and should be preferred for many common business intelligence dashboards and analyses. Because OBIEE integrates map views as a native view type, once a BI administrator has configured OBIEE to use maps, they can be added in a manner of minutes. Maps reveal patterns and relationships in data sets that are simply not available in other view types. Map views are ideal for integrating external data sources and providing important contextual information for internal organizational data. It is highly recommended that map views be included in every OBIEE implementation.

CHAPTER
5

Advanced Visualizations

This chapter includes topics that we have loosely collected under the term "advanced" for a few different reasons. Some of the material is challenging and truly represents advanced techniques. Other material isn't advanced in that it is difficult, but rather that it is somewhat unusual and is not often included in OBIEE implementations. Additionally, some of the material may not be advanced from a configuration or visual interpretation perspective, but it may require significant computing resources and should not necessarily be seen as default visualizations. Also included are some visualizations such as gauges that require a fair amount of effort to configure, but offer questionable value from the perspective of human cognition and may not represent a "best practice" presentation of data. However, because many business intelligence dashboards include these types of views and many executives request them, this chapter explains how to configure them as well as how to respond for requests for their inclusion.

In short, various topics in this chapter have been included because they "go beyond" normal implementations in some way. With that being said, business intelligence systems are growing and becoming more integrated into their organizations in many ways. As organizations integrate BI and analytics into their internal processes and into the way they understand and "sense" their business, the systems themselves morph and evolve and become more differentiated. There is a natural tension between a desire to use "out-of-the-box" settings and avoiding the overhead of maintaining custom extensions of systems, and the desire to customize the system to the specific needs of the organization. Customization increases the cost of implementing upgrades, increases implementation time and expense, complicates the process of debugging systems and fixing problems when they occur, and raises the risk associated with the departure of key development personnel (who may not have done a good job documenting code extensions and customizations). However, all organizations are unique and require some degree of adaptation of BI software. Much of this book is centered on the premise that investments made in improving data visualizations from out-of-the-box, default settings generate significant organizational returns because data and evidence are much better understood.

Another way in which BI systems are evolving is from a more static notion of "business reporting" based on historic reports or even "business intelligence" that is centered on interactive dashboards toward the notion of "business analytics," in which automated analytical processes are integrated into business operations. Some of what is talked about in this chapter is seeing how those "business analytics processes" are creating momentum for an evolved business intelligence system and are pointing toward the future of BI. More systems today are seeking to integrate predictive analytics alongside more traditional historic business intelligence reports. Whereas BI dashboards might normally include measures such as Sales Current Year, Current Year Sales Forecast, and Last Year Sales, more organizations now want to show Predicted Sales Next Year (in essence, a forecast for next year that uses sophisticated algorithms to continuously update the prediction as new data arrives).

In fact, we the authors are doing more work combining the power of OBIEE and the Oracle Advanced Analytics option of the Oracle Enterprise Edition Database, which includes Oracle Data Mining and Oracle R Enterprise. As more and more analytically complex information is included on OBIEE dashboards, the need to think carefully about how to graphically represent that information becomes vital. The opportunity to include and involve the "data scientists" (otherwise called "statisticians," "actuaries," "researchers," "scientists," "economists," "data miners," and so on) in enterprise business intelligence systems pays huge dividends because they are typically accustomed to thinking deeply about data and how to present it.

Trellis Charts

Trellis charts are like a table of graphs. Visualizations are organized and aligned and presented as a unit.

As you can see in Figures 5-1 and 5-2, trellis charts are relatively "dense" as visualizations and can convey a large amount of data in a condensed space. Trellis

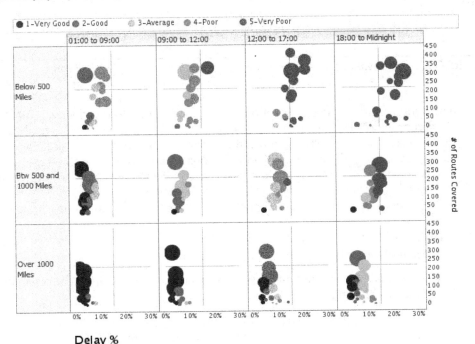

FIGURE 5-1. *A simple trellis chart showing multidimensional pattern*

Cross-Trended Analysis
By Month by Top Carriers

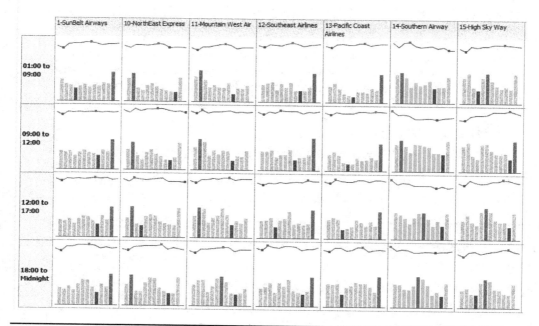

FIGURE 5-2.   *An advanced trellis chart showing multiple graph visualizations*

charts require care in their conception and design in order to be effective. Although they can provide a high level of value (and we the authors are enthusiastic about their inclusion on OBIEE dashboards), they are not for every situation and can often create cascading challenges in real-world implementations. Above all else, trellis charts should be compared to other alternatives and used only when they are likely to provide higher value to specific roles and user groups.

Consider using trellis charts when at least one of the following situations exist:

■ A need exists to show granular information for different dimensional values simultaneously.

■ Small graphs and patterned views are important to communicate a larger pattern or trend.

■ It's easier to perceive a situation or trend through the simultaneous presentation of multiple, granular views than it is through summary measures.

- Detail is required more than summary for the accurate understanding of the organizational situation.

- Granular detail along multiple dimensions is required to recognize outliers, phase transitions, and other nonlinear patterns. (These can be extremely difficult to recognize without the aid of visualization.)

CAUTION
Trellis charts can be computationally demanding:

- *Trellis charts may increase the need for a powerful presentation server.*
- *Trellis charts may create complex SQL queries and thus impact server performance.*

There are two types of trellis charts in OBIEE: simple and advanced. You can think of them as Type 1 trellis charts and Type 2 trellis charts because they have different characteristics (there's really nothing terribly "simple" about simple trellis charts, and advanced trellis charts don't have broader or deeper capabilities—they are just different). Trellis charts are an extension of the rows and columns method of organizing data. Simple trellis charts are a table of graphs. Advanced trellis charts are more like sparklines (commonly used in Microsoft Excel) and are limited in the visualizations that can be used inside each cell. The biggest difference between them is that simple trellis charts share a common scale, whereas advanced trellis charts are individually scaled. When creating a trellis chart, think about which type you want to create before you invest a lot of time in creating it; you cannot transform a simple trellis chart into an advanced trellis chart, and vice versa.

Trellis charts also support interactivity such as drill, sort, rollovers, and action links. Because of their complexity compared with more simple visualizations, it may not be obvious to many users what the interaction effects will be. When trellis charts are used as a "summary" visualization on "explanation" dashboards, a narrative view should be included showing additional information and interaction options. See Figure 5-3 for an example of a narrative view that adds important information and analytical context for a trellis chart. Trellis charts should have their own analysis and not be included as one of several views in a single analysis. Trellis charts can be computationally intensive for both the presentation server and for the BI server. Avoiding the inclusion of other views with trellis charts can help in diagnosing performance issues. Additionally, column interactions such as drilling on a result in a trellis chart can surprise and confuse users in some cases. Column interactions should be carefully designed in trellis chart views for both visualization and performance reasons. The settings and choices that make sense for a trellis chart may not make sense for other more standard views, so it's generally best to isolate them.

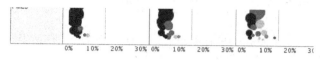

Delay %

Trellis Chart Notes

Each colored bubble represents an individual airline's performance for that flight distance and departure time. Rollover bubbles to see the details of number of routes included, number of total flights, the average flight performance delay percentage, and its relative rating.

Note the strong correlation between Distance Group and Departure time. Long flights that depart in the morning have the least amount of delay while short flights that leave in the evening have the highest amount of delay.

Drill on the departure time at the top of the chart to open a Trellis Chart in a new window with flights detailed by 1 hour increments.

FIGURE 5-3.   *Narrative views add important information for trellis charts.*

Simple Trellis Charts (Type 1 Trellis Charts)

Simple trellis charts share the same scale of data for an entire matrix of like visualizations or microcharts (whereas advanced trellis charts use individual scaling for each cell of the matrix). Simple trellis charts should be used where the comparisons between different cells in the matrix are more important than the individual patterns that exist within the microchart visualizations themselves. The Airline Performance Matrix bubble chart trellis chart in Figure 5-1 is a good example of this. The comparison of the different bubble charts directly leads to the insight that flight delays are correlated with both distance and time of departure. A large number of microchart visualizations are available for inclusion in simple trellis charts—choose from vertical bar, horizontal bar, line, area, line-bar, pie, scatter, and bubble.

Generally speaking, all the recommendations made in Chapter 3 regarding graph types and when to use them apply for determining which visualizations to use in trellis charts. Line graphs that show the progression of a measure over time can be very effective. Remember, however, that we as humans are not as good at comparing angles and size/volume as we are at comparing height/level. We are fairly good at comparing the relative difference between immediately adjacent colors, but relatively poor at determining the absolute value of colors and grayscale because our perception is skewed by the surrounding visual objects. It is critically important to consider what the major point of a trellis chart presentation is and to consider what tradeoffs exist.

In Figure 5-4, we can see what is similar to a pivot table of microcharts. Scales can either be shown or not shown in simple trellis chart views. In this case, the scales are not shown, because of the complexity of utilizing dual vertical axes and emphasizing relative patterns that compare a total of 16 different combinations of dimension values (four different geographical regions by three different time of day periods and a total day column). A tremendous amount of information is presented in a very compact space. Each cell shows 52 different bars and 52 different week performance measures, for a visualization total of more than 1,600 individual data points and thousands of comparisons. Here, the emphasis is on the relative patterns and value representations rather than the individual data points. We can immediately perceive that the West Region has a smaller number of flights compared to the South Region. By studying the trellis more closely, we see that shorter-distance flights (shown in the leftmost series of microcharts) have poorer performance than the longer flights. When comparing the rough patterns of the Delay Performance % measure shown as a line, we see that the West and Midwest Regions had more significant problems at the end of the year than did other regions (notice how the line trends dramatically higher in the far right of the microcharts). When small line graphs are used, make sure the x-axis (horizontal axis) for the line is Time (calendar units or time units) or another continuous measure. If you use another continuous measure, make sure this is clear because many users will presume the x-axis is Time.

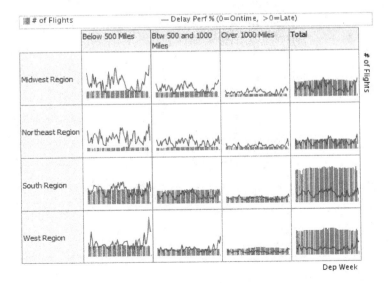

FIGURE 5-4. *Simple line and bar combo trellis chart with a common scale*

The layout interface (shown in Figure 5-5) for simple trellis charts is relatively straightforward. The Columns and Rows settings are defined for the matrix/table of microcharts. Typically, these are dimension columns that modify or parameterize measures displayed on the graphs. A microchart is displayed for each combination of these row and column dimension values. The number of measures displayed/required is different for different visualizations. Notice that a Display Format dropdown menu (shown in Figure 5-6) is included for dimensions in both columns and rows. This offers the ability to add conditional formatting as well as to fine-tune the appearance of the titles and the cells. The prompts that appear inside the Visualization box depend on the specific visualization chosen. The line bar combo graph allows for different measures for two y-axes (vertical axis) and the choice of a Group By field that determines what dimension is used for the x-axis inside each microchart (for example, Departure Week). In this example, we can see the bars represent the number of flights whereas the line represents the delay performance percentage (a "normalized" index related to the amount of time in delays relative to flight time).

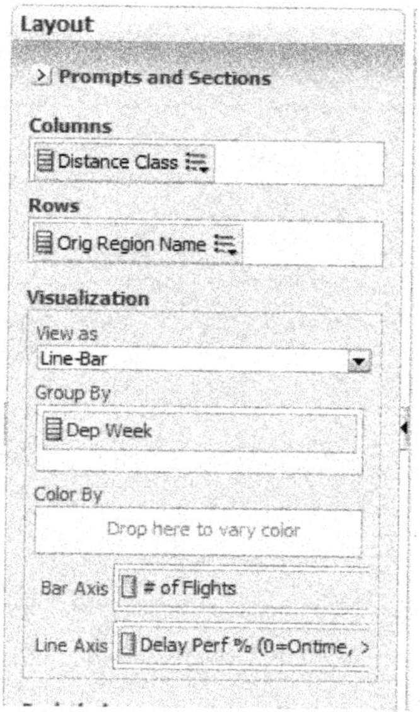

FIGURE 5-5. *Layout editor pane for trellis charts*

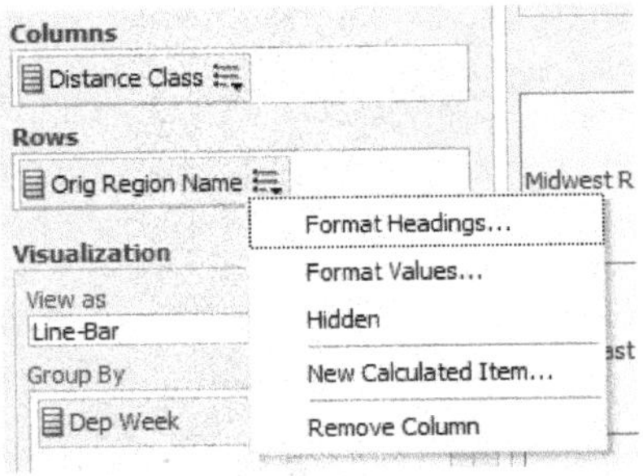

FIGURE 5-6. *Drop-down menus enable formatting for trellis rows and columns.*

Advanced Trellis Charts (Type 2 Trellis Charts)

Advanced trellis charts make use of what are called "spark" charts. This term was popularized by Edward Tufte ("sparkline" was the original term). According to Tufte, "A sparkline is a small intense, simple, word-sized graphic with typographic resolution." The concept behind this is to show a word-size graphic and a pattern with no scale—it is the trend that's shown in a spark chart. Different measures can use different visualizations within the same matrix. Advanced trellis charts should be used where the simultaneous presentation of multiple related visualizations provides tremendous value. Advanced trellis charts should not be used where the cells of the matrix are meant to be compared to one another (which, quite frankly, is rather common and sometimes unavoidable). Because the individual scales between different cells in the matrix are likely to be different, a narrative text explanation of that difference should generally be included in all advanced trellis chart presentations. Advanced trellis charts may be effective when it is generally understood that the individual cells should not be considered together. Let's say that we are looking at the share price quotes for different publicly traded stocks. We know that the discrete dollar change in price for each share stock is somewhat meaningless to compare to one another (that one stock increased $10 whereas another increased $100 has no comparative value). The same may be true for the relative sizes of divisions within a corporation where there is a preexisting understanding of the context of the data. In situations like these, the differently scaled cells may not mislead or misinform users, because there is an understood context regarding the nature of the data or the situation.

Scales do not appear on the microcharts, but when the user rolls over a microchart, the Start, Maximum, Minimum, and End values can be shown. These values can also be highlighted in different colors. In Figures 5-2 and 5-7, the maximum is shown in green and the minimum is shown in red. Each individual microchart visualization style has its own individual formatting and measure. For most of these visualizations, Time should be the x-axis dimension. This helps ensure that visualizations are not misinterpreted. Even so, trellis charts should be accompanied by an explanatory narrative view, as shown in Figure 5-3, that helps explain the chart and its main objectives. Legend views may also help clarify, but even more than with traditional charts, trellis charts should be kept simple so that they are fairly easy to interpret visually.

It can take a lot of experience and expertise to "read" graphs and charts that have many dimensions and many visual representations. There is a real danger using graphs with a lot of complexity in trellis charts. If the message of a single cell requires a lot of study, it may be very difficult for the user to then discern a pattern by comparing multiple iterations of that complex graph. Use trellis charts when the user needs to see multidimensional charts all at the same time, so they can easily look for patterns across one or two dimensions. Because trellis charts are already more difficult to understand, err on the side of keeping the individual graphs simple. If you need a complex visualization, perhaps you should use a regular graph and make sure it is big enough to understand.

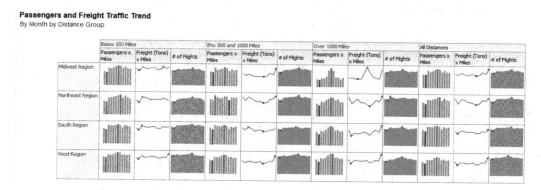

FIGURE 5-7. *Advanced trellis charts are individually scaled.*

Gauges and Dials

Gauges and dials may be the archetypal visualization for dashboards simply because they are so ubiquitous in cars and mechanical systems. What we have to remember, however, is that gauges and dials evolved in a physical, analog world where they were measuring a mechanical difference. That is, most dials and gauges revealed some type of pressure or voltage difference, and they incorporated springs and included a single pivot point. They used angle to visually show difference because that was the simplest way to design something mechanically. Also, they had to show immediate change in a highly varied and dynamic environment. Most business functions are not like driving a car, where constant and immediate corrective action is necessary from individuals (although some "frontline" positions can have this requirement). Circular dial gauges, like pie charts, tend to require a fair amount of screen real estate.

Gauges can be effective when the metaphor for the measurement has a direct connection with a gauge or if the gauge is related to a familiar object. For example, if a resource is limited and declines with use until it is replenished (like a tank of gas), then a gauge view that reflects the percentage of remaining resource (from 100 percent to 0 percent, or empty) can be useful. Of course, more and more vehicles are using distance in miles/kilometers or even time to empty rather than percentage remaining so the metaphor is becoming less and less applicable. It's also instructive that many modern vehicles are now showing amount of gas left in the tank as a bar graph instead of a dial. Likewise, a measure that is showing throughput rate or speed can be modeled as a gauge view because most people will interpret it as such.

We the authors are generally not big fans of performance gauges with stoplight colors. We'd much prefer to use performance tiles, bar charts, or even small table views with conditional formatting in most use cases.

Vertical bar–style gauge views can be effective, particularly in series. The vertical level reading of a bar-style gauge is similar to a bar graph. The relative height of the value bar can be effectively compared across multiple gauges, although perhaps not as easily as with other visualizations. Bulb-style gauges are somewhat similar to performance tiles in that they offer a spot of color that indicates a relative "state" or value. They are not capable of displaying text as a part of the colored "bulb." Careful attention should be paid to the adjacency of elements when placed in series or side by side because they tend to be viewed first as "whole" and only later as individual parts (indeed, that is one of their advantages). Figure 5-8 shows the collect-to-bill ratio for three different product brands. Figure 5-9 shows the settings for this particular style of gauge. Threshold values in gauge views can be expressed in a wide variety of ways, including Dynamic (useful for "high/medium/low" or "good/average/poor" representations), Custom Value, Variable Expression, and SQL Query. Gauges can also be set to respond to the threshold values of other measures, much like conditional formatting for a particular table column can respond to another column or measure.

FIGURE 5-8. *Bulb-style gauge view*

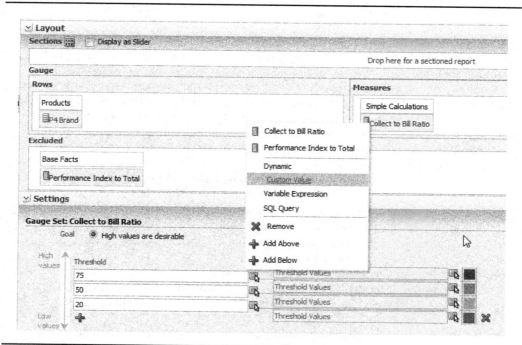

FIGURE 5-9. *Threshold value gauge set for bulb gauge view*

When clients insist on having needle-style gauges (shown in Figure 5-10), you should always try to always use a 180-degree dial arc length (shown set in Figure 5-11) and generally avoid data labels. Try to avoid multiple series of dial- or needle-style gauges because the comparison of the angle of the needle from gauge to gauge is difficult to visually interpret quickly. When multiple readings are required, then a better choice is to use performance tiles, bulb gauges, or even a small conditionally formatted table.

FIGURE 5-10. *Needle-style gauge view*

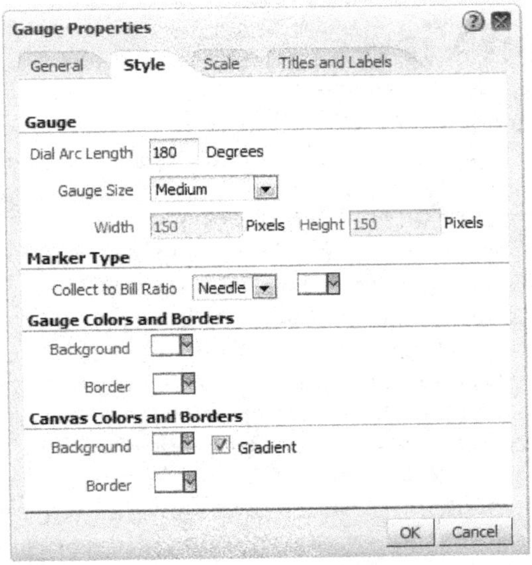

Gauge Properties
General
Style
Scale
Titles and Labels
Gauge
Dial Arc Length
180
Degrees
Gauge Size
Medium
Width
150
Pixels
Height
150
Pixels
Marker Type
Collect to Bill Ratio
Needle
Gauge Colors and Borders
Background
Border
Canvas Colors and Borders
Background
Gradient
Border
OK
Cancel

FIGURE 5-11. *Set Dial Arc Length to 180 Degrees for dial gauges.*

Vertical bar gauge views are colorful, but their data values are more difficult to interpret than other bar charts because the visual emphasis of the graph is on the color threshold values and not on the "bar" that reflects the value of the measure. Figure 5-12 shows an "indexed" value for revenue that compares the normalized results for brand revenue against a common index. This type of indexing strategy is useful for comparing values that are widely varied in scale and cannot normally be compared.

Revenue Performance to Index Total
2.0
1.5
1.0
0.5
0
BizTech
FunPod
HomeView

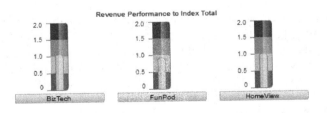

FIGURE 5-12. *Vertical bar gauge view with index scale*

Extending Native OBIEE Data Visualization Views

Because OBIEE has a web-based front end, it's possible to incorporate several different methods of extending the normal "menu" of data visualizations. The following several sections provide a quick overview of some of the capabilities that OBIEE possesses and highlight some of the tricks that can be employed to meet some requirements that exist with more advanced analytics situations. There is a tremendous amount of excitement and new developments in the open-source data visualization community. Given Oracle's long-held strategy of integration of and support for the open-source community, the future is very bright for new visualizations and techniques being made available to OBIEE. It must be mentioned that a tremendous number of resources are available for many of the languages and techniques mentioned in the rest of the chapter. Entire libraries of books, thousands of websites, extensive repositories of code, and countless online videos and courses explain and teach how to use R, JavaScript, D3, and Oracle's ADF.

Although there is undoubtedly great power in using these extended capabilities, there is often an accompanying burden of some additional work in maintenance and a strong requirement for documentation. Therefore, organizations should maintain a list of "extended" visuals that should be tested when they want to upgrade to new releases, upgrade hardware and deployments, or otherwise significantly modify the implementation. There are few things more frustrating to users than when a favorite or important dashboard is "broken" and can't be fixed because the original developer is no longer around and no one else can figure out what has been done.

Don't feel as though you have to be an expert to utilize some of the languages and techniques shown in this section. You don't have to take months of training before you can produce some interesting and beneficial results. Indeed, developers are often much better off having a specific idea of what they are trying to accomplish and learning what they need to know to realize that objective than they are trying to learn an entire new language from scratch (of course, some basic "grounding" explanations in an entirely new environment can go a long way to reducing frustration and avoiding basic mistakes). Look for code that is "close" to what you are wanting to accomplish and then edit it and extend it to fit your specific use case rather than trying to code everything from scratch. The OBIEE SampleApp is particularly good at supplying interesting and useful examples.

Showing Data Distributions Using Tricks with OBIEE Stacked Bar Graphs

OBIEE 11*g* does not have a boxplot or whisker plot graph as a native view that charts the distribution of a measure, but that just means we have to employ a few tricks to conjure up a whisker-style boxplot. Figure 5-13 employs a line bar graph combo view to reflect the full distribution of a measure for a particular dimension.

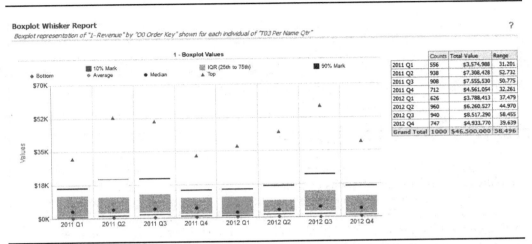

Boxplot Whisker Report ?

Boxplot representation of "1-Revenue" by "OO Order Key" shown for each individual of "TO3 Per Name Qtr"

	Counts	Total Value	Range
2011 Q1	556	$3,574,988	31,201
2011 Q2	938	$7,308,428	52,732
2011 Q3	908	$7,555,530	50,775
2011 Q4	712	$4,561,054	32,261
2012 Q1	626	$3,788,413	37,479
2012 Q2	960	$6,260,527	44,970
2012 Q3	940	$8,517,290	58,455
2012 Q4	747	$4,933,770	39,639
Grand Total	1000	$46,500,000	58,496

FIGURE 5-13. *Configured whisker boxplot*

Boxplot graphs typically shows the "inner quartile range" (IQR) for a data series. There are four quartiles: 0 to 25 percent, 25 to 50 percent, 50 to 75 percent, and 75 to 100 percent. The IQR consists of the two quartiles starting at 25 percent and ending at 75 percent. This means you need to have a bar "floating" in the middle of the graph representing the data from 25 percent to 75 percent. See Figure 5-14 for a detailed view of a whisker boxplot. In general, you can create bar graphs with "floating bars" by graphing the difference between each bar with the background color in a normal stacked bar chart. For example, you can achieve this effect by placing a colored bar that ends at the 75 percent mark and then stacking on top of it another bar in the same color as the background whose top is at the 25 percent mark (in our example, the background is white and the bar placed on top it also white). Voila! The colored bar appears to "float" in the middle of the data range. Note that additional lines (or "whiskers") were added at the bottom 10 percent mark and the top 90 percent mark. Then there's the inner quartile range bar and two lines, one at 10 percent and one at 90 percent. This is done by adding two more bars for each line: a thin colored bar and a "background color" bar. Figure 5-15 shows a total of six bars—three are colored and three are white). Notice also that the "white" bars separating the IQR bar from the 90 percent mark sometimes cover the $18K gridline.

Top
90% Whisker
IQR
10% Whisker
Bottom
2012 Q2
2012 Q3
2012 Q4

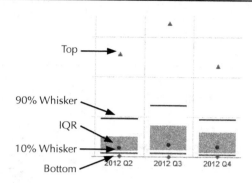

FIGURE 5-14. *Detailed view of whisker box plot*

Although a "line-bar" graph is employed, there are four different values that are actually presented on the graph as graphics, not lines (the diamond shows the bottom or lowest value, the top circle shows the average or mean value, the bottom circle shows the median value, and the triangle shows the top or highest value). Although the IQR bar and the 10 percent and 90 percent lines establish the ranges, the four graphics show specific values. It is the distance relationship between these different values that offers a sense of the distribution of the data. For example, when the average or mean value is higher than the median value, we know that the distribution of the data is skewed and that there is a larger number of smaller values, along with some large values that "pull" the average higher.

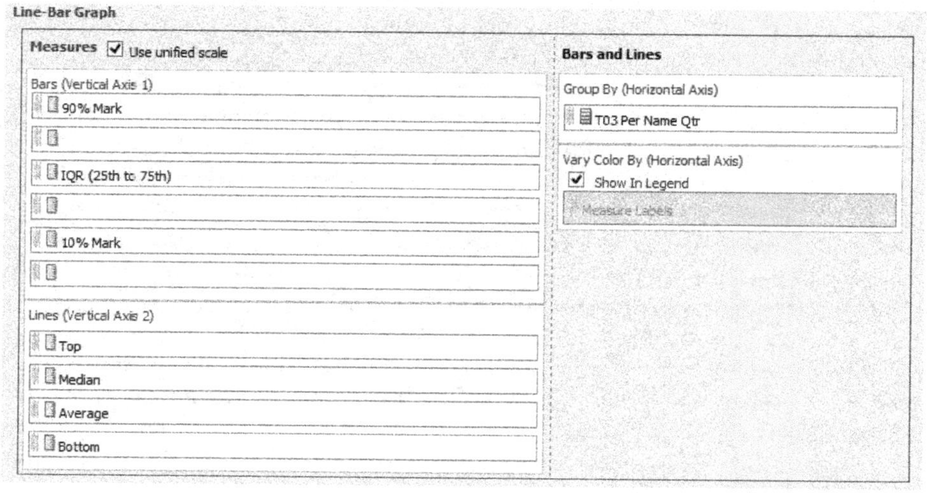

Line-Bar Graph
Measures
Use unified scale
Bars (Vertical Axis 1)
90% Mark
IQR (25th to 75th)
10% Mark
Lines (Vertical Axis 2)
Top
Median
Average
Bottom
Bars and Lines
Group By (Horizontal Axis)
T03 Per Name Qtr
Vary Color By (Horizontal Axis)
Show In Legend
Measure Labels

FIGURE 5-15. *Line bar graph measures for bars*

Figure 5-16 offers insight into the strategy for defining the columns on the Criteria tab for the query. The key insight to the formula is to recognize the use of the **ntile** function. This function subdivides a data set into buckets (here, it's setting 100 buckets and then finding the max of the 75th bucket and the minimum of the 25th bucket and using those to establish the value range). Each of the columns has its own formula that establishes its range.

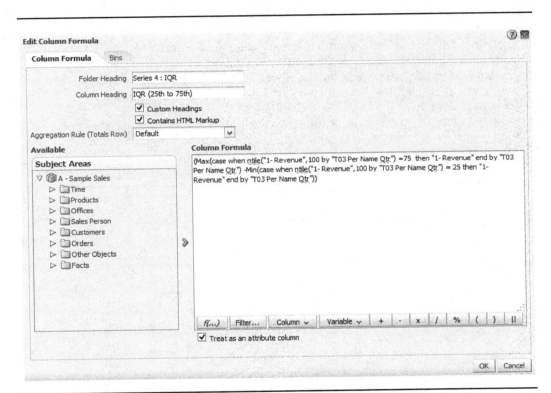

FIGURE 5-16. *IQR column formula*

This is a relatively "dense" visualization, and one that is most appropriate for data analysts who will study the distribution of data and draw insights from it. This kind of view would be excellent to show the range of purchase transactions that might otherwise be hidden in more aggregated "sales analysis" views or obscured in large tables of numbers. If you are working with functional managers or executives who want to deeply understand specific data sets, see if you can spark their interest in learning to read a visual presentation of the distribution of the data and how those distributions change over time. This is particularly important for evaluating customer purchase behavior, cost accounting for complex manufacturing operations, and frontline customer-facing functions with high variability. For example, in Figure 5-13, notice that for 2011 Q2, a single top order of 52K pulls up the average. If you were to simply focus on the "average order," you would lose this nuance in the data.

In this example, we can easily see the highest value for each month and its pattern across time as well as the range of order values and how those ranges differ across time. We can also compare quarters with one another and evaluate the change of the measure over the full time period. It is much faster to visually scan the graph and get a sense of the distribution of the data than it is to scan the table in Figure 5-17. The value of a well-done boxplot with whiskers graph makes it worth the additional time to find and modify the code needed to accomplish the visualization. However, whenever there are seven different values per column to understand, users will need some practice and patience when they are first exposed to and before they get full value from data visualizations like these. Placing a visualization directly next to a table can be a good way to help "sell" the value of the visualization. Try to come up with insights such as "a few very large orders are pulling up the average when compared with the median order" from the table of numbers in Figure 5-17.

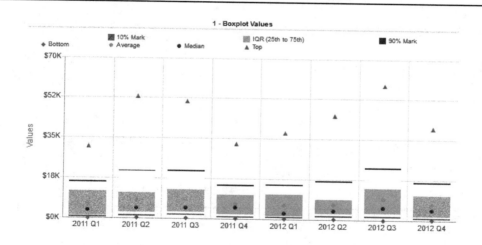

	Counts	Total Value	Range	Bottom	10% Mark	25% Mark	Median	Average	75% Mark	90% Mark	Top
2011 Q1	556	$3,574,988	31,201	117	399	745	3,566	6,429.8	11,170	14,903	31,318
2011 Q2	938	$7,308,428	52,732	225	1,004	1,982	4,303	7,791.5	10,494	19,665	52,958
2011 Q3	908	$7,555,530	50,775	317	1,385	2,281	4,631	8,321.1	11,836	19,847	51,092
2011 Q4	712	$4,561,054	32,261	303	736	1,477	5,000	6,406.0	9,974	13,591	32,565
2012 Q1	625	$3,788,413	37,479	195	558	934	2,681	6,051.8	10,326	14,006	37,674
2012 Q2	960	$6,260,527	44,970	212	1,132	1,965	3,885	6,521.4	8,300	15,665	45,182
2012 Q3	940	$8,517,290	58,455	158	1,286	2,465	5,360	9,060.9	13,030	21,583	58,613
2012 Q4	747	$4,933,770	39,639	210	621	1,243	4,270	6,604.8	10,169	15,554	39,848
Grand Total	1000	$46,500,000	58,496	117	1,385	745	4,434	7,280.4	13,030	13,591	58,613

FIGURE 5-17. *It is easier to scan this graph than to interpret the table below it.*

Oracle ADF Visualizations

Oracle's Application Development Framework (usually referred to by its acronym ADF) is a framework for developing applications in Java that marry data from a variety of sources with a variety of front-end environments, such as HTML5 websites, and mobile applications. ADF allows integration with SQL, PL/SQL, JavaScript, and HTML, to name a few. JDeveloper from Oracle is a software application that is often used to develop applications using ADF. If you're interested in learning more about writing your own custom SOA visualization applications, you'll want to dig further into both ADF and JDeveloper. ADF Essentials and JDeveloper are both free from Oracle. You'll find lots of code and tutorials and examples to help you out.

Figure 5-18 shows an Open-Hi-Lo-Close graphic with two visualizations. A simple line shows the highest and lowest price for a stock during a period of time, along with two "whiskers" that show the opening and closing price. A bar graph underneath it shows the total volume for stock trades during the period of time. The graph is running in a separate application and is integrated into the OBIEE dashboard. Whatever a developer wants to accomplish in the code can be shown on an OBIEE dashboard (this includes highly interactive features and animations). A simple pop-up is shown on the graph, but this could also be coded to move over time and to "play a movie" of the data. The OBIEE dashboard uses the Embedded Content object type (as shown in Figure 5-19) to call the results of the application. In this particular case, the application is using the OBIEE BI server as a data source and is also running in the same WebLogic domain. This is typical of highly specialized customer visualization applications that are integrated with OBIEE.

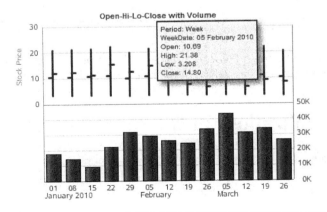

FIGURE 5-18. *Open-Hi-Lo-Close chart with bar chart*

FIGURE 5-19. *Embedded Content dashboard object calls the ADF visualization application.*

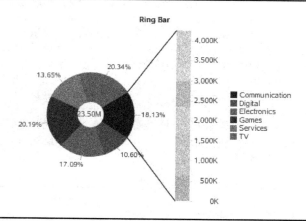

FIGURE 5-20. *Ring bar chart rendered by ADF application built with JDeveloper*

The ring bar chart shown in Figure 5-20 shows the same line of business groups as percentages in the ring and as values in the stacked bar. The range of visualizations that can be rendered with ADF is very extensive.

Using R Visualizations in OBIEE Dashboards

More and more organizations are wanting to integrate predictive analytics into their OBIEE environments. The Oracle R Enterprise component of the Oracle Advanced Analytics option for Oracle Database offers an excellent opportunity to execute highly advanced predictive modeling and statistical analysis. R is an open-source scripting language and environment for statistical computing and graphics. It is popular, powerful, and comprehensive. R is not only excellent for developing data-mining models and all flavors of data analysis, but it also has powerful and wide-ranging data visualization capabilities at the cutting edge of data science. By using R, we can expose all sorts of data visualizations, especially those that are not natively available in OBIEE.

Data values or selections made by users on OBIEE dashboards can be passed back to an Oracle database and processed as part of predictive model. The predictive model results can be sent to OBIEE for visualization and presentation, meaning that highly interactive "what-if" analysis systems, estimations, and even Markov Chain Monte Carlo systems can be built. These advanced visualizations from Oracle R Enterprise can be leveraged by OBIEE utilizing two different methodologies:

- Bring in R images as a serialized BLOB in an Oracle database as a column in an OBIEE table. Create a table in the OBIEE repository with three columns (Name, ID, and Image) that calls the image from your R environment (this is something that your OBIEE administrator will have to configure). You will use a simple table view to show the R PNG visualization. R and OBIEE have powerful scripting capabilities, so it is possible to pass dashboard prompt values, session variables, and other inputs back to R for a highly interactive visualization. This works for representing images as BLOBs, where each row of the result set is its own PNG image (and has its own ID).

- Bring in R images that have been encoded in R as an XML string to an OBIEE dashboard through the BI Publisher interface. This works well when you want to visualize both structured data and image results together.

Figure 5-21 shows an ARIMA times series analysis visualization (ARIMA is a statistical forecasting algorithm often used to make predictions in data sets where growth, seasonality, and variability all have influence). The dark line shows a data series. The solid white line starting at time value 200 shows the prediction computed by the R ARIMA model. The peach area inside the dashed line to the right shows a 95 percent confidence interval range, both high and low.

Figure 5-22 and Figure 5-23 show how simple the modeling is in OBIEE Answers. All the visualization work is being done in the back-end database. OBIEE is simply receiving the results of that output as a column in a table and publishing the extremely simple table view on the dashboard. Note that the query definition includes only three columns. A narrative view is used to publish the PNG output (a table view could also be used).

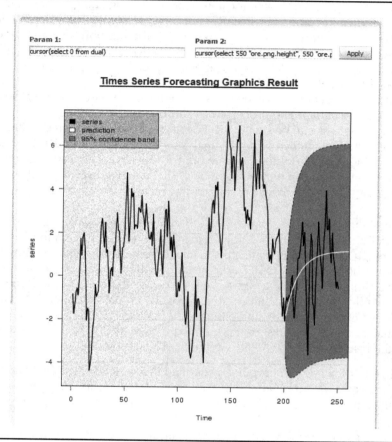

FIGURE 5-21. *R visualization brought into an OBIEE dashboard as a BLOB image*

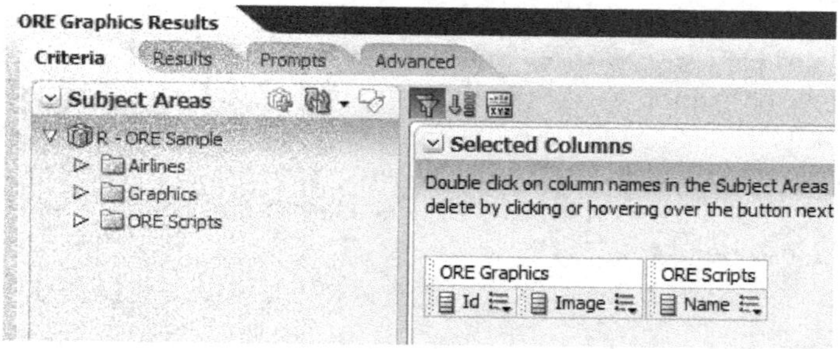

FIGURE 5-22. *Criteria tab for R visualization*

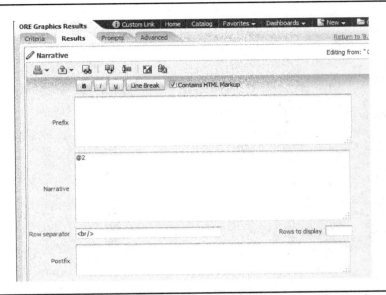

FIGURE 5-23. *Narrative view publishing a PNG image rendered in Oracle Database using Oracle R Enterprise*

In this case, the @2 code is saying to OBIEE, "Publish the contents of the second column (the image column) on the Criteria tab." Those contents happen to be a PNG image that was generated in the Oracle database. This image was brought into OBIEE through the BI Server repository file (see your OBIEE admin for more information on how to integrate images from other data sources). Narrative views are particularly flexible and can be used to not only to render HTML, but also to bring in other information. For example, they can be used to render custom code in OBIEE's web front end. The advantage is that the code is isolated to that particular query or analysis. Of course, the disadvantage is that the code is isolated to that particular query or analysis.

Figure 5-24 shows a combined view of graphic results and structured data selections that function as dashboard prompts. The visualization produced by R is another example of a whisker boxplot, functionally similar to the one in Figure 5-13. We can compare the middle inner quartile range that represents 50 percent of the flights and the whisker lines for years 2000 and 2008. This advanced visualization allows us to compare not only average delay values for the five airports, but also the distribution of the flight delays across the entire year.

Figure 5-25 shows the BI Publisher data set for the ORData data model. The script takes the parameterized values from the dashboard prompts and passes them back to the database (and ultimately, R) for execution of the XML visualization. A fair amount of configuration is required both in BI Publisher and in the OBIEE

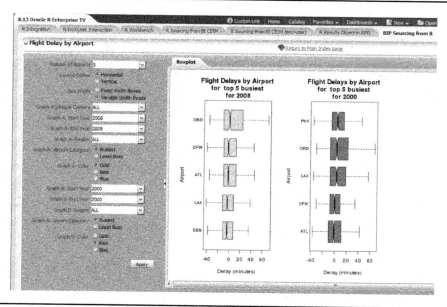

FIGURE 5-24. *BI Publisher–rendered visualization from Oracle R Enterprise*

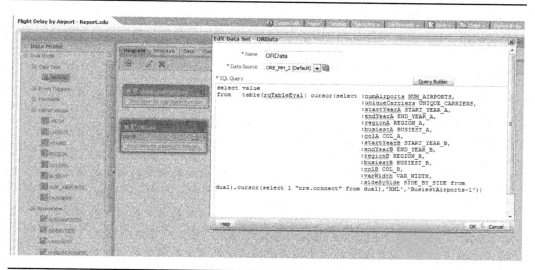

FIGURE 5-25. *BIP data set definition for ORE box plot graphic*

repository file to enable this kind of functionality. The power, however, to realize complex graphics and interaction with and visualization of structured data in an enterprise BI system with extensive dashboard capabilities greatly extends the visualization capabilities of the OBIEE platform.

Using the Third-Party Visualization Engine D3

D3 is an open-source Java library for advanced visualizations that can be installed in the same WebLogic environment with OBIEE and made available to the OBIEE front end through the use of narrative views. D3 stands for "Data-Driven Documents." D3 can be used for those situations where clients require a visualization that is not available natively in OBIEE. Examples of popular visualizations that D3 can be used for include word clouds (shown in Figure 5-26), tree maps, and other visualizations that require display of the distribution of data sets such as bullet graphs and thermometer charts. There are other JavaScript-based visualization libraries and systems, but D3's advantages are that it is open source, standards based, flexible and extensible, and has a comprehensive set of advanced visualizations.

NOTE
Consult with your OBIEE administrator to install and configure the D3 libraries. Although calls can be made to external web services, this involves sending data streams outside of the OBIEE environment for rendering/processing and is not recommended for most implementations that require data security.

FIGURE 5-26. *Word cloud from D3. Sales rep name size is relative to volume.*

D3 employs a Document Object Model (DOM) framework that allows data to be bound to objects generally. Manipulation of the visualization is enabled through changes in the data and the joins to the objects and the container. Instead of telling D3 how to render everything, you tell D3 what you want to render and then join data to it. In this way, D3 is somewhat different from other graphics engines. This strategy also enables highly dynamic visualizations that respond to changes in data selection (for example, with dashboard prompts) and facilitate animations and transitions between data states. Styles, attributes, and other properties can be specified by data, not just constants. D3 is more declarative in nature rather than imperative (procedural). It's helpful to have some background in JavaScript, and for large implementations, you should pass your code by an experienced programmer and test it for scalability before deployment.

Figure 5-27 shows one of the more commonly requested visualizations that is not available in older releases of OBIEE and is rendered on an OBIEE dashboard through the use of D3. Tree maps are made up of blocks that are proportional in size to a chosen metric (the algorithm recursively subdivides an area into rectangles). This tree map responds to the prompts shown at the left side of the dashboard, demonstrating the interactivity that is possible between OBIEE and D3.

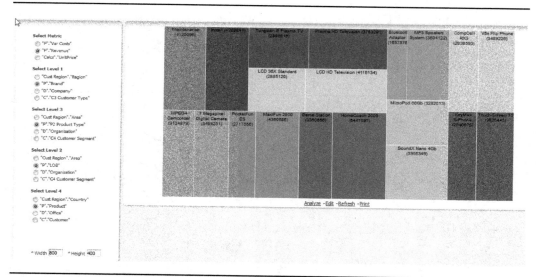

FIGURE 5-27. *D3 tree map visualization*

Figure 5-28 and Figure 5-29 show the relative simplicity of passing parameter information from an OBIEE dashboard to the D3 graphics engine. Each of the formulas for the levels and the metric are nearly identical to the formula shown for Level 1. The formula consists of a prompt value (**{Dim01}**) and a default value (**{"Products"."P4 Brand"}**).

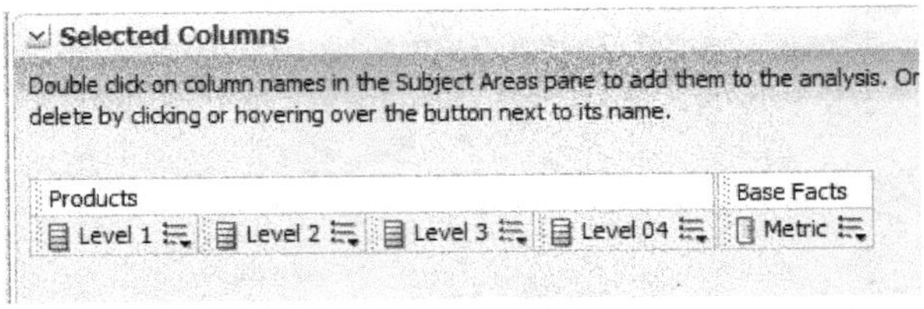

FIGURE 5-28. *D3 tree map Criteria tab*

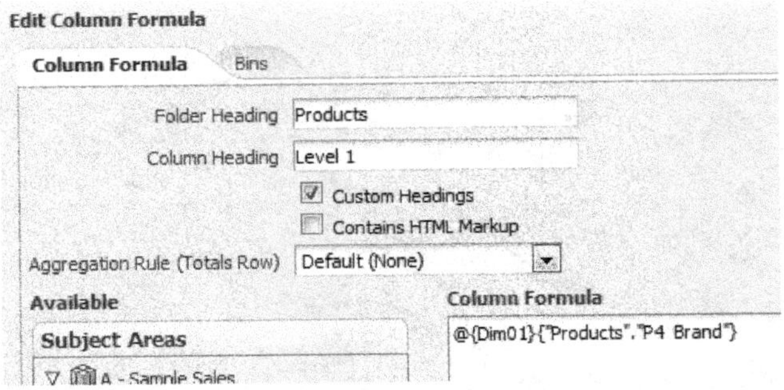

FIGURE 5-29. *D3 tree map formula example*

Figure 5-30 shows how a narrative view in OBIEE is used to render D3 visualizations. Notice that the Contains HTML Markup box is selected. All the real work is being done in D3. The code in the Postfix field is only partially shown in the figure (because it is 75 lines in length), but is shown in its entirety in Listing 5-1. Notice how the Prefix code is calling the D3 program installed in the WebLogic domain and initializing the script. The Narrative field is used to push the data to the array **mydata**. Finally, the Postfix field does the real work, looping through the **mydata** array and building up the variable **jsonStr**, which is evaluated and ultimately passed on to D3 for rendering. The point here is not to explain how D3 works in detail, but to show that OBIEE can leverage the extended capabilities of a fully formed data visualization engine like D3 and do so in a highly interactive manner.

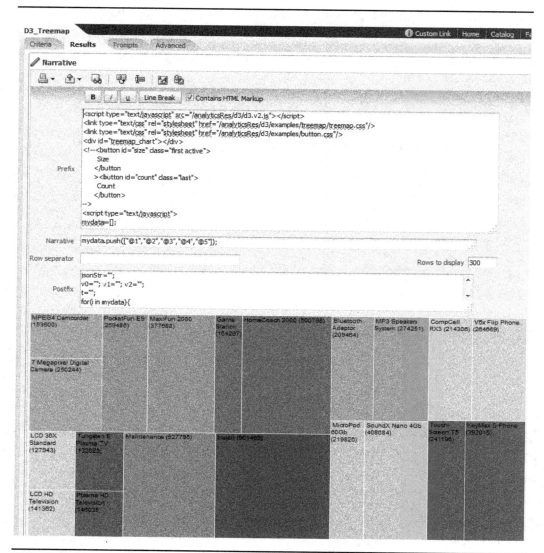

FIGURE 5-30. *D3 tree map narrative view with code*

Listing 5-1. *The Code in the Postfix Field*

```
jsonStr="";
v0=""; v1=""; v2="";
t="";
for(i in mydata){
    found=0;

    if(v0!=mydata[i][0])
       {found=1;  endMarker="]}]}]}";}
    if(v1!=mydata[i][1] && !found)
       {found=2;  endMarker="]}]}";}
    if(v2!=mydata[i][2] && !found)
       {found=3;  endMarker="]}";}

    if(i!=0 && (found>0))          jsonStr+= endMarker;
      if(i!=0)  jsonStr+=",";

    if(v0!=mydata[i][0]){   jsonStr+=
       "\n{\"name\": \""+mydata[i][0]+"\",\"children\": [";}
    if(v1!=mydata[i][1]){   jsonStr+=
       "\n\t{\"name\": \""+mydata[i][1]+"\",\"children\": [";}
    if(v2!=mydata[i][2]){   jsonStr+=
       "\n\t\t{\"name\": \""+mydata[i][2]+"\",\"children\": [";}

    jsonStr+="\n\t\t\t{\"name\": \""
           +mydata[i][3]+ "\", \"size\":" + mydata[i][4] + "}";

    if(v0!=mydata[i][0]){ v0=mydata[i][0];}
    if(v1!=mydata[i][1]){ v1=mydata[i][1];}
    if(v2!=mydata[i][2]){ v2=mydata[i][2];}

    if (i==(mydata.length-1)) { jsonStr+="]}]}]}" };
}
jsonStr = "{\"name\": \"All Products\", \"children\": [" + jsonStr + "]}";
var myDataObject = eval('(' + jsonStr + ')');

var width = @{Width}{800},
    height = @{Height}{400},
    color = d3.scale.category20c();
var treemap = d3.layout.treemap()
    .size([width, height])
    .sticky(true)
    .value(function(d) { return d.size; });

var div = d3.select("#treemap_chart").append("div")
    .style("position", "relative")
    .style("width", width + "px")
    .style("height", height + "px");

json=myDataObject;
```

```
    div.data([json]).selectAll("div")
        .data(treemap.nodes)
        .enter().append("div")
        .attr("class", "cell")
        .style("background", function(d)
            { return d.children ? color(d.name) : null; })
        .call(cell)
        .text(function(d)
            { return d.children ? null : d.name+" ("+d.size+")"; });

  d3.select("#size").on("click", function() {
    div.selectAll("div")
        .data(treemap.value(function(d) { return d.size; }))
        .transition()
        .duration(1500)
        .call(cell);

    d3.select("#size").classed("active", true);
    d3.select("#count").classed("active", false);
  });

  d3.select("#count").on("click", function() {
    div.selectAll("div")
        .data(treemap.value(function(d) { return 1; }))
        .transition()
        .duration(1500)
        .call(cell);

    d3.select("#size").classed("active", false);
    d3.select("#count").classed("active", true);
  });

function cell() {
  this
      .style("left", function(d)
          { return d.x + "px"; })
      .style("top", function(d)
          { return d.y + "px"; })
      .style("width", function(d)
          { return Math.max(0, d.dx - 1) + "px"; })
      .style("height", function(d)
          { return Math.max(0, d.dy - 1) + "px"; });
}
</script>
```

JQuery

JQuery is another general-purpose JavaScript library that has some visualization capabilities, although it is not as focused on data visualization as is D3. JQuery is one of the "workhorses" of the Web, and it is likely that most of the web developers in your organization will be familiar with it (they may or may not be familiar with D3).

Figure 5-31 shows a sparklines-style table somewhat similar to a trellis chart. This was rendered using JQuery. Figure 5-32 shows the Table Layout editor in the Results tab. Once again, we see that most of the work is done via scripting. There is a column on the far right where the column heading name has been replaced with a single space. This is the Spark Functions Definitions column (shown in Figure 5-33) that converts the code to visualizations. The column is necessary (and shown to the right of the Bullet column in Figure 5-31) but has no data to show in the table (that's why there is a single space). If we kept the column heading name, there would be a wide empty cell.

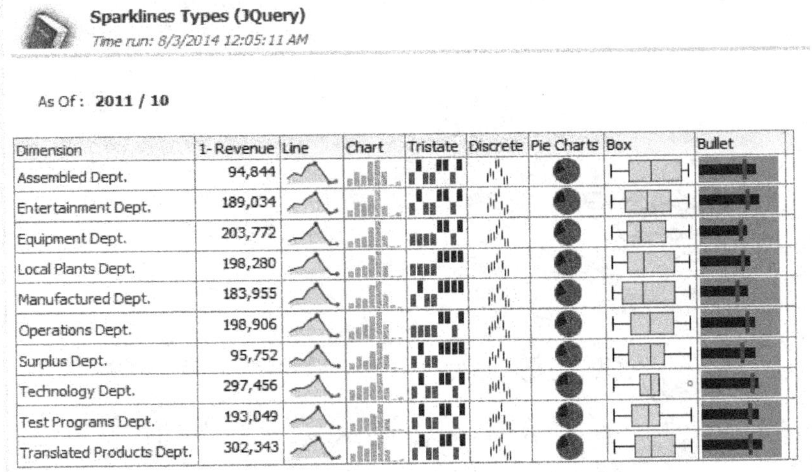

FIGURE 5-31. *Sparklines JQuery table*

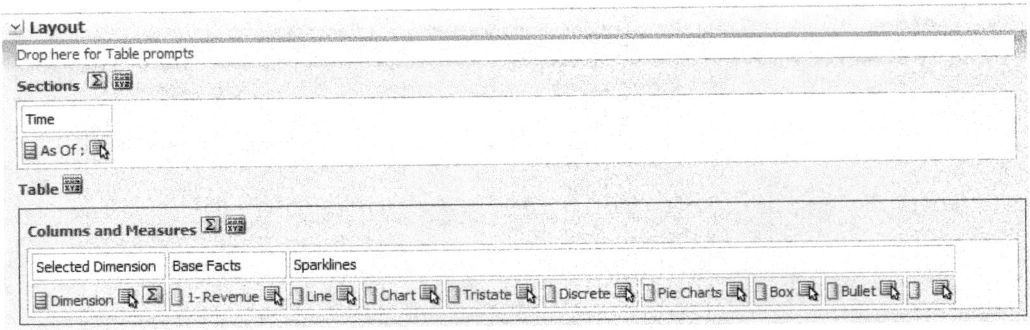

FIGURE 5-32. *Table layout for JQuery sparklines*

Selected Dimension	Time	Base Facts	Sparklines
🗐 Dimension ☴	🗐 T02 Per Name Month ☴	🗐 1- Revenue ☴	🗐 Spark Functions Definition ☴ 🗐 Line ☴ 🗐 Chart ☴ 🗐 Tristate ☴ 🗐 Discrete ☴ 🗐 Pie Charts ☴ 🗐 Box ☴ 🗐 Bullet ☴

FIGURE 5-33. *Criteria tab for JQuery sparklines*

Figure 5-34 shows the code that is entered directly in the Column Formula field for the Sparklines Functions Definition column. This provides the definitions used by all the columns. Figure 5-35 shows the code that is entered directly for the Chart column. This serves as an example for all of the sparkline columns.

Edit Column Formula

Column Formula   Bins

Folder Heading Sparklines

Column Heading Spark Functions Definition

☑ Custom Headings
☐ Contains HTML Markup

Aggregation Rule (Totals Row) Default

Available

Subject Areas

▽ 🗐 A - Sample Sales
  ▷ 🗀 Time
  ▷ 🗀 Products
  ▷ 🗀 Offices
  ▷ 🗀 Sales Persor
  ▷ 🗀 Customers
  ▷ 🗀 Orders
  ▷ 🗀 Other Objects
  ▷ 🗀 Facts

Column Formula

```
'<script type="text/javascript" src="/analyticsRes/SampleApp/Scripts/jquery-1.4.2.min.js"></script>
<script type="text/javascript" src="/analyticsRes/SampleApp/Scripts/jquery.sparkline.js"></script>
<script type="text/javascript">
/*
   This defines bar chart functions (one for each row of report)    */ $(function() {
$(".a'||cast(rcount(1) as varchar(3))||'").sparkline("html", {type: "bar", barColor:"#CBC29F"}); });
/*
   This defines line functions (one for each row of report)    */$(function() { $(".b'||cast(rcount(1) as
varchar(3))||'").sparkline("html", {type: "line", width:"40px", minSpotColor:"red",
maxSpotColor:"green"}); });
/*
   This defines tristate bar functions (one for each row of report) */$(function() {
$(".c'||cast(rcount(1) as varchar(3))||'").sparkline("html", {type: "tristate", negBarColor:"red" ,
posBarColor:"green"}); });
/*
   This defines discrete chart functions (one for each row of report) */$(function() {
$(".d'||cast(rcount(1) as varchar(3))||'").sparkline("html", {type: "discrete"}); });
/*
   This defines pie chart functions (one for each row of report) */$(function() { $(".e'||cast(rcount(1)
as varchar(3))||'").sparkline("html", {type: "pie"}); });
/*
   This defines box chart functions (one for each row of report) */$(function() { $(".f'||cast(rcount(1)
as varchar(3))||'").sparkline("html", {type: "box"}); });
/*
   This defines bullet chart functions (one for each row of report) */$(function() {
$(".g'||cast(rcount(1) as varchar(3))||'").sparkline("html", {type: "bullet"}); }); </script>'
```

| f(...) | Filter... | Column ⌄ | Variable ⌄ | + | - | x | / | % | (|) | || |

OK   Cancel

FIGURE 5-34. *Sparklines Functions Definition column formula for JQuery sparklines*

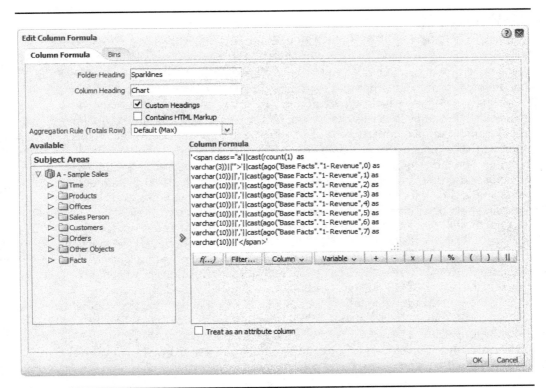

FIGURE 5-35. *Chart column formula for JQuery sparklines*

It's relatively straightforward to see what's being done. The chart column formula uses a simple **span** statement and casts each column input as a **varchar (10)**. The Spark Functions Definition code specifies the eight bars that are displayed in the Chart column. The argument to the **ago** function varies from 0 to 7 to provide the last eight periods of data. This is a good example of specialized code that is buried in the definition of the query.

Bear in mind that although JQuery (and other advanced visualizations not built into OBIEE) provides additional flexibility in displaying data, it comes at the cost of additional complexity and maintenance. Imagine the number of places that would have to be modified if the name of the column changes from "1-Revenue" to just "Revenue," or the changes required if you want to display 10 bars instead of 8 bars.

Summary

Data visualizations in OBIEE can be extended using several different methodologies, languages, and techniques. There is virtually nothing that can be done in other web-based systems that can't be done in OBIEE. Trellis charts are tables of small charts that are organized by columns and rows. Simple trellis charts (or "Type 1" trellis charts) have a common scale across all mini charts of the same type. Advanced trellis charts (or "Type 2" trellis charts) are individually scaled and should not be used for direct value comparisons, but rather for overall pattern detection. Gauges have many challenges from a human cognition perspective and should be used carefully. Some of OBIEE's native visualizations can be extended beyond their immediate use case, although at the risk of additional complexity and maintenance. For example, line bar combo graphs can be extended to show tremendous detail regarding data distribution in a "whisker boxplot"–style graph.

Oracle ADF provides a flexible and extensible capability to develop data visualization applications that can be called from OBIEE dashboards. The language R is taking the predictive analytics world by storm and has tremendous native data visualization capabilities. OBIEE can show native R visualizations rendered in an Oracle database as BLOB objects. BI Publisher can also be used to create an XML-based visualization that allows for parameterization and interactive capabilities with R scripts in the Oracle database. OBIEE can use JavaScript to render visualizations. D3 is a particularly powerful open-source JavaScript library, and JQuery is a common, general-purpose JavaScript library that many web developers are familiar with. It can be used to render custom graphics in OBIEE.

CHAPTER
6

BI Publisher

From a data visualization perspective, there are things that can be done with BI Publisher that are more difficult to do with standard OBIEE. That being said, there are also some complications and nuances that BI Publisher presents. BI Publisher could be the subject of its own book, so we'll confine ourselves to a limited discussion. (Indeed, virtually every chapter in this book could be replicated using BI Publisher as the main interface rather than OBIEE.) All the general guidelines on visualization design from Chapters 1 through 5 apply to visualizations created in BI Publisher.

Oracle BI Publisher is an enterprise reporting product from Oracle that is a standalone product and is fully integrated into OBIEE 11*g*. As Oracle states, "BI Publisher is the reporting solution to author, manage, and deliver all your reports and documents." BI Publisher provides the ability to create and manage highly formatted reports from a wide range of data sources and render them as "pixel perfect" reports (with a high degree of control over exact placement of report elements). Oracle BI Publisher also allows you to create reports from different types of data sources, such as Oracle Database, files, OBIEE, and Web Services.

The Power of Pixel Perfect Visualizations

In many use cases, you'll want to specify exactly how a visualization appears, down to every pixel. In such cases, it's sometimes best to utilize the powerful templating abilities of BI Publisher. For example, you might want to reproduce an exact version of a profit and loss (P&L) or balance sheet financial statement, complete with extensive formatting that would be painful to replicate in the standard OBIEE analysis editor.

BI Publisher Contrasted with OBIEE

Although BI Publisher started out as a standalone product (and is often still used as such in many Oracle application environments), it has been in the process of being integrated into OBIEE for several years across many releases. OBIEE and BI Publisher have overlapping capabilities, and because BI Publisher is "a part" of the OBIEE Foundation Suite and comes not just bundled as a companion application but as an integrated set of features, it can be challenging to differentiate where it exactly starts and stops. BI Publisher was developed with a "print this report on a page" mindset, whereas OBIEE Answers was developed with a "publish this query on a dashboard screen" mindset. BI Publisher has a "print this result like this" mentality, while Answers has a "fit these results on a web-based dashboard" mentality.

The original name for BI Publisher was "XML Publisher" (a name still used sometimes when it is bundled with other Oracle applications). BI Publisher is on the cutting edge of Oracle's approach to visualization as its elements form the foundation of BIMAD (BI Mobile App Designer), the latest module of BI Foundation Suite. In most field implementations, BI Publisher has a definite "printed document" mentality and its strengths are particularly suited to that purpose. For example, BI Publisher is often used for printing invoices, accounts receivable statements, highly formatted weekly "update" reports, and even checks. Basically, when you have a document and want to add "fields" containing numbers or names or other images, BI Publisher is a good solution. You can almost think of it as "mail merge" on steroids. Suppose you have a standard form letter, but need to add calculated measures and visualizations based on who you are sending it to. BI Publisher is your answer. Of course, this is only one set of use cases, but this explanation is helpful when people need to know the difference between BI Publisher and OBIEE. BI Publisher also supports XBRL, a special form of XML that attaches tags for financial data and allows the efficient transfer of financially formatted data between applications. This specialized functionality has particular importance in situations where formatting carries both meaning and relevance for interpretation, such as with financial statements. Figure 6-1 shows a traditional use case for BI Publisher in which data fields are defined on a template document and a "merge" function places the correct values into the fields. Figure 6-2 shows a "typical" use case for BI Publisher in which a document is produced with BI data and visualizations.

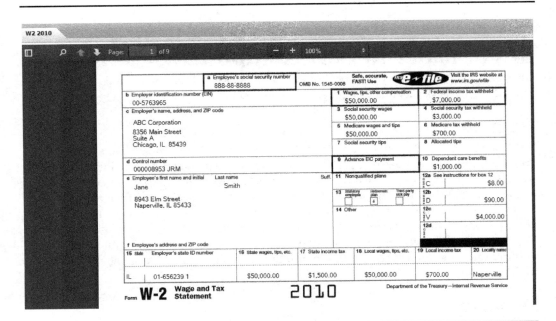

FIGURE 6-1. *Traditional use case for BI Publisher*

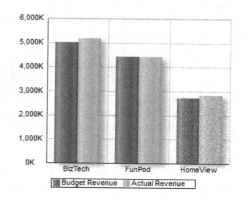

FIGURE 6-2. *Typical use case for BI Publisher*

BI Publisher Report Components

The three components of a BI Publisher Report (Data Model, Template, and Properties) all work together to deliver a finished report.

Data Model

The "data model" component is where data sources and selections are made. BI Publisher thinks of this data model as just a stream of XML data. Historically, this was a series of relational tables. Because data can come from multiple sources, you can use BI Publisher as a sort of easy data federation engine. Starting in release 11.1.1.6, BI Publisher can use OBIEE's BI server repository file as a data source. This deepens the integration of BI Publisher into the Oracle BI family of products because you can capitalize on the work done in the RPD file when using BI Publisher reports. You can even use the result of an OBIEE analysis as a data model for BI Publisher.

Template

The "template" component establishes the basic layout into which data fields are placed. This template can be created in Microsoft Word, Adobe Acrobat, Microsoft Excel, or BI Publisher's Layout Editor.

Properties

And finally there is a set of properties attached to the layout that are specific to the report. These properties establish important display attributes for the layout and include many display choices such as borders, chart colors for data series, and more.

Layout Editor Is the Major Interface

The Layout Editor component is the major interface for BI Publisher in OBIEE and provides a "WYSIWYG" editor for web-based outputs. Here's where thinking of BI Publisher's historic roots can help. Suppose you have a data set (model) and want to merge it into a document (template) and produce an individualized version for each record in a data set and then distribute individualized reports electronically on a scheduled basis. When the output is an HTML screen rather than a printed piece of paper, the thinking gets a bit more complex. The Layout Editor is like a template editor for the Web. (Of course, web pages can then be converted into different output formats, such as .pdf, .rtf, and so on.)

Bi Publisher has very powerful output capabilities; however, we the authors are usually not very big fans of the "out-of-the-box" default settings in BI Publisher. As you can see in Figure 6-3, there are too many 3-D effects, garishly bright graphs, and effects that distract from the message of the data. The good news is that the output can be highly configured through the interface.

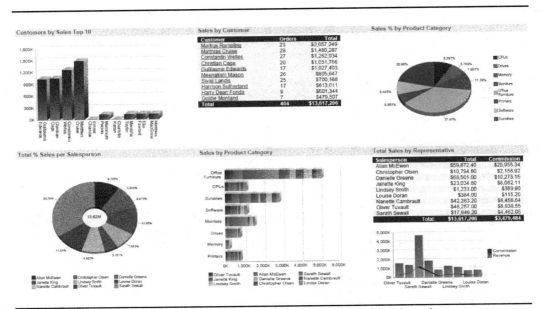

FIGURE 6-3. *Typical BI Publisher layout with 3-D effects and bright colors*

Although layouts can be created in Microsoft Word and saved as .rtf layouts, we'll focus on the Layout Editor interface that is presented as part of OBIEE because OBIEE is the subject of this book. Additional information on inserting the appropriate XML tags and configuring the file .rtf docs can be found in the Oracle Fusion Middleware Report Designer's Guide for Oracle Business Intelligence Publisher 11*g*:

http://docs.oracle.com/cd/E23943_01/bi.1111/e22254/create_rtf_tmpl.htm

Interacting with BI Publisher

You really have three different "levels of interface" with BI Publisher when designing tables, graphs, and visualizations. These levels are described in increasing complexity and degree of customization possible. The first level is the "selector" level, where you drag and drop and select which features from a limited set you want to use. The second level is the visual GUI for an XML script coder. The layout and structure of this interface is organized similar to the way XML scripts are organized. The third level is where you edit XML code directly.

Figure 6-4 shows the Layout Editor interface for an airline passenger count report. The Layout Editor can be thought of as combining certain elements of OBIEE

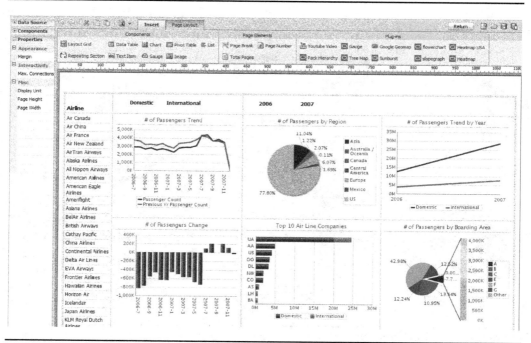

FIGURE 6-4. *BI Publisher Layout Editor*

in one interface: the dashboard builder in OBIEE, where we use columns and sections to organize and align objects; the Criteria tab in Answers, where we define the data to be used in analysis; and the Results tab in Answers, where we edit and refine analysis views. In the far left panel we see three different menu groups: Data Source, Components, and Properties. Data Source shows the data model that is used for the report. You can add a data value, series, or label by dragging it from the Data Source panel to the designated drop zone on the layout.

Components are objects on the layout. The biggest difference between OBIEE dashboard layouts (covered in Chapter 7) and the BI Publisher Layout Editor is the Layout Grid. Although grid cells are similar in concept to columns in the OBIEE dashboard builder, it's possible to drag the edges of the grid lines to the position you want (much easier than using a dialog and entering pixel numbers). It's also possible to place grids inside of grids so that you can align objects within a section and keep your layout organized. Also, grids cells can be merged. This provides you with a tremendous amount of flexibility and capability when designing layouts. You may find that this is similar to the process of laying out a web page with tables inside of tables, which is prevalent in many web page design tools.

The ribbon at the top provides a contextualized list of actions. The tabs that are displayed are dependent on the active object selected in the layout. Figure 6-5 shows basic items that become available when the chart is selected in the layout. The list of chart styles in the drop-down shows a range of color selections for a bar chart. Again, be careful of just using the default, out-of-the-box selections. See your OBI administrator to add your own color ramps and selections to the list of available options. Figure 6-5 shows the drop zones for values, labels, and series.

You'll likely find that you do the majority of your editing by using the Properties panel on the far left because it offers more granular control of the output results. Most of these menus are fairly intuitive and follow the approximate order of the final XML output (that is, if you were to open the .xdm file in a text editor such as Notepad, you'd find the code sequenced from top to bottom of the sections of the Properties panel). Many of the interfaces in BI Publisher Layout Editor are relatively intuitive and easy to understand. Clicking in the Margin area brings up the Margin interface shown in Figure 6-6. Notice that the "Margin" definition in the interface is highlighted and the other options are all clearly shown (otherwise, the difference between margin and padding might be confusing). The only "trick" in using the GUI interface is knowing to click the "..." button near the property you want to edit. Making adjustments to refine results is exactly what BI Publisher is all about.

The Properties | Chart menu allows you to select different types of charts. You'll find all the types included in OBIEE, plus a few more. The ribbon on top has a nice "fly-out" menu that shows thumbnail examples of the graphs. Figure 6-7 shows the selections for bar graphs. We'll look at some of the more useful and unique graphs in the "BI Publisher Dual-Y Graph Types" section of the chapter a little later.

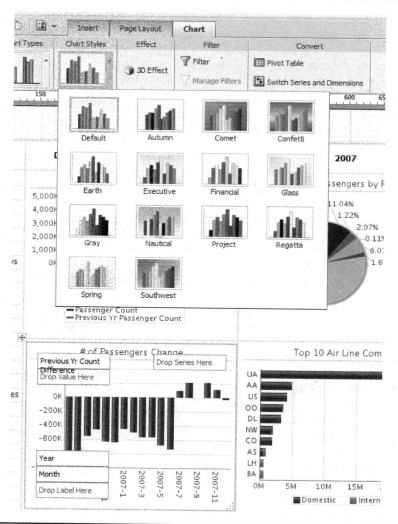

FIGURE 6-5. *BI Publisher ribbon and drop zones*

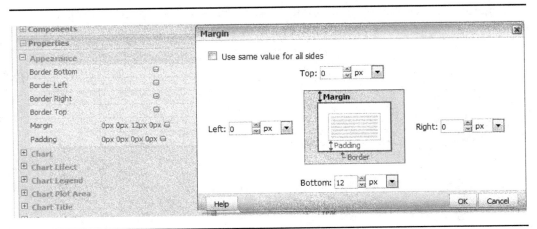

FIGURE 6-6. *The Margin interface in the Properties panel*

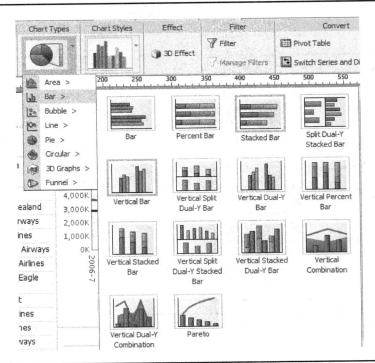

FIGURE 6-7. *Bar chart selections available in BI Publisher Layout Editor*

Figure 6-8 shows the selections for line charts. The "Dual-Y" options also offer some very interesting possibilities.

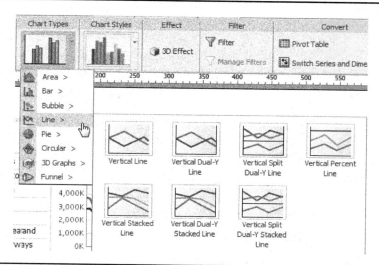

FIGURE 6-8. *Line chart options in Layout Editor*

Figure 6-9 shows the bubble chart options. This section includes scatter plots. These are some of the most useful charts in BI Publisher Layout Editor.

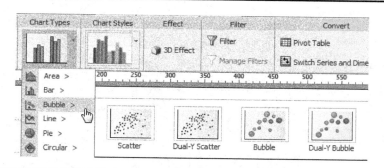

FIGURE 6-9. *Bubble chart options in Layout Editor*

Figure 6-10 shows the pie chart options in BI Publisher layout editor. Pie charts are one of the most common visualizations in business today, even though they are not particularly strong from a human cognition perspective. The "fly-out" information available with Pie-Bar and Ring Bar charts can help bring attention to a particular data selection/group. This disrupts the overall story of the comparison of the various pieces to the whole, but also has the positive effect of making a particular element more prominent within the context of a larger situation. While both pie charts and ring charts suffer from similar problems of lack of consistent interpretation, they can be effective in some circumstances. As stated in Chapter 3, you should avoid 3-D effects and stick with the "flatter" visualizations.

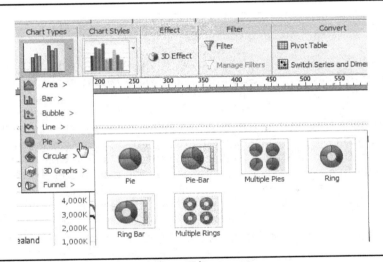

FIGURE 6-10.   *Pie chart options in Layout Editor*

Figure 6-11 shows the circular chart types available in Layout Editor. Line radar charts are best used for dissimilar measures (see radar graphs in Chapter 3). Polar charts can be useful when significance is attached to the presence of a data element in the different quadrants.

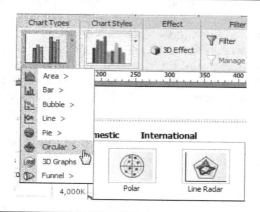

FIGURE 6-11. *Circular chart types in Layout Editor*

Figure 6-12 shows the 3-D graph types in BI Publisher Layout Editor. These graph types should mostly be avoided because they are problematic to implement well, partly because the "depth dimension" necessarily causes the data to overlap. This can work if you only have two or three dimension values in the "depth dimension" and when the data is sorted so that the larger numbers are farthest from the screen, but the presentation is still problematic. When you have multiple dimensions to the data and you want to show them, you'll need to work hard to find what the "main" message is of the analysis and how best to present it. There are usually better alternatives. If you must represent multiple dimensions on a screen, an array of smaller graphs is often superior to trying to represent all the data in one graph.

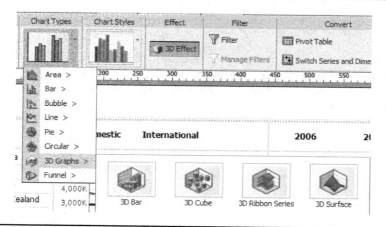

FIGURE 6-12. *3-D chart options in Layout Editor*

Figure 6-13 shows the area chart options available in BI Publisher Layout Editor. Area charts are colorful, and people love them. They can work well when they are limited to one or two data elements in the selection (the Vertical Split Dual-Y option can also be used). When more than two data elements are included in a "stack," however, interpretation becomes problematic.

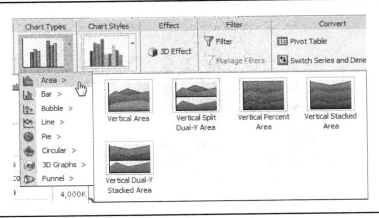

FIGURE 6-13. *Area chart options in Layout Editor*

BI Publisher Dual-Y Graph Types

The most useful of the additional graph types are the vertical dual-Y bar, the split dual-Y stacked bar, and the vertical split dual-Y bar. We'll walk through a use case where a traditional stacked bar chart fails to show important data that is "swamped" by the size of the rest of the data sets. There are many other examples where a second y-axis adds to meaning and eases interpretation.

In Figure 6-14, we want to show how many passengers there were by airline terminal. However, the three main terminals had passenger counts in the millions of passengers, but an "Other" category had a handful of passengers in two of the years—that's why the Other bar doesn't show up. Let's say that the passenger counts for the "Other" terminal were not incidental to the business, but rather were significant and needed to be brought to attention in the visualization. You can run into situations like this all the time when dealing with real data where some of the data categories exist at a completely different scale but represent important information to management and need to be represented. The typical answer is to create two different graphs with two different scales and to reflect in their position and design that they should be consumed at the same time. The vertical split dual-Y bar graph shown in Figure 6-15 addresses this need by putting all values in the same graph and showing them at two different scales (one on the left y-axis and one on the right y-axis).

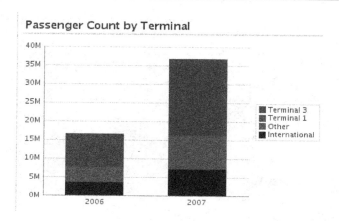

FIGURE 6-14. *Traditional stacked bar chart*

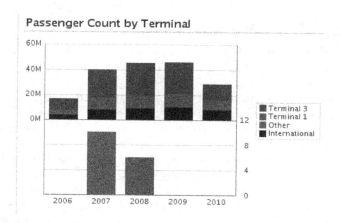

FIGURE 6-15. *Vertical split dual-Y bar*

Although using a split dual-Y bar graph solves this problem, bear in mind that dual-Y axis scales are fraught with challenges in interpretation. In this example, the Other category actually dominates the graph from a visual attention perspective. This gives it an "outweighed" presence in the analysis. The facts are that there were very, very few passengers that didn't depart through one of the main three terminals. If you want to point out the differences, it's very difficult to do with a traditional bar graph. The Other category "disappears" at the scale of millions of passengers. The vertical split dual-Y axis graph allows a story to be told, but it's told by consciously distorting the visual presentation of the data. Generally speaking, dual-Y axis charts and graphs should be employed in analyst role dashboards and should be avoided in general executive and enterprise summary dashboards unless the context of the data is clearly obvious and there is little potential for misinterpretation.

CAUTION
Make sure the cognitive benefits of presenting data using a graph with a dual-Y axis scale outweighs the cognitive cost of requiring users to interpret a more complex graph.

Dual-Y axis graphs can also bring sharp attention to trends in otherwise familiar graphs. Although these are traditionally done in separate graphs, there can be some benefit to adding the "insight" to a graph on second y-axis. Whereas in the first example we saw the benefit of using two y-axes to represent two different scales of the same series, in this example we'll use different measures (and no "series" field). Figure 6-16 shows a traditional "this year" and "last year" graph. The interpretation of the widening variance between the two years is left to the user to see (at first glance, it just seems that this year is following the same trend as last year). However, because the overall scale of the graph is relatively large compared to the change, the trend is missed. But it's hard to miss the "diverging" lines shown in Figure 6-17. Even though it can take some effort to figure out which line is attached to which axis the first time, managers and executives become accustomed to reading patterns in graphs quite quickly. Often, important insights contained in "difference" and "percentage difference" measures are missed because either they are left to interpretation due to only discrete values being graphed or they are not highlighted in a clear manner.

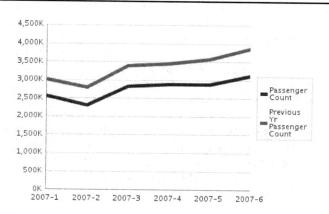

FIGURE 6-16. *Traditional "this year versus last year" graph*

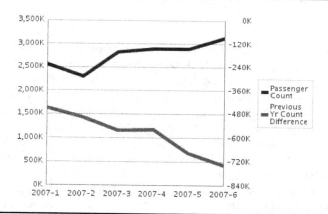

FIGURE 6-17. *Vertical dual-Y line graph shows two different measures with two different scales*

Figure 6-18 shows the "drop zone" values for the chart shown in Figure 6-17. Note that there are two different measures in the "Drop Value Here" field; the top measure equates to "Series 1" and "Axis 1" on the far left y-axis and the lower value equates to "Series 2" and "Axis 2" on the right. When three measures are included, two will be grouped together on a single axis (start with Axis 1 on the far left and add related measures before finally adding the measure that is intended to be on Axis 2). Taking away clear insights from dual-axis graphs when there are more than two lines is a significant challenge and is best suited for situations where no ambiguity exists about which lines are which. Adding more and more information to single graphs gets counterproductive in most cases.

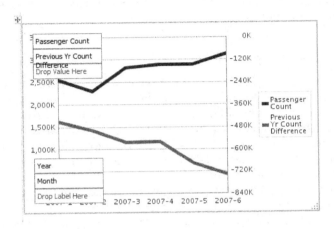

FIGURE 6-18. *Drop zone for vertical dual-Y line chart*

Figure 6-19 shows the "drop zone" values for a vertical split dual-Y bar chart. Notice that there is only one measure, but that it also includes a "group by" attribute in the "Series" drop zone (in this case, Terminal). Although it's possible to add more than one attributes to the "series" and create a "nested" group by attribute, this should be reserved for special use cases.

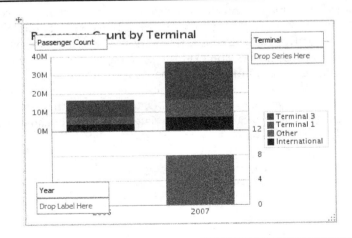

FIGURE 6-19. *Drop zones for vertical split dual-Y stacked bar chart*

Although for OBIEE charts developed in Answers it may be possible to navigate to the Advanced tab in Answers and edit the XML for a particular analysis, this is not recommended. Too many parts of the code are automatically generated by other parts of OBIEE, and editing the wrong piece of XML will break your analysis. This is not necessarily true in BI Publisher.

Bursting Reports

One of the features in BI Publisher used most is its bursting capabilities. For example, suppose you want to send an open orders report each week to each of your salespeople. This report should be highly formatted so that it can be shown to the customer. You also want to e-mail the report to each of the salespeople to minimize their time spent in using OBIEE—all they have to do is look at their e-mail. Each salesperson is only to receive orders for his or her customers. This requires a separate PDF file for each salesperson.

The ability to run a report once and then generate a separate file when some value changes is called "bursting." The term originated when computer printouts needed to be "bursted," separating the "burst page" or cover page that identified the recipient of the report. When reports are designed to be bursted, each person can receive his or her page(s) separately. Today, this means delivering a separate file for each person automatically, often by including the name (or number) of the field that changes in the filename.

Figure 6-20 shows a PDF file that is designed to be bursted. Each page is complete and shows orders for a single customer. Indeed, we could have created a separate file for each customer and designed this to be delivered directly to the customer. A good example of this operation would be a BI Publisher report that generates invoices for each customer.

The process for generating reports to be bursted is exactly the same as for regular reports, except you need to specify what data fields to burst by and deliver by. From a visualization perspective, the main difference in designing reports for bursting versus regular reports is the lack of context from prior pages. Indeed, it may be inappropriate to provide page numbers, or perhaps page numbers need to start over. Special attention must be given to headers and footers that must supply all of the information to place the information in context. Data selection transparency is critically important. Also, you should be sure to date each page, because files can be preserved and can lose the natural context of "today's date."

CUSTOMER ORDERS REPORT
Current Date: Aug 18, 2014

ORACLE
BI PUBLISHER

Customer Name:	Martin Geraldine
Customer ID:	116
City:	Detroit
State/Province:	MI
Country:	United States of America
Order(s) Grand Total:	32,307.00

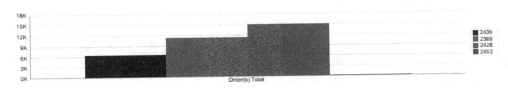

Orders Summary

Customer Name	City	State/Province	Country	Order ID	Channel	Order Total
Martin Geraldine	Detroit	MI	United States of America	2436	direct	6,394.80
Martin Geraldine	Detroit	MI	United States of America	2369	online	11,097.40
Martin Geraldine	Detroit	MI	United States of America	2428	direct	14,685.80
Martin Geraldine	Detroit	MI	United States of America	2453	direct	129.00
					Total	32,307.00

Hardware and Software, **Engineered to Work together**
About Oracle | Legal Notices | Terms of Use | Subscribe | Contact Us

Oracle **BI Publisher**
More Information | Feedback

Page 1 of 19

CUSTOMER ORDERS REPORT
Current Date: Aug 18, 2014

ORACLE
BI PUBLISHER

Customer Name:	Landis Sivaji
Customer ID:	144
City:	Cedar Rapids
State/Province:	IA
Country:	United States of America
Order(s) Grand Total:	160,284.60

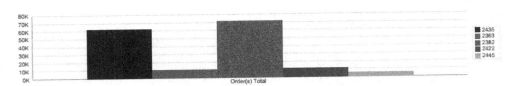

FIGURE 6-20. *BI Publisher PDF file showing bursting*

Summary

BI Publisher presents a powerful alternative to building dashboards in OBIEE. BI Publisher excels at producing pixel-perfect reports, where you want fine control over the exact layout of graphic and text elements. It was especially developed for printed reports and uses templates to incorporate data (which can be from multiple sources) into a page that you can lay out with a GUI editor. This GUI editor provides a powerful capability for laying out a page to your exact needs. You can use the bursting feature to deliver reports to multiple recipients at once, with different content going to each recipient.

You may want to incorporate BI Publisher reports into your dashboards if you need some of the unique graph types (especially dual-Y graphs). You will find that the specific methods of working with prompts, laying out a dashboard, and data selection are a bit different with BI Publisher than the rest of OBIEE, but the visualization concepts are exactly the same.

CHAPTER
7

Dashboard Design
and Mechanics

We the authors usually begin our training session on dashboard design by encouraging the participants to think of OBIEE dashboards as websites. The usual response is, "Wait a minute, I thought we're here to learn about business intelligence and business analytics systems, not websites." That's exactly right. We feel free to leverage many of the best practices that have been developed over the past two decades in website development exactly because they often have direct applicability to business intelligence dashboard development.

Here is our preferred definition of a business intelligence dashboard:

A dashboard is a visual presentation of current summary information needed to manage and guide an organization or activity.

The following definition comes from Stephen Few of Intelligent Enterprise:

A dashboard is a visual display of the most important information needed to achieve one or more objectives, consolidated or arranged on a single screen so that the information can be monitored at a glance.

Many business intelligence dashboard definitions emphasize the need to understand the content of the dashboard "at a glance." Although this may be true for real-world dashboards in fighter aircraft, nuclear power plants, security systems, and other highly dynamic environments in which dashboard users must make split-second determinations and respond immediately, most business intelligence dashboards do not share this need. Think of dashboards as a place where people go for news, insights, and understanding. These all should be communicated in an efficient and effective manner. Think of the way that newspapers are organized. They have sections with themes for readers with specific interests. Headlines provide summary information that allows a reader to scan for articles of particular interest or importance. The best newspapers strive for a consistent tone and never compromise quality or professionalism in their writing and insist on objectivity and a lack of deliberate slanting of the truth in their presentations.

OBIEE has a "democratic" soul when it comes to business intelligence. Every user automatically gets a dashboard called "My Dashboard" in which they can place their favorite analyses, graphs, tables, and other objects. Additionally, users can save their customized dashboard settings and apply them quickly and easily. We will cover this more in Chapter 8, after we discuss various dashboard prompts. In most organizations, a central group creates the broad organizational dashboards, but there is also a need for individualized presentations of information, and for many users, that means doing it yourself. The same basic principles apply to all dashboards, no matter if they are personalized.

BI systems (and new implementations in particular) can be very effective "truthsayers" in organizations. BI systems with a Common Enterprise Information Model (like OBIEE's repository file) often expose "dirty data" and inconsistent or incorrect data flows in business processes, leading to legitimate work in determining what the true data is. We often uncover situations in the "testing" phase of new OBI implementations where historic "gold standard" reports have inaccuracies or falsehoods. For large organizations with extensive audit and reporting procedures, this can be an issue. We always encourage organizations to invest the work to get the foundational data correct/consistent so that future analytics work can be developed with confidence. BI systems and new implementations of them must be managed carefully not only from a technical perspective, but also from an organizational impact perspective. New insights, visualizations, analyses, alerts, and presentations may fundamentally change the way positions, roles, people, and functions are seen and understood within organizations. Data visualization is a very powerful tool, and choosing how data (evidence) is presented and emphasized can be a source of friction and perceived unfairness within an organization.

Exploration vs. Explanation

Differing needs and perspectives inform the decisions that should be consciously made when you are designing business intelligence dashboards. Exploration dashboards are all about developing new and previously unknown insights into data sets. In contrast, explanation dashboards are about communicating known information to a group of people so that they understand it better and so that a shared, common foundation of knowledge is established. Fundamentally, exploration is an individual or small group activity. Sharing those discovered insights to a broader audience is what "explanation" is all about. There are several strategies (some mutually exclusive) that guide dashboard design.

Exploration strategies include the following:

- Go fast, see everything.
- Go slow, capture everything.
- Go to the blank spots (high-return, high-uncertainty, tolerant driven).
- Go for low-hanging fruit (low-risk driven).
- Go for bang for the buck (high-value, low-uncertainty driven).

Explanation strategies include the following:

- Maximize information comprehension by all (serve lowest common denominator).
- Maximize the density of data presentations (lower cost of searching).
- Provide extensive contextual information to communicate richness of scenarios.
- Minimize unnecessary contextual information so key points can be perceived at a glance.

- Require others to learn to interpret data presentations as leaders do.
- Minimize information that new members of the organization must learn.
- Limit the number of dashboards to minimize the amount of time spent searching for and viewing different dashboards.
- Provide a large number of dashboards to address needs of multiple roles within the organization.
- Use dashboards to persuade and support a particular strategy or perspective.
- Use dashboards as a purely objective communication medium.

Roles of Dashboard Users

Dashboards should be designed according the needs of the role a user or group plays within an organization. The organizational responsibilities, the expectations for awareness and knowledge, and the information needed for decision making are all critically important for determining the presentation and organization of the information for a particular user or group of users. There are many tradeoffs in data visualization and dashboard design; there is no such thing as "maximize everything."

As organizations grow, they naturally develop different interpretations of organizational position and performance, resulting in different priorities and perspectives. These organizations need coherence and coordination to avoid developing conflicting strategies. Broad use of common dashboards combat these tendencies and provide that coherence and a "shared understanding."

One of the biggest challenges for BI dashboards is the diverse needs of people that they must serve. Obviously, different people see and interpret presentations of data differently. They have different expectations, different levels of experience, different backgrounds, not to mention the differences in individual cognitive processes. However, a key point of large enterprise BI systems is to deliver consistent interpretations across diverse user populations. This means designing analyses and dashboards for a large percentage of the people occupying the role for which the dashboard is intended. Figure 7-1 shows a landscape with mountains and valleys representing the interpretive ability of a large user population and where height equates to value (you can think of this as a type of "fitness landscape"). Some might be tempted to design for the highest peak, but if it is surrounded by deep valleys, then the average value may be lower than it should. Designers should ideally aim for a high plateau with low variability, but good average height. Although it may not be the ultimate highest peak, it does provide a high expected value across the user population along with a strong sense of shared interpretation and organizational coherence.

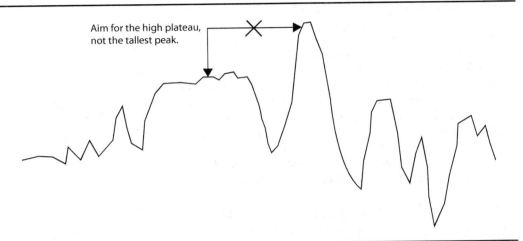

Aim for the high plateau, not the tallest peak.

FIGURE 7-1.   *Diagram with height showing interpretive ability across a large, diverse set of users*

Dashboard content should be customized for the role of the user. If many users have the same exact role, they should use common dashboards. When users (especially executives) have overlapping responsibilities (as they so often do when it comes to organizational performance and results), they should share common dashboards (or at least common analyses, even if they are on different dashboards) so that they have the opportunity to see the same data presented in the same manner. If they do not have the same data presented in the same manner, it is less likely that they will share a similar understanding of the organization's performance and position.

When we are referring to dashboard roles, we are referring to the position and responsibilities that a person has within an organization, not their ability to execute select statements in a database schema.

When designing dashboards for particular roles, ask the following questions:

- What decisions do the people with this role make?

- What data (evidence) and contextual information is needed to support those decisions?

- Who else shares this information in the organization?

- What level of interaction is needed for this information?

- Which is the dominant use of this dashboard: exploration (search for previously unknown insights) or explanation (delivery of "discovered" data for understanding)?

This emphasis on roles also helps reinforce the central importance of business use cases as opposed to personal preference. Organizational dashboards are not about "taste" or "opinions" or what someone believes "looks good." They are about objectively communicating information or a common strategy.

Obviously, decision making should be centered on evidence and not "gut feel" or opinion (as it too often has been). A hyper attention on "decisions" can mean that other important goals of business intelligence dashboards are lost, particularly the goal of shared understanding and organizational coherence. When people share a common understanding of an organization's position and performance, they are more likely to agree with, support, and reinforce the choices that others in the organization make. This issue of organizational coherence is most apparent when it is lacking in a serious way and groups (often aligned by function) oppose one another.

Common Roles in Organizations

Although your organization may define roles differently, commonly the following roles are found in organizations: executive, analyst, manager, and frontline employee, as well as customer, supplier, and other.

Executive

Executive dashboards should communicate information quickly. They should be designed to minimize the time required to develop an understanding of an organization's position and performance. Executives should have access to additional dashboards that others in the organization may use. Executive dashboards should not wait for any queries to execute or visualizations to render. All views, reports, and messages should be nearly instantaneous. Executives often have deep experience in organizations along with an extensive knowledge of organization-specific information (names, acronyms, business units, and so on) and may not require as much contextual information as less experienced employees. Executives new to the organization often require extensive support and often benefit from individualized training in the firm's OBIEE implementation. The effective use of OBIEE by executives can yield massive returns to the organization. Ineffective or misinterpretation of business intelligence dashboards and reports by executives can be disastrous. Executives often benefit from "portal" operations that allow additional outside information and activities to be provided or controlled from OBIEE dashboards. Exception reports must be carefully weighed and balanced on executive dashboards to avoid being distracting. Forward-looking exceptions, forecasts, and predictions should be prioritized. When you're designing executive dashboards, bear in mind that some executives will insist on information being presented via alternative vehicles, such as PDF files or PowerPoint files that are e-mailed. This may affect the screen resolution you can use and the amount of interactivity you can presume.

Analyst

Analysts are primarily in the role of developing insights. Their dashboards should be designed for data exploration activities and include a wide variety of views, reports, alerts, exceptions, and external data sources. Analysts require the highest range of parameterization and can better tolerate complexity and information-dense or unusual visualizations. Analysts typically have the highest degree of skill and technical knowledge. Analysts should all undergo extensive training in OBIEE so that they can leverage its full power in the pursuit of discovering new insights. Analysts should also receive extensive training in data visualization so that they can effectively design tables, graphs, dashboards, interactive components, filters, prompts, and views for use by others in the organization.

Manager

Line managers are important users of OBIEE dashboards. Their dashboards should be highly structured so that they establish patterns of use and find important information quickly with minimal technical training. Reports should be organized around themes, times (schedules), and exceptions. Exception reports should provide for interactivity and guided navigation. Dashboards for managers should be conceived and designed as "continuously monitored dashboards" or conceived and designed as "occasional update dashboards."

Frontline employee

Frontline employees often need very specific data very quickly so that they can interact effectively with customers, processes, and associates. The key to designing effective dashboards for frontline employees is to understand their specific needs and to maximize the return on the most important activities. The principles of Situational Awareness that have been developed for real-world dashboards (for fighter planes and so on) often have direct applicability for frontline employee dashboards. Action links can be used to take specific actions that benefit the organization by enabling more efficient workflows.

Customer, Supplier, and Other

More and more organizations that have implemented OBIEE are looking to leverage their investment by providing portal connectivity and access to OBIEE dashboards (they often monetize access to create new sources of income). Although data filtering is an obvious need, these dashboards can provide tremendous value to outside stakeholders. You can also gain important insights by analyzing usage-tracking statistics on what dashboards and analyses these people access.

Importance of Dashboards Depends on Roles and Usage

We tend to spend differing amounts of time designing various dashboards. Each dashboard has something of an "importance metric" that could be expressed as the summation of the importance of each user multiplied by the need for coordination that their role has across the different functional areas of the organization and down the different levels of responsibility within an organizational hierarchy:

Dashboard Importance Score

$$= \sum_{1}^{n} \text{importance of dashboard user} \times \text{organizational coordination requirement of user's role}$$

Although executive dashboards may not have a high number of users, their importance level is very high and the need for coordination may be very high if the summary dashboard is being used to communicate overall organizational performance and position. These dashboards warrant a tremendous amount of care in their design. Likewise, a dashboard that is seen by hundreds or thousands of users (even if they do not have high "individual importance" scores) will also warrant a high importance metric simply because of the large numbers of users. Dashboards that do not score as high tend to be departmental dashboards with specific views of information for a defined group that is already highly coordinated. The effort for these types of situations tends to go into the design of the analyses themselves (including an extensive look at calculated measures and comparison metrics) and deep visualizations that include multiple dimensions. These visualizations tend to be difficult for more occasional users to understand.

Dashboard Content Can Vary by User

As you design dashboards, bear in mind that dashboard content can vary by user. For example, in Figure 7-2 you can see Paulo Rodney's view of a table of data. This differs from the view presented to Daniel Noonan, shown in Figure 7-3, using the "acting as" feature. Notice that Daniel Noonan can only see two of the organizations and the total changes appropriately. In addition to data content changing for each user, visibility of dashboard pages, dashboard content, and data elements can all vary by user. When you capitalize on this feature, be sure that users are aware of the differences between users so they are not confused due to results that differ by user.

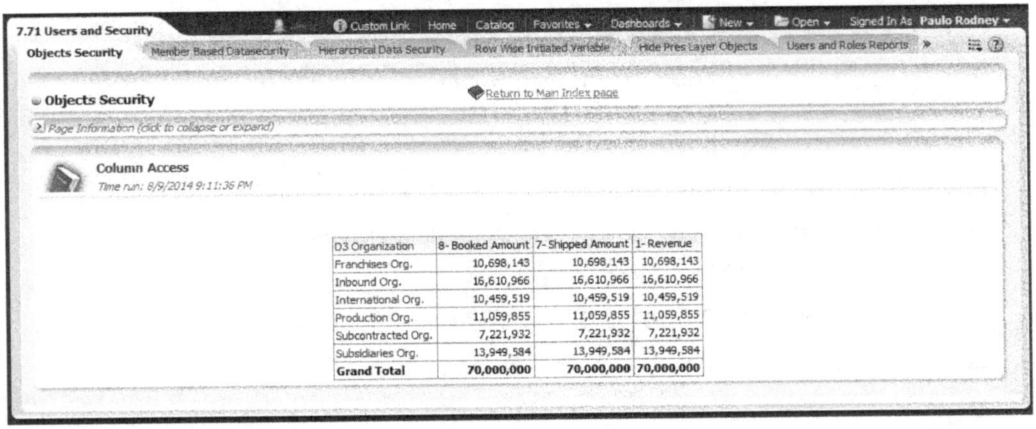

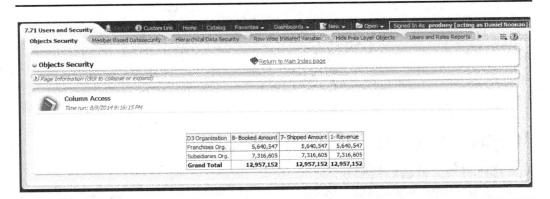

FIGURE 7-2.   *Dashboard viewed by Paulo Rodney*

FIGURE 7-3.   *Dashboard viewed by Daniel Noonan shows a subset of data.*

Dashboard Standards and Style Guides

We the authors are strong believers in developing standards and using style guides
for large business intelligence systems and find that they provide tremendous value
to the organizations that employ them. From a visual design perspective, we often
review an organization's web style guide and adapt elements of it for business

intelligence dashboard design. Standards and style guides provide many advantages, including the following:

■ Consistency in presentation and interpretation

■ Efficiency and speed in the development and design process

■ A stronger professional look and feel to dashboards

■ A reduced chance for misrepresentation of data and jarring visuals that draw attention not because of their importance, but because of their appearance

■ A stronger sense of organizational coherence and alignment

■ An increased chance that data visualization best practices are employed

■ A coordinated opportunity for engagement in the process of making choices between alternatives and justification for design choices that otherwise might be challenged

As stated before, it is helpful for people to think of OBIEE dashboards as websites. One of the advantages of this approach is that it helps reinforce the patterned and structured appearance of common data elements, which is central to most website design strategies. That is, certain types of content are located in the same area on multiple pages so that users become accustomed to certain patterns. You should take a similar approach in designing basic dashboard layout strategies for OBIEE.

Important OBIEE Dashboard Considerations

OBIEE dashboards dynamically respond to the size and shape of the analyses that are published on them. These analyses are defined in the "Answers" portion of OBIEE. It is not possible to edit the analyses in the dashboard interface; you have to do this in the analysis editor interface. You end up iterating a lot using these two interfaces as you develop BI systems.

Basic Layout

OBIEE dashboards consist of pages, columns, and sections. Objects that are placed on the dashboard are generally referred to as "content." See Figure 7-4 for an example of the relationship between these layout objects.

Dashboard objects   Dashboard pages

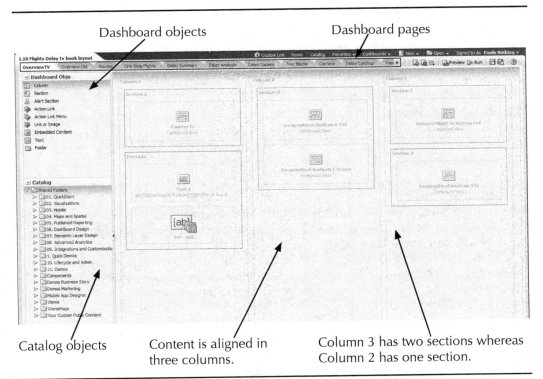

Catalog objects   Content is aligned in   Column 3 has two sections whereas
                         three columns.   Column 2 has one section.

FIGURE 7-4.   *Dashboard builder interface for editing dashboard layouts*

Dashboard Pages

Dashboards typically have multiple pages. These pages are generally conceptually related through function, theme, perspective, flow, outcome, or some other commonality. Just as websites often have multiple pages of linked content, so do dashboards. This becomes important when applying the scope of prompts, which can be set either to "page" or to "dashboard." When the scope of dashboard prompts are set to "dashboard," all column prompts set to "is prompted" will apply their filter conditions according to setting of the prompt, even if it appears on another page on the dashboard. You should visually differentiate between action links, dashboard links, and other navigational objects that take a user to a different page on the same dashboard, to another dashboards within OBIEE, to another part of OBIEE, or to another HTML site outside of OBIEE.

CAUTION
The scope of dashboard prompts can be set to "dashboard" or to "page."

Dashboard Columns

Columns are used to align content on a dashboard page. They are extremely flexible and can be arranged to appear side by side, above or below, or in different sized "blocks." They should really be thought of as "super-sections." A given column can have multiple sections.

Dashboard Sections

Sections are placed within columns and hold the actual dashboard content. Sections are used to group content together within a column or "block." A given section can hold multiple objects.

Dashboard Content

Content includes catalog objects such as compound layouts of analyses with multiple views, prompts, and alerts and dashboard objects such as links, folder views, embedded content, and text.

Different versions of OBIEE have different levels of flexibility in the adaptability of columns and sections. Understanding the interactions and auto-adjustment characteristics of columns and sections is important to understanding how to achieve the desired layout results.

NOTE
Columns are typically used for alignment. Sections are used to group content objects within columns.

Include Contextual Information on Dashboards

Many BI analyses and reports are interesting and useful only when they are accompanied by contextual information that provides perspective and relevance. A good example of "context" is evaluating current year-to-date sales figures with previous year-to-date sales figures for the same period of time. The previous year's figures provide the context in which the current year's figures are understood. Context is a funny thing. Without it, many people will interpret raw data differently and draw entirely different conclusions (not always a bad thing, but not a good thing if you are trying to increase organizational coherence and understanding). Also, a lack of context for some information means that interpretations don't just differ, but that each individual has to apply a great deal of effort to interpret raw data.

Context guides users and provides a setting that furthers comprehension and understanding. Timestamp information stating when a report was run is a good example of context. Although this information is extremely important for report-based systems in which updates are impossible (such as paper-based systems), it may not be important for dynamic dashboards that are continuously updated. In these situations, "report run" timestamps may be somewhat irrelevant and serve only to clutter the interface. On the other hand, for data warehouses that are updated periodically, the date the data is "as of" can be critically important; what does "year to date" mean?

What date? Today? Yesterday? Last week? Other "contextual" information such as what filters and selection steps were applied are critically important to understanding and the interpretation of analysis results. Sometimes context for analyses is woefully underdeveloped in BI systems and the evaluation of context is lacking in the conscious design process. It is important to integrate analyses with one another, to signal relationships between contextual information (such as graph legends) and analyses, and guide dashboard users. The key then is for the dashboard designer to understand the role and uses for the dashboard and to provide the appropriate contextual information that supports the intended understanding.

Dashboard Format and Placement of Contents

OBIEE dashboards have always been relatively responsive to analysis results and have dynamically adjusted their height and width, depending on the specific selections at a moment in time. This bias toward dynamic response versus static report publishing and designing "in parts" so they can respond to individual content requests carries forward. Indeed, the approach of formatting containers separate from content is evident throughout OBIEE and occurs at several different levels. Although this strategy at times seems to add layers of work and abstraction, it also provides structure along with the opportunity to build consistency.

Not all portions of a dashboard have equal visual prominence. Most languages are read from left to right and from top to bottom. (Situations and user roles that don't apply to these generalizations should leverage similar insights from this section, but adapt them to the needs of their specific circumstances.) The visual prominence of objects on dashboards is influenced by several different factors. For example, is the object stationary or moving? Motion draws the eye to a far greater degree than any other factor. If you want people to look at something, make it move. If you don't want to draw attention to an object, do not make it move. We the authors have seen implementations where designers wanted to fit a large amount of text onto an OBIEE dashboard, and to make it fit within a limited space befitting its importance, they created a scrolling, ticker-style field. The intent was to diminish its importance, but it in reality it was given accidental extra prominence by putting in motion! Collapsible sections (see Figures 7-15 and 7-16 later in the chapter for an example), text fields, and even new browser windows are better solutions in this situation than scrolling ticker fields.

Color, size, position, and shape all contribute the relative visual prominence for dashboard objects (but pale in comparison to motion). The degree to which each of these factors contributes to the visual prominence of an individual object varies in relation to the contrast and alignment with other dashboard objects. When color is used sparingly (which is recommended), color stands out as a powerful visual attractor. If bright colors are used all over, it's more difficult for a particular color (even a bright one) to stand apart and demand attention. Likewise, when many objects are visually aligned, an object "breaking" the line will draw attention to itself. The more similar, aligned, and near objects are to one another, the more they appear to be a part of a "whole" and less distinct and individual.

Imagine a dashboard page as being made up of "zones." These zones do not have hard, defined edges, but rather are general regions that are influenced and shaped by the content and appearance of the content on a particular dashboard page. Figure 7-5 shows an idealized portrayal of the relative weight of these zones. One element often seen on initial dashboard designs is the placement of the company logo in the upper-left quadrant of the dashboard. Think of pixels on a dashboard as a limited commodity. Although many like to see their company name prominently displayed (and it is difficult to advise against featuring the logo), most people are aware of where they work. This space is often prime screen real estate that can add a tremendous amount of value to a dashboard page. If some sort of corporate branding is desired, you should find a special "logo font" that can be incorporated into a header, place the logo in a footer at the bottom of the page (which provides a visual "foundation" for each page), or use a small logo in the upper-right corner. The upper-left corner is best reserved for summary "context" information that applies to the entire dashboard or dashboard page or for prompt selections. Because OBIEE dashboard content sections respond dynamically to the size of the data request and presentation, they expand leftward and downward. This means that objects anchored on the top and the left side of the dashboard are more or less "fixed" in their position.

FIGURE 7-5. *Darker areas of screen are more prominent.*

Form Follows Function

Content should be organized to help users understand, interact with, and derive meaning from the information that is presented. This means that it should be consciously designed to reflect the needs of the user role and show the data according to the nature of the data. Information should not be placed just anywhere on a dashboard. Each pixel placement on the dashboard is a unique location. Although there are always tradeoffs between different alternatives, the physical layout of the dashboard should not influence the choice/placement of the data visualization. We sometimes hear a justification such as, "This graph fits in this space perfectly! Let's put it there." Not the best reason for the placement of a graph, to say the least. The convenience of the physical layout is not more important than the needs of the users. We the authors actually heard the statement, "It's easier for the BI admin team if all the tables are on one page, so the users will just have to get used to flipping back and forth between the graphs page and the tables page." Although creating layouts and thinking through them takes time, the design of the dashboard should be driven by the role of the user and primary uses of the data. Of course, it will also be influenced by the prompts and other navigation controls. At times these become important considerations as well.

Alignment, Grids, and Structure

Alignment facilitates scanning a page quickly, signals a relationship between dashboard elements (what goes with what), and helps create a sense of order and cohesiveness. Just as tables are easier to read when the data elements and headers in them are aligned, entire dashboards are easier to read when their elements are aligned. OBIEE has strong tools for creating alignment (even when content changes size dynamically with data selection) through the use of columns. Although horizontal alignment is advised (especially at the top of the dashboard page), it's more important to align elements vertically when possible. Large related visuals should be "stacked" on top of one another, and users should be asked to scan vertically rather than horizontally; horizontal scrolling is not intuitive in most interfaces.

You should place dashboard prompts along the left side of the dashboard in a consistent position so that users become accustomed to finding them easily. For "mobile friendly" layouts, group prompts along the top of the dashboard page. See Chapter 10 for important considerations regarding designing dashboards for mobile devices.

Dashboard Layout Mechanics

The dashboard page in Figure 7-6 has three columns that help organize the content of the page and place it into a context. The far-upper-left corner contains micro-sized analyses that offer summary context for the selections made in the dashboard prompts immediately below them. The very small narrative view shows the total number of flights in the system (6,235,242) and the number of flights included in the current selection or report. The prompts are organized into their own section that visually stands out because of its border. Although borders are sometimes employed too often and can block the visual flow between dashboard objects, when used selectively and purposefully, as they are in this example, they can be effective.

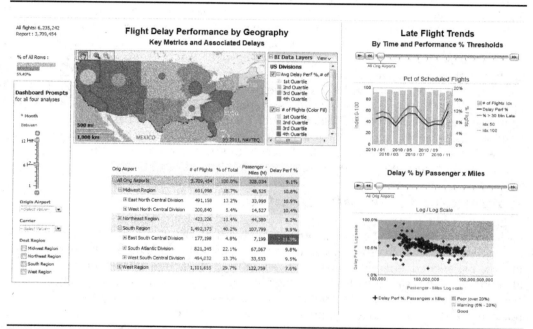

FIGURE 7-6. *Typical dashboard layout shows several of the key concepts discussed so far.*

The four analyses are grouped into two major groups that are organized vertically. Prominence is given to the map view (maps should generally be placed in the center-top position on dashboards). The table view below it provides specific information in support of the map view and allows for vertical expansion as users navigate the geographical hierarchy. Conditional formatting in the Delay Perf % column gives strong visual emphasis to categories that fall below threshold limits. If placed above the map, the vertical expansion of the table would tend to push the map off the bottom of the dashboard and would place too much visual emphasis on the conditionally formatted cells.

The levels of the hierarchy are colored with a slight background color so that their level and relationship within the hierarchy can be understood at a glance. In general, you should place the most important and relevant visualization for a dashboard page in the upper center-left region. In this case, the overall pattern of flight delay data in combination with the level of flight activity (as measured by the number of flights) is best communicated by the summary map. More detailed information is shown both below the map (in table form with conditional formatting) and in the right-side column titled Late Flight Trends. The right-side column is visually separated with the use of a light rule, thus giving it its own space. Two different dense visualizations (a dual-axis bar and line combo graph) and a scatter plot graph provide additional insight regarding flight delays. Both are relatively advanced visualizations and are intended for a more sophisticated user such as a data analyst. The repetition of the graph section sliders reinforces the concept that the two views are related, but independently parameterized by their respective sliders. The log/log scale of the scatter plot graph is called out more than once so that users are aware of the nonstandard data scales for both axes.

Dashboard Property Page Size

The dashboard property Page Size can be set to one of the following options when it comes to dashboard content:

■ Fit Content

■ Fill Browser Window

Although this is a property of a dashboard, it especially is applicable for dashboard columns that are set to Best Fit (see later in this chapter). When you choose Fit Content, the size of the container will expand and contract dynamically according to the size needed to display the content with no wrapping. Dashboard columns are sized by the largest section in the column. Any additional space in the browser window is added to the right of the content. Content within columns and sections is aligned to the left by default.

When you choose Fill Browser Window, when there is additional space, the size of column/containers will expand proportionally to fill the full browser window. Dashboard columns are again sized by the largest section in the column. Content within columns and sections are aligned in the center by default.

The difference between the two settings largely occurs with the treatment of "white space" when the content is smaller than the browser window. When the content is wider than a browser window, a horizontal scroll bar is added to the dashboard. Likewise, when the content is longer than a browser window, a vertical scroll bar is added for the dashboard. When you're working in organizations, it's best to design dashboards with an "ideal" screen resolution in mind. Once you have the analyses, views, and initial layouts determined, you can go back and set the container properties to a specific size for the element that is determining the width of the largest section in the dashboard column. According to W3Schools (w3schools.com) on August 1, 2014 (shown in Figure 7-7), the most common single-screen resolution is 1366×768 (this is significantly wider than 1024×768, the former most common screen resolution).

Obviously, different organizations have different standards, but don't automatically assume that most non-mobile users will be low resolution (we'll cover designing for mobile devices in Chapter 10). For example, let's say that you have a large table using column selectors and it's uncertain how wide the table may get. You may want to limit the pixel count of the table to 800 pixels in width so that scroll bars will be added to the table rather than to the dashboard when it gets really wide.

Screen Resolution Statistics

As of today, 99% of your visitors have a screen resolution of 1024x768 pixels or higher:

Date	Other high	1920x1080	1366x768	1280x1024	1280x800	1024x768	800x600	Lower
January 2014	34%	13%	31%	8%	7%	6%	0.5%	0.5%
January 2013	36%	11%	25%	10%	8%	9%	0.5%	0.5%
January 2012	35%	8%	19%	12%	11%	13%	1%	1%
January 2011	50%	6%		15%	14%	14%	0%	1%
January 2010	39%	2%		18%	17%	20%	1%	3%

FIGURE 7-7. *W3Schools screen resolution statistics as of August 1, 2014*

Laying Out Dashboard Columns

Figure 7-8 shows the OBIEE interface that is used for editing the dashboard shown in Figure 7-6.

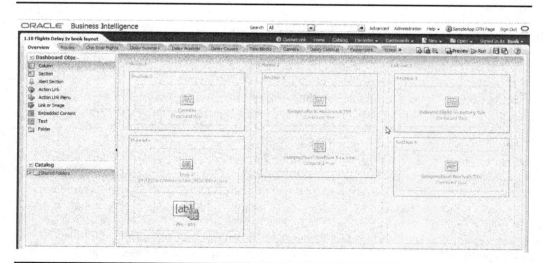

FIGURE 7-8. *Dashboard builder/editor for the Flights Delay dashboard*

The dashboard builder has a similar feel to OBIEE Answers in that objects are dragged from the left panel to the layout editor. Sections are separate containers within columns that hold specific objects. Objects are either added from the catalog or are created using the dashboard builder itself.

As you can see, there are three distinct columns for this dashboard page. Within each column are one or more sections. Columns are roughly analogous to iframes in that they organize areas of dashboard pages. As shown in Figure 7-9, the size of columns can be set to one of three different settings:

- Best Fit

- Specific Size

- Minimum Size

Learning how these size choices influence the appearance and the dynamic display of data is important to designing effective dashboards.

Dashboard Column Size Set to Best Fit

Best Fit is the default setting for all new columns. It sizes columns dynamically, depending both on content to be displayed and on the settings that are established for the overall dashboard properties. Best Fit is often the easiest and fastest setting to use to get a sense of how certain content is going to fit with other content onto a dashboard page. You might want to develop analyses with multiple views and even more than one default layout. This way, you can place your content onto dashboard pages into a single column using the Best Fit option and try out different arrangements to see what insights are suggested and revealed with different adjacencies and placements. This also can provide you with alternatives to show to stakeholders/users. You will get much better guidance when you ask stakeholders/ users to state preferences between alternatives rather than trying to state what "their needs are." (Hint: they don't know what they want until they see it and often don't know what is wrong with a given layout, but will be less inclined to use it if it is "wrong.")

Although Best Fit will arrange everything on a dashboard page just fine, it doesn't necessarily align content. Organization and clean lines nearly always aid dashboard users in scanning and drawing insight from BI dashboards. It sometimes is easier to determine the best alignment and placement strategies as a secondary or even tertiary step in the design process. This is especially true for major "executive dashboards," which are viewed by very senior people and large numbers of people within an organization. These dashboards are so important that they require extra time and attention in their design. Even if you start with a single "Best Fit" column, important dashboard pages often evolve to include multiple columns and employ one of the other column settings.

Some dashboard designers are loath to have "empty space" on dashboards and actively encourage content to be expanded and fill all the white space. However, negative space (empty white space) is as much a design element as positive space. Don't fall into the trap of believing that you need to fill every corner of every dashboard. Make sure that your choices have purpose behind them. In other words, use blank space consciously to help organize and draw attention to the elements on the dashboard that users are viewing.

Dashboard Column Size Set to Specific Size

As shown in Figure 7-9, the Specific Size option provides for more specific control of the size of a column. Dashboard columns can be set to be a specified number of pixels in width (the default interpretation of a number). Numbers with a suffix of "pixel" or "px" or no suffix will be interpreted as pixel counts. If you want to specify the proportional distribution of space for dashboard columns when using the Fill Browser Window option, specify a percentage for the column in the Column Properties dialog. For example, "33%" will override the calculated proportion and set the amount of allocated blank space for the column to 33 percent of the browser window. Scroll bars are added to the column when the size of the content exceeds the space specified in the Column Properties dialog. As mentioned before, large tables pose many challenges, both in terms of data interpretation and understanding. Although many executives have gotten used to looking at large tables of numbers during their careers, deriving insights from comparisons of discrete values across very wide and down very long tables is difficult and yields inconsistent results across users (different insights and understandings of the same data sets across user populations lessens organization coherence). It is sometimes okay to add scroll bars to large tables when the alternative is to have them push other content off of a dashboard screen. Setting the column width to be a percentage of the browser window allows for a more balanced presentation of content on denser dashboard pages for deployments where users have large differences in screen resolution.

TIP
Use the Preview button shown in Figure 7-10 often to check your dashboard layout while designing.

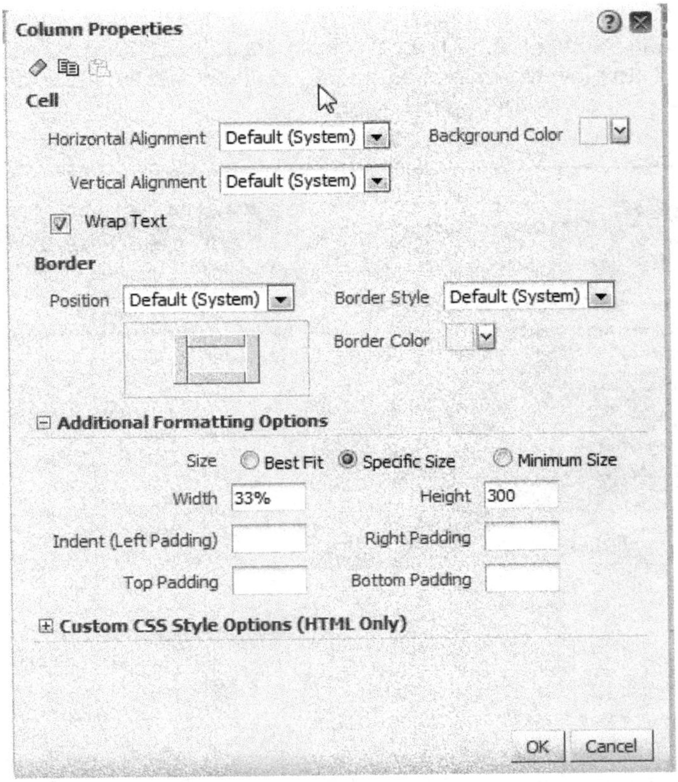

FIGURE 7-9. *Specifying the size of a dashboard column*

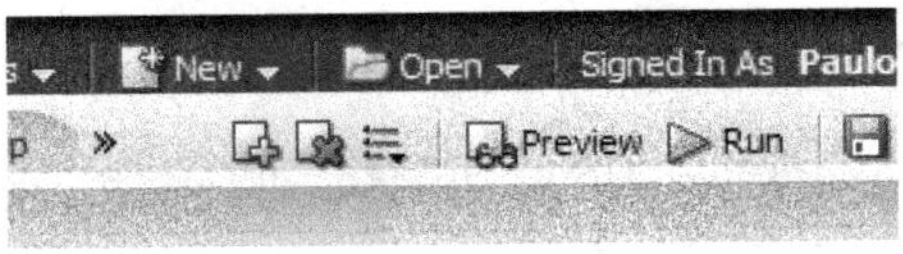

FIGURE 7-10. *Preview button (glasses icon) for checking the dashboard layout*

Figure 7-11 shows the Flights Delay Overview dashboard page redesigned for 1024×768 screen resolution. The section of Column 2 (the middle column) is set to be 450 pixels wide. Notice the horizontal scroll bars at the bottom of the section that are necessary to view the map legend and would be needed if the table was expanded wider by a user's drilling behavior.

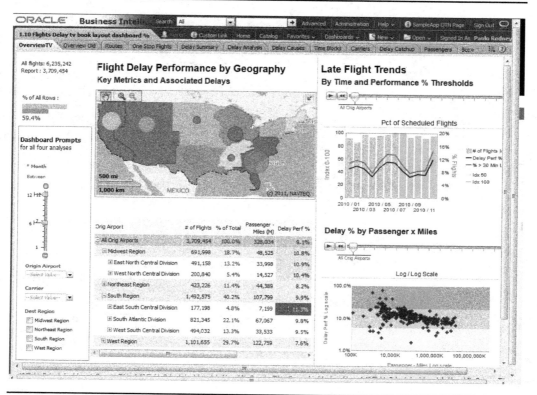

FIGURE 7-11. *Dashboard redesigned for a 1024×768 resolution*

This is partly where balancing the advantages and disadvantages of alternative presentations comes into play. Many dashboards are viewed on mobile devices and at a wide array of screen resolutions. Although dashboards could be built to a "lowest common screen" resolution, doing so may compromise their display on larger screens. Understanding the role of the most important users comes into consideration here. It may be better to design a particularly dense dashboard for large screens and allow it to be somewhat "compromised" (that is, include scroll bars) on smaller screens. In general, designs intended for mobile displays should be smaller and less dense than designs intended for general office viewing.

Although the "percentage of browser window" option is available, it can also be more frustrating at times due to all the other influences in browser behavior. The fixed pixel amount, where columns are given pixel specifications, allows a direct mapping of the size of the view specified in the Analysis/Answers interface and the dashboard interface. Scroll bars are added when the size of the content is larger than the specified size of the container, as shown in Figure 7-11. Figure 7-12 shows how the size of Column 2 is set to 450 pixels in width.

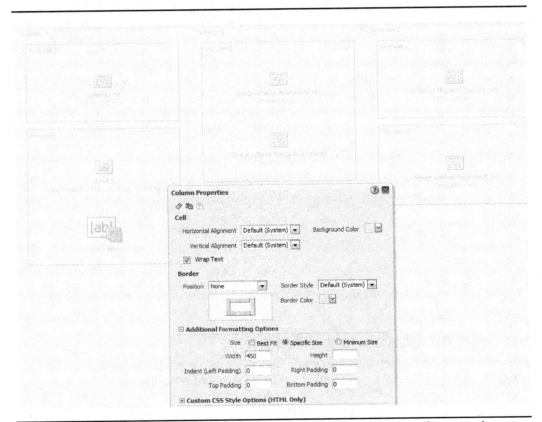

FIGURE 7-12. *Column properties for Column 2 set to a specific size of 450 pixels*

Dashboard Column Size Set to Minimum Size

Columns can also be sized to "Minimum Size." This setting means that the column container will always show at least the specified pixel or percentage size regardless of the state of the content. When the content is larger than the specified minimum width, the container will expand in size to fit the content. No scroll bars will be added to the container.

Freeze Column Setting "Anchors" a Column to the Left or Top of a Dashboard Page

Starting with version 11.1.1.7, it is possible to use the Freeze Column setting to visually anchor the leftmost column against the upper or left side of a dashboard page. A column that has had the Freeze Column setting applied will always remain in view (see Figure 7-13 for appearance of the Freeze Column setting link). Other columns will have scroll bars added if the viewing window is not large enough to fully display their content. This is useful for columns containing dashboard prompts, where seeing their configuration adds to the transparency of the data selection for different tables and graphs. This also becomes potentially important for dashboards that are viewed on mobile devices because scrolling is more prevalent in mobile applications. Because these "frozen" columns are constantly viewed, they should be limited in size so that enough screen real estate is available for other content.

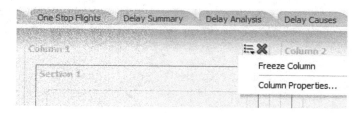

FIGURE 7-13. *Freeze Column setting appears directly above the Column Properties link.*

Laying Out Dashboard Sections

Sections are used for organizing content within columns. Sections can be set to place multiple objects either horizontally (side-by-side) or vertically (stacked) within the section. Figure 7-14 shows the rather unintuitive interface in which the vertical layout is selected (and therefore grayed out) and the icon for a "horizontal" layout for a section is highlighted as a different potential option. No rollover shows for the currently selected "vertical layout" when you mouse over it because it is already selected and you cannot switch to it.

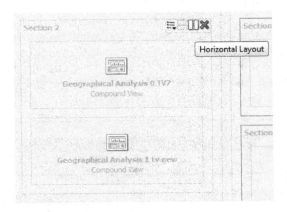

FIGURE 7-14. *Vertical layout of sections*

Like columns, sections are also containers and can also respond dynamically to the content placed inside them.

Formatting Sections

You can use colored borders on columns and sections to indicate relationships between various objects on dashboards (more on this in the Master-Detail and Dashboard Prompts sections in Chapter 8). Although additional color can introduce a certain amount of distraction from the visual presentation of the data (tables and graphs), the additional clarity showing which objects are controlling or parameterizing other objects through prompts or master detail linking connections improves the interpretation of the data and provides additional transparency of intent.

The placement of prompts is challenging. In general, they should be physically close (if not adjacent) to the views they are parameterizing, but you could also place them in a consistent location common to most of the organizational dashboards so that a pattern of use is established and users know where to look for prompts without having to "hunt" for them. Try to place prompts either in their own vertical column on the left side of the dashboard (most common) or in their own column along the top of the dashboard spanning the entire width (add a column break after "Column 1" so that your next columns will move to the left side of the page). We cover dashboard prompts in Chapter 8.

Formatting sections is mainly a question of alignment (making the dashboard cleaner and more organized) and the placement of analyses and views that are related by the data sets that they use and the insights that they offer.

Using Collapsible Sections for Help Text

It is helpful to create a collapsible section named "Expand to see help text for this dashboard" that contains only text. The SampleApp application uses this technique to give information about a dashboard. If a user wants to get it out of the way, he or she can simply collapse it. For example, in Figure 7-15, a column has been added at the top of the dashboard with a collapsible section for help text. Figure 7-16 shows how collapsed sections take up little space on a dashboard.

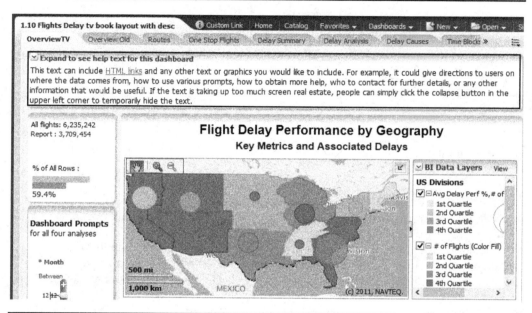

FIGURE 7-15. *Sections can include collapsible text.*

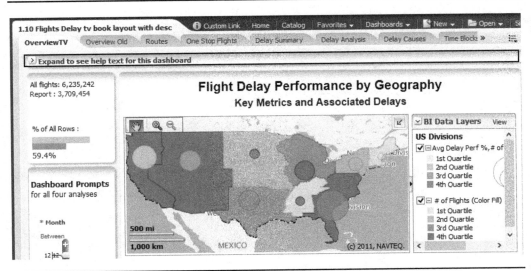

FIGURE 7-16.   *Collapsed sections take up little space.*

Summary

Dashboards need to reflect the goals of the organization. Because various needs differ, you may have to create different dashboards for the different roles within the organization, even if the content is similar. Spend the most time on those dashboards that influence the most number of people. Also, add contextual information on dashboards.

Designing the layout of dashboards can seem like a "messy" process, but it is critically important. Keep your dashboards clean. Design for an "ideal" screen resolution. Use columns for alignment and sections for logical organization. Anchor columns at the top and left to maintain their visibility when users must scroll. Use the Best Fit option initially and then optimize important dashboards with finer-grain settings. Don't be afraid of white space; instead, use it as a design element.

CHAPTER
8

Dashboard Interactions

One of the major features of OBIEE 11*g* is its support for interactions, customizations, and parameterizations. The more users interact with dashboard elements, the more likely they are to understand the data selections, accurately interpret the visualizations, and draw logical inferences. One of the major mistakes made with OBIEE implementations is the creation of largely static dashboards. This typically results from well-intentioned IT implementation staff doing "requirements analysis" in which they collect hundreds of Excel spreadsheets (read "tables of numbers") that OBIEE is to replicate. Someone dutifully re-creates the hundreds of spreadsheets, sometimes placing one report per dashboard page (or even worse, one report per dashboard). Users are left scrolling through endless lists of names (also copied from the legacy system) trying to find the one report they want. Almost invariably, most all the reports are variants of a few basic reports with different parameters selected for different dimension values.

On the other hand, in some implementations there are so many prompts on the dashboard pages that users are overwhelmed with the number of choices. This "extreme" parameterization adds tremendous complication to the front-end system and makes it virtually impossible to construct meaningful visualizations. After all, it's one thing to slap some columns together in a table view; it's quite another to meaningfully express or represent data sets in a visualization. Visualizations show or demonstrate relationships, trends, comparisons, and insights related to data. The style of the visualization chosen, the data range for different axes, the methodology for representing different metrics and dimension values are all dependent on the major purpose and intended use case for the visualization. Dashboards should help users understand and explore a particular perspective or view of organizational data. Replicating the full depth and complication of a subject area on a dashboard through the use of too many prompts seldom adds value. You're better off training users how to create their own analyses so that they can construct meaningful queries and views than you are trying to place lots of prompts on a dashboard. In many of these situations, OBIEE becomes a glorified "ETL" tool, where users construct tables to download into Excel. OBIEE was not designed to do this, and, quite frankly, there are better ETL tools for scripting extracts from a data warehouse. Remember, you should be striving for a split of roughly 60 percent visualizations to 40 percent table views. This entire chapter is devoted to the concept of helping your users select, sort, drill, link, navigate, zoom, pan, run, control, manage, and generally interact with OBIEE, especially as it relates to dashboards. See the Interactions section of Chapter 11 for information on specific interactions within an analysis.

Users Already Know about Interactions

Users are becoming more exposed to and comfortable with interaction and selection interface elements. Most users now know how to use drop-down menus and recognize the major user interface paradigms that OBIEE employs. In short, the restrictions that exist today for interactions with dashboards in OBIEE implementations have far less to do with user training and perceived levels of sophistication in user audiences (an issue that has historically been trotted out to lessen the "complexity" of dashboards and only do the bare minimum) and far more to do with a general reluctance on the part of traditional IT departments to spend project resources on front-end design and user interfaces. They far prefer to spend time and external consulting dollars on the "back-end" design of data warehouses, ETL, and repository design. Although all of those are admittedly important, so is the design of the front end. The other typical situation occurs when the full complication of the warehouse and data sources are brought into the font end, leaving users with the responsibility to learn complex interactions, join patterns, data definitions, and other modeling nuances. The analytical needs of the users should drive the design of the data structures in the subject areas that are built in the repository file.

Organizations are better off and will achieve greater value starting with three well-designed dashboards that have strong interactivity features than they will with 300 static dashboards. The power of interaction cannot be oversold when it is compared with static reports as a standalone replacement. Many managers in organizations like to receive a static report on a regularly scheduled basis (such as weekly or monthly). However, these static reports should be produced as .pdf files and be delivered to their intended audience. They can also be archived and collected into directory structures and be made available through dashboards, but generally they should not form the foundation of OBIEE systems.

Dashboard Interactions Are about Engagement

Dashboard interactions are all about engagement with the audience. There is something fundamentally satisfying about a system that responds to you and something unsatisfying about a system that is completely static and cannot be changed. When users interact with data, they are much more likely to understand it and derive insights from it than when merely viewing it. Part of the key to designing effective dashboards, then, is to guide users effectively in how to make changes to primary data selections, visualizations, and contextual information that exist on dashboards and to accurately reflect the relationships that exist between different selection/interaction objects and data visualization objects.

You may be concerned that dashboard users will not know that selections can be changed or how to change the selections for a given dashboard. If one dashboard page is titled "Western U.S. Sales" and another dashboard page is titled "Eastern U.S. Sales," users know where to go for their reports and can avoid having to change a Region prompt to Western or Eastern. However, this practice belittles the intellectual capacity of many users. Further, it leads to an explosion of dashboards and analyses and complicates maintenance of an OBIEE system. With an effective series of prompts and interactions, you can combine Eastern and Western U.S. Sales dashboard pages into one page, save on maintenance, and design a more functional dashboard. Different users can even customize the Region prompt to default to individualized regions; see the section titled "Creating and Applying Saved Customizations" later in this chapter for more information. The key is making it clear what prompt controls what portion of the screen.

There are two primary ways to visually indicate that objects on a dashboard are associated with one another:

- They can be physically grouped together.

  - Space between "clustered" objects indicates similarity within a cluster and difference between clusters.

  - A border can be drawn around the group to indicate inclusion.

  - A background color can be added behind the area including the related objects that differentiates them from other elements on the dashboard.

- They can share a common visual element.

  - The related objects can have their own borders with the same color.

  - The related objects can share a common background color.

  - They can share a visually strong "style" such as font treatment, color scheme, or icon that identifies them as being related and different from other parts of the dashboard.

Perhaps the most important relationship to reflect on dashboards is the relationship between dashboard prompts and the analyses and views they parameterize. Because prompts directly filter data selection, it is particularly important to signal visually the relationships between the prompts and their associated analyses. It is also important that not only does an individual user receive feedback about the prompt values being selected, but also that all viewers of business intelligence systems understand the data selections being presented. In large systems, filters can become complex. The physical act of making a selection involves the user with the data-filtering process and thus increases the transparency of the data set (and limits the amount of exposition that might otherwise be necessary to explain what data is included).

Dependent relationships can also be signaled through visual intensity. For example, it may make sense to use a heavy line weight or a darker background color for a prompt, whereas the objects it modifies use a lighter weight line or lighter background color.

The specific techniques employed will depend on the intended audience and their role in the organization (see the section "Common Roles in Organizations" in Chapter 7), the nature of the visualizations, and the overall organizational "look and feel" and style of dashboards.

Master-Detail Linking

The process of Master-Detail linking allows multiple views to be set to the same parameters simultaneously and thus improve the interpretation and understanding of data by showing multiple views.

Master-Detail linking parameters are broadcast on a "channel" to which other views can "tune in" (including views for the same analysis as well as views associated with other analyses). The "master" views are associated with the analysis containing the column that is configured to broadcast its parameters. Detail views are configured to "listen" to the broadcast channel and automatically update themselves based on user selections within a master view.

There are some slight differences between the ways measure columns, attribute columns, and hierarchical columns function in Master-Detail views. When functioning as a master, measure columns pass all associated metadata when a particular data cell (in the case of a table) or region (in the case of a map or graph) is selected and broadcast to the detail views, which are listening to the channel. Attribute columns pass the metadata at the current level in the hierarchy and "above" to the associated detail columns. Hierarchical columns set as master columns broadcast contextual information, depending on their expanded level and the expansion level of any detail hierarchical columns set to listen to the broadcast channel. Interaction such as drills can also be sent, but visualizations should be designed to accommodate data presentations at different levels. If you are new to designing Master-Detail strategies for dashboards, you should start with using measure columns.

Although these prompts that are functioning as filters can have broad scope and can control analyses across many dashboard pages, you should replicate the prompts on each dashboard page so that users can see what selections are filtering the data. If dashboard space is at a premium, ensure that a filter view or a narrative view with the prompt definitions appears on the dashboard page. Starting with version 11.1.1.7, it is possible to hide slider prompts on detail views—just make sure that the user is aware of the parameterization being set by the master column selection.

Configuring Master-Detail Linking

You can configure columns to broadcast their selection to all views that are configured to listen to user selections. Figure 8-1 shows how selecting a specific LTV (Life Time Value) bin for customers on either the Customer by LTV Bins bar graph combo or the Cust Predicted LTV table sets the slider prompts in the four combo visualizations on the right side of the dashboard.

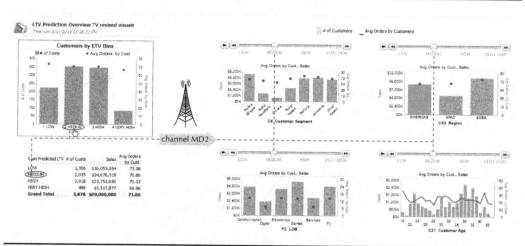

FIGURE 8-1. *Master-Detail linking for Oracle Data Mining customer Life Time Value*

The process of setting up Master-Detail linking involves a few steps, but greatly enhances the coherence of business intelligence dashboards. In Figures 8-2 and 8-3, a specific column in an analysis is configured to broadcast using Master-Detail Event Channel MD2. When a selection is made on a view for this analysis that includes this column, the other views on the dashboard page (as shown in Figure 8-4) that are configured to listen to Master-Detail Event Channel MD2 will automatically adjust their selections to reflect the choice that the user just made.

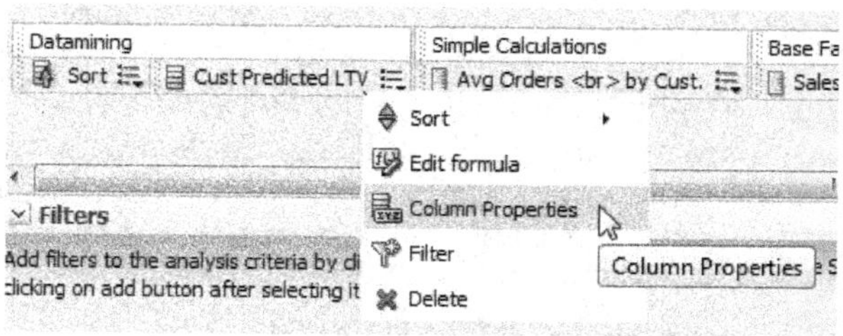

FIGURE 8-2. *Start with Column Properties on the Criteria tab*

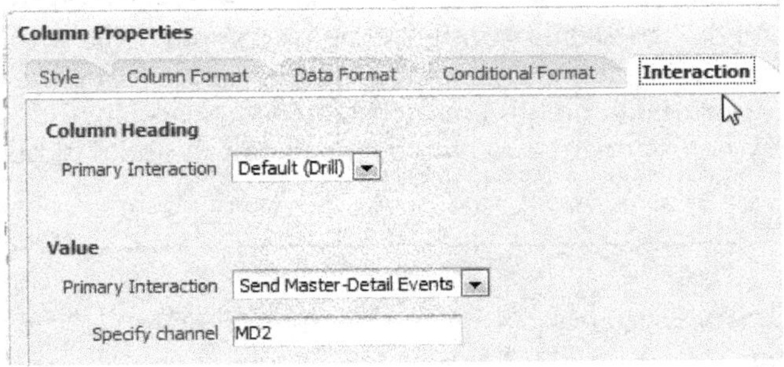

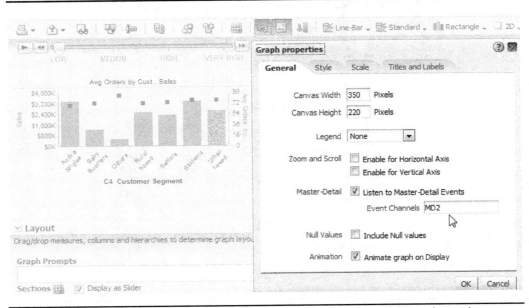

FIGURE 8-3. *Specifying a "broadcast" channel for Master-Detail linking*

FIGURE 8-4. *Setting graph properties to listen to a Master-Detail event channel*

Formatting Views with Master-Detail Linking

Notice that in Figure 8-5, bold italic formatting helps communicate Master-Detail broadcast capability; although the appearance is rather subtle (compare it to Figure 8-6), it does look different. It is amazing how effective slight formatting differences can be when standards are employed in analysis and dashboard design.

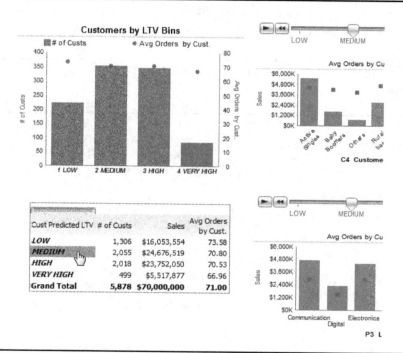

FIGURE 8-5. *Bold italic formatting helps communicate Master-Detail capability.*

Cust Predicted LTV	# of Custs	Sales	Avg Orders by Cust.
LOW	1,306	$16,053,554	73.58
MEDIUM	2,055	$24,676,519	70.80
HIGH	2,018	$23,752,050	70.53
VERY HIGH	499	$5,517,877	66.96
Grand Total	**5,878**	**$70,000,000**	**71.00**

FIGURE 8-6. *Default formatting of Cust Predicted LTV values*

When everyone uses fonts or formats consistently to communicate a certain kind of relationship (or lack thereof), users become quite accustomed to them. We could also use a color, a border, or even a graphic treatment to indicate a Master-Detail linking broadcast capability, but because it is so common, a more subtle treatment is recommended that most dashboard users will adapt to over time. Remember, the more pronounced an effect is visually, the more it calls attention to itself and the more it detracts from other "attention-deserving" elements on the dashboard. Also, the more color is used on a dashboard, the less effective additional uses of color will be. We the authors tend to err on the conservative side of using color only when another alternative is not available. In the current example, we believe that the bold italic font setting works well to indicate Master-Detail linking capability. Finding the correct balance between the different effects and their relative importance for the intended audience and its role is a careful balancing act.

Slider Prompts with Master-Detail Linking

Graph prompts displayed as slider prompts are particularly effective as detail views, as shown on the right side of Figure 8-5. Note that graphs can listen to more than one channel (separate them with commas). The master column must be displayed in the body of a view that you want to act as a master view and not on the edge or in a slider prompt. Conversely, the opposite is true for detail views. The column that is responding to the "master" should appear on the edge or in a section/graph prompt. Think of it this way: you are asking detail views to respond to a data selection made in another view. You can refer to the Oracle documentation for more information.

Map Views as Detail Views

One of the most interesting and engaging additions to OBIEE 11.1.1.7 is the ability to designate maps to listen to a Master-Detail channel and to respond by panning and zooming automatically to a particular data selection based on a data selection in a master column in a master view. This means that if you are displaying worldwide sales and want to zoom into a particular country, you can automatically update all the views (including your map) with a simple double-click.

Figure 8-7 shows a global view using a map view with choropleth fills of sales by country and a detail annual sales bar graph and pie chart with country slider prompts.

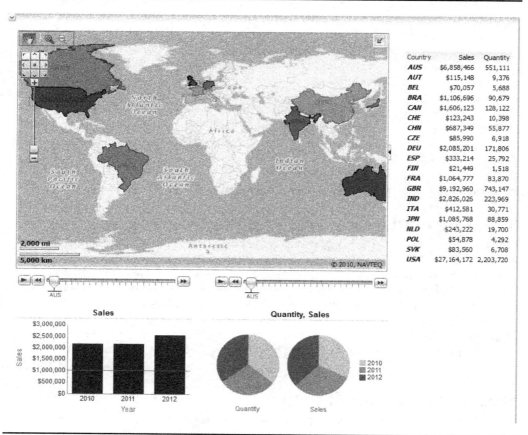

FIGURE 8-7. *World sales with global view*

It can be laborious to scroll through all the different countries of the world. In Figure 8-8, France is selected in the table view and all the views have automatically updated to reflect this selection. Notice how OBIEE zoomed and centered the map view on France. Again, the Country column in the table is formatted with a bold italic font to indicate to the user that this is a master column. Although map views can also act as excellent "master views," the new ability to listen to Master-Detail channels and automatically respond makes maps even more powerful.

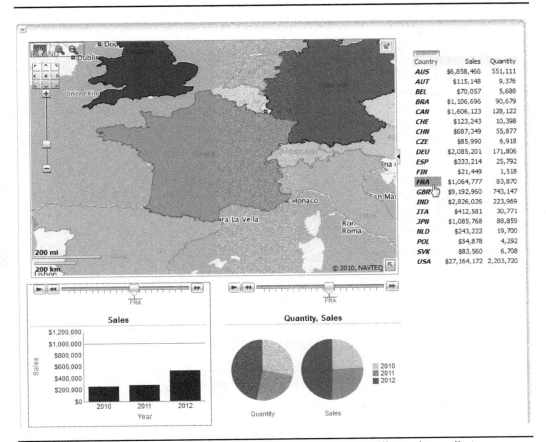

FIGURE 8-8. *The selection of France in table view automatically updates all views.*

Dashboard Prompts

The word "prompt" is used in different ways for different types of objects in OBIEE
11*g*, so don't be confused if you perceive some inconsistencies in the details.
Prompts always refer to an object in which selections are made by users. Sometimes
the prompts are integrated into a particular view or analysis (an "inline prompt"),
and sometimes they exist as separate catalog objects. A "drop-down" selector can
be a graph prompt that controls only a single view, or it may be a dashboard prompt
that controls dozens of views across multiple dashboard pages (see the section
"Important OBIEE Dashboard Considerations" of Chapter 7 for a discussion of the
scope of prompts). A dashboard column prompt is a specific kind of filter that is able
to pass filter definitions to all or some of the analyses or scorecard objects on a

dashboard (can be the same dashboard page on which the prompt appears or across all the pages that make up a dashboard). We'll review the several different options for presenting dashboard prompts visually along with the best practice uses for each.

Standard Prompts

Figure 8-9 shows the creation of a new dashboard column prompt. The prompt types shown in Figure 8-10 appear in the following order from left to right: List Box, Radio Buttons, Check Boxes, Choice List, and Text Field. We will describe each one of these types of prompts and their common uses.

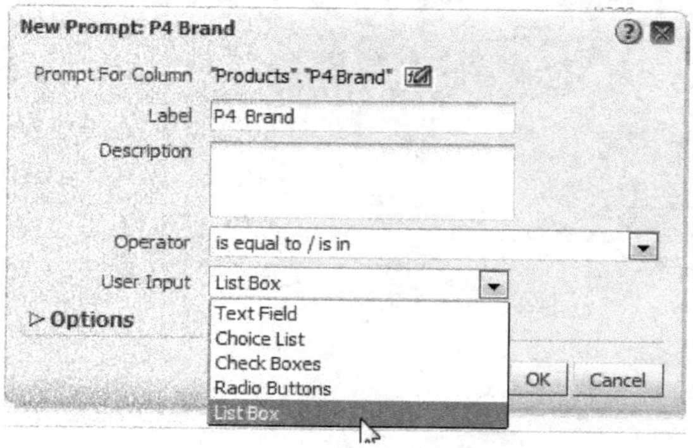

FIGURE 8-9. *Types of dashboard column prompts*

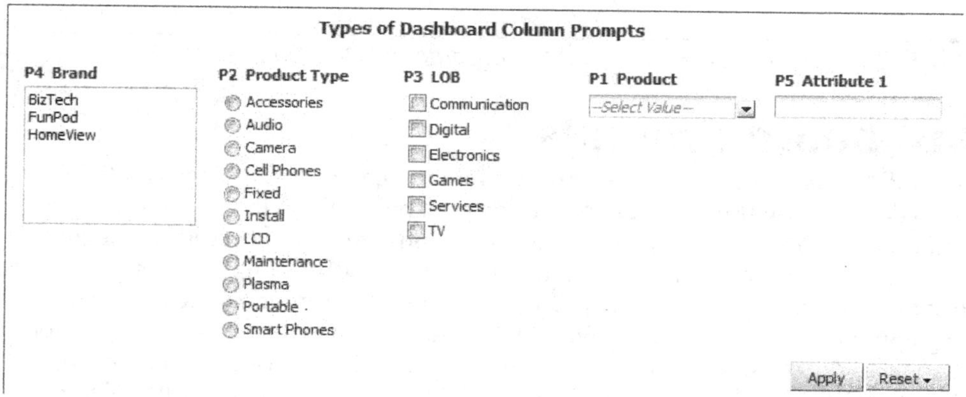

FIGURE 8-10. *Types of dashboard column prompt examples*

TIP
Generally speaking, dashboard prompts should have defaults of the most common or most sensible values to avoid unnecessarily requesting large amounts of data. These defaults values should be communicated to users.

List Box

The List Box prompt type presents a list of values to the user and allows the user to make single or multiple selections using the SHIFT and CTRL keys. There is also a great deal of flexibility in configuring the values included in the list (for example, custom groups from selection steps can be included), and all the filter definition operator options such as "is not equal to," "less than," and "greater than" are also available. Refer to the Oracle Fusion Middleware User's Guide for full information. List boxes are very flexible and configurable and are an appropriate option for relatively long lists of selections where giving users the ability to see all selections simultaneously and to multiselect using the SHIFT and CTRL keys are more important than preserving the substantial space that list boxes can require. Be aware that there are limited formatting options for changing the appearance of selection choices. You can use string formulas in the SQL function argument to change the values to uppercase, append each value with a custom string, and so on.

Radio Buttons

The Radio Buttons prompt type presents a list of values to the user and requires the user to make a single selection. As in most modern user interfaces, radio buttons can only be used to select a single value, so use this option when you want users to consciously choose between mutually exclusive alternatives. This makes most sense when the visualizations are designed as comparisons with a non-additive or custom comparison value such as comparing individual salespeople with a mean value for the sales team. For example, it would not make sense to compare more than one selection with an average value.

Check Boxes

The Check Boxes prompt type presents a list of values to the user and allows the user to make single or multiple selections, but the selections must be made for each item in the list (you cannot use SHIFT or CTRL key to multiselect). It is very similar to the Choice List option, but rather than showing active choices through highlighting, it shows them with a checked or unchecked box. Check boxes require more width than do choice lists, but they can be clearer (especially when a background color is used in the prompt field and highlighting is problematic). It is generally clearer to use a check box for a default value for a prompt because it is very clear which items are selected. Check boxes are good for full-list multiselection purposes because of their visual clarity. Because the box for each member must be individually clicked, check boxes are more appropriate for smaller and shorter lists than choice lists. As with choice lists, there is also a great deal of flexibility in configuring the values included in the list (for example, custom groups from selection steps can be included), and all the filter definition operator options such as "is not equal to," "less than," and "greater than" are also available. Refer to the Oracle Fusion Middleware User's Guide for full information.

Choice List

The Choice List prompt type is perhaps the most common, mainly because it takes up the least amount of screen real estate. Initially, choices are collapsed to a single line with a drop-down arrow, but when a user clicks the drop-down arrow, a list of values similar to the check boxes is presented to the user and allows the user to make single or multiple selections (again, like the check boxes, one at a time). For lists that are too large to display, an internal scroll bar appears to scroll the list. As shown at the bottom of the box in Figure 8-11, a "Search…" choice allows the user to search to "Select Values." The Select Values interface shown in Figure 8-12 allows users to find specific values through a search interface and to shuttle multiple values from the available list on the left to the selected list on the right. This provides a strong ability for users to navigate long lists.

FIGURE 8-11. *Choice list*

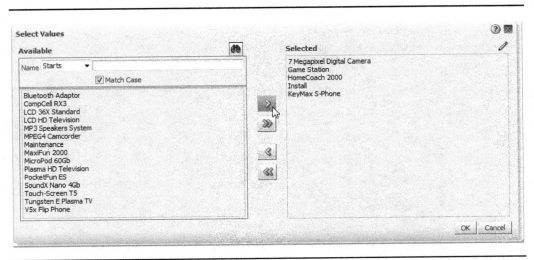

FIGURE 8-12.   *Select Values interface*

Text Field

The Text Field prompt type requires the user to enter a single value. This value must precisely match a value in the column (options are not presented from which the user can select). The primary use case for this prompt is for the entry of names where the full set of selections is not present or exposed. When using a Text Field prompt, consider providing hints to the user such as "Enter in all caps" or example entries. A good way to provide these hints is via the Description box when creating a prompt. Text entered in the Description box appears when the user hovers over the prompt. This works for each of the prompt types, but is especially important for the free-form Text Field prompt type.

Calendar Prompt

When you create a column prompt for a column that has a data type of date, an option to create a prompt with a special calendar selection tool appears, as shown in Figure 8-13. This is an intuitive selector (shown in Figure 8-14) that functions like many calendar tools in other programs. You can either create a single date selector (is equal to, less than, greater than, and so on) or use an "is between" option (shown in Figure 8-15) to select values in a date range.

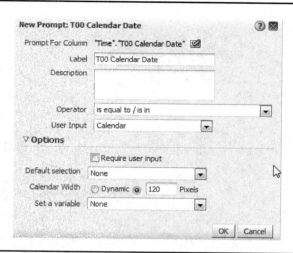

FIGURE 8-13. *When the data type is a date, the Calendar option will appear in the User Input field.*

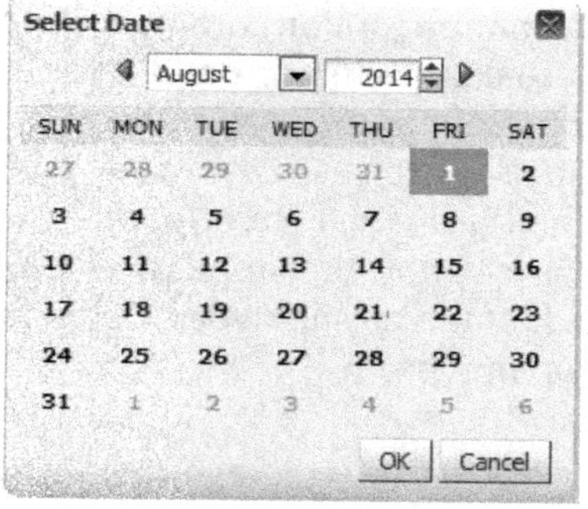

FIGURE 8-14. *Calendar selector tool for date column prompts*

Date
Between 08/01/2014 — 08/31/2014

FIGURE 8-15. *"Is between" date prompt*

Slider Prompt

Slider prompts are used for selecting numeric inputs for ranges defined by "is between." The visual advantage of slider prompts is that they provide information about the relative nearness and farness of the data selections to the overall range. This is potentially useful in many cases when you want to give users some sense of the proportion of the data selection being made versus the overall scale of the range of data.

Users can click the buttons/bars and drag them to the position required, or they can click directly on the number line. They can also type precise numbers in the field. This is useful for round threshold values such as customers with sales between $500,000 and $1,000,000 or months 4 through 10 as shown in Figure 8-16.

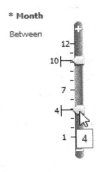

FIGURE 8-16. *Provide figure caption.*

Image Prompt

Image prompts are selection mechanisms that respond to user interactions on an image rather than a field. We'll discuss two primary use cases for this, although there are sure to be plenty more. The first is a small image of a map, as shown in Figure 8-17. To be honest, this is becoming less common with the integration of native map views in OBIEE and the powerful editing tools in Oracle MapViewer, Map Builder, and Oracle Maps.

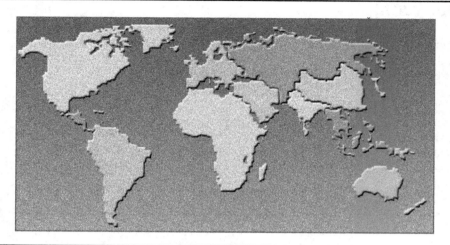

FIGURE 8-17. *Image prompt: clicking a world region outline is the same as selecting from a drop-down prompt menu.*

The second is in the inclusion of product images in tables. Many firms struggle with long names, non-intuitive product numbers, and complex indexes for large product catalogs. A relatively small thumbnail image of the product can provide users with an interface that can be scanned quickly for immediately recognizable selections. This method can be preferable to text-only names in drop-downs and other lists.

Always Visually Communicate the Role of Dashboard Prompts

The inner wiring and inner workings of prompts in OBIEE can get quite complex. You can set prompts to respond to or to be modified by other prompts. You can have prompts interact with filters, selection steps, other analyses, variables, and more. The question addressed in this book is not so much "How do you do logically program the interface?" but rather "How do you visually communicate the relationships that you program into the interface so that users understand them?" As described in Chapter 7 on dashboard layout, the physical location of prompts and their nearness to the analyses and views that they influence are critically important.

One of the simplest ways to indicate a direct relationship is to use a common background color for a prompt and the analysis that it modifies. Figure 8-18 shows this effect. The Contribution Waterfall Members radio button prompt on the left controls the Contribution Waterfall visualization on the dashboard. Whereas the rest of the prompts interact with all other dashboard elements, the singular connection between the Contribution Waterfall visualization and its prompt is emphasized with the gray background color. These two objects are placed into different columns on the dashboard (both set to Best Fit) and their alignment may change due to the expansion or contraction of other dashboard objects. However, given their physical nearness and especially the common background color, their relationship should always be easy to see.

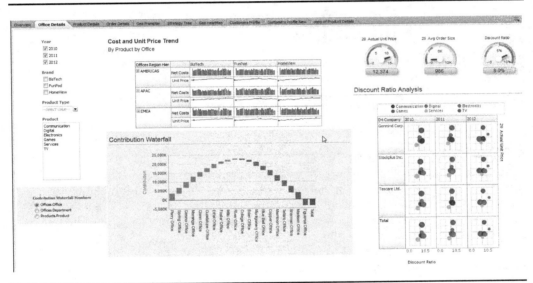

FIGURE 8-18. *Prompt and analysis share a common background color.*

If the visual weight of the background color is too dominant and distorts the importance of the objects relative to other objects on the dashboards, colored borders can also help signal a relationship between the items. In Figure 8-19, the relationship is still apparent, but the weight of the visual presentation is not as strong. In other situations, we have used colored lines or bars on the sides or bottom/top of visuals to indicate commonality and connectedness. Generally speaking, the more intrusive or obvious a visual clue is, the more it draws attention to itself and is understood.

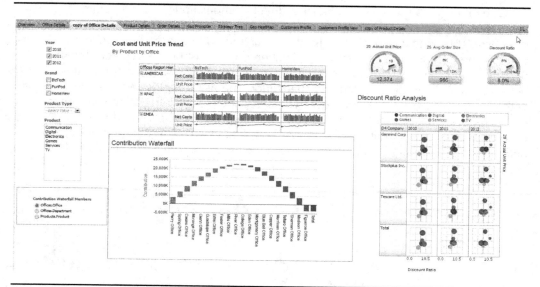

FIGURE 8-19. *Prompt and analysis share a common border color.*

Cascading Prompts

Cascading prompts are ones whose values are limited by the selections in other prompts. These enable users to interact with much larger lists of values by limiting the presentation of members by another column (typically a "parent" column in the same hierarchy). Although it is possible to use hierarchical prompts (prompts directly against a hierarchy that modifies the selection steps for a particular view), they do not restrict the amount of data. Cascading prompts do act as filter definitions, but the interaction relationship between the prompts should be communicated visually. Cascading prompts should be given a background color (or a border at a minimum) to signal they belong together and interact, and explanatory text should also be added. Cascading prompts are generally designed in a left-to-right format, as shown in Figure 8-20.

Select Region First to Limit List of Countries Shown

Region --Select Value-- ▾ Country --Select Value-- ▾ Apply

FIGURE 8-20. *Cascading prompt*

As always, the tradeoffs for different alternatives should be evaluated. There are advantages in establishing strong and consistent conventions, and there are limits to how much information can be conveyed easily. Identification of which design elements to prioritize is critical; it's not possible to prioritize everything. Emphasizing one element necessarily means de-emphasizing others.

Creating and Applying Saved Customizations

Dashboard prompt values and user-configured settings can be saved by individual users and applied at later dates. They can even be shared with other users and can be saved as the default for dashboards and dashboard pages. This is extremely useful in large organizations with complex prompts. Once users set all the prompts to the values they want, they can drop down the Page Options toolbar on the dashboard and select Save Current Customization. They can either select for use by "me" or for use by "others." Figure 8-21 shows how a previously named set of selections can be applied.

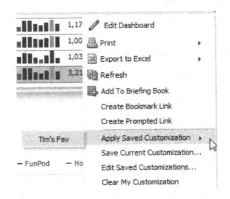

FIGURE 8-21.   *Saving and applying dashboard customization, including prompt selections.*

Navigation

Supplying information within an understood or anticipated context is one of the differentiators between a well-designed business intelligence system and a traditional reporting system. Although the objective for data visualization is to guide users intuitively through the interface and the capabilities of the interface, a small amount of end-user training and orientation can go a long way toward giving users the confidence to engage in interactive behavior with the system. (One of the biggest impediments to users interactively engaging with BI systems is their fear that they will "break" something or harm the system through a lack of knowledge.) This is why it's best to err on the side of adding directional text to dashboards that tells users what to do rather than assuming that they will understand. That being said, filling a dashboard with directional text rather than investing time in interface and visualization design will seldom yield good value.

Well-designed BI systems guide users to additional information and new insights within the context of their current place within the system. As BI systems get larger and more complex, designing navigational aids and visually indicating their presence becomes more and more important. All of these navigational aids can also be configured to appear on a conditional basis. These rules allow for clean and easy-to-scan interfaces when an organization is experiencing "normal" results and for fast navigational aids to appear when thresholds are met or conditions are exceptional. These business rules and this action framework add a higher level of sophistication to dashboards.

Primary Navigation Actions

The primary "navigation" actions are as follows:

- **Link**   Change browser address to a new web page.

- **Drill**   Add new detail information to a specific view.

- **Zoom**   Change the resolution of the current view to show more detail.

- **Open**   Open a new browser page.

Link

Links change the address of the browser session. The (nearly) universal format for displaying a link in a web interface is to underline the text. Therefore, you should reserve the underline format only for links and not use it to signal emphasis. There are several ways to add a link on OBIEE dashboards and analyses, and understanding the differences between them can help. Remember that you can think of an OBIEE dashboard as a website (often, a very large complex website). Adding contextual navigation helps users find important information that otherwise might be buried in a data warehouse. Just as links in and between websites enriches online data, navigational aids in OBIEE add tremendous value to the data stored in large enterprise BI systems. There are several "navigational objects" that you can place directly onto OBIEE dashboards (in addition to the interaction capabilities embedded within analyses). These are shown in Figure 8-22.

FIGURE 8-22. *Linking objects available for insertion on OBIEE dashboards*

Although there are overlapping capabilities of each one of these options, they also have best-practice use cases and visual presentations. Exposing a directory structure directly through the inclusion of a folder view can both speed general navigation and familiarize users with the structure of catalog objects. Plenty has been written elsewhere on how to logically organize and structure directories. Of particular note is the importance of anticipating the expansion of your directory, because changing the depth and path to catalog objects can break links and require "rewiring" of dashboards, prompts, views, links, and other objects. That is, you should anticipate expanding your directories down (in depth) and across in terms of new folders and try to avoid changing the location of existing objects. We also discuss catalog structure in the section "Working with BI Catalog" in Chapter 12.

Typically, you should place a folder view for linking to the OBIEE catalog structure at the bottom of the far-left column (typically a column that holds prompts). This practice encourages users to look in a familiar place for links to the catalog and allows users to view the catalog structure without leaving a dashboard (a surprisingly handy feature, particularly for power users and developers). The bottom-left corner is a "purpose-driven" location on the dashboard and is typically not one of the most immediately visible spots. You should place the folder view at the bottom so that its level of visibility on the dashboard itself is dependent on the other content on the dashboard. Alternatively, you can place the folder view at the bottom-right corner of the dashboard. This is also a convenient location that gives users a consistent place to navigate to for access to the directory. We the authors slightly prefer the bottom-left corner because folder views seldom take much width, and there are fewer issues with alignment and logical organization.

Actions provide functionality to navigate to related content and to invoke operations, functions, and processes in external systems. They are highly configurable "code" objects that can be configured for navigation and to invoke processes. They can be programmed to respond automatically to conditions (such as threshold and logical operators) and new data feeds. Agents (formerly called "iBots") include scheduling capabilities and configurable delivery actions. Closely associated with actions are action links and action link menus. Action links are more flexible than standard web hyperlinks and a very attractive element of OBIEE. The visual appearance of action links cannot be configured easily in the standard user interface, so important conditional dashboard action links should be placed in their own dashboard section. This section should then be formatted to help convey the level of importance, need for immediacy of response, and rarity of occurrence. You can also add a text message (which can be formatted with HTML tags) and use a font size for the level of importance as well as use a background color for immediacy of response (these situations call for the use of bright colors so that they visually standout from other objects on the dashboard; if bright colors are used elsewhere, it diminishes the impact they have for action links) and exclamation marks and symbols for rarity. In general, you should place important conditional action links separately, near the analyses to which they are associated, rather than always embedding them within a column name or view.

 TIP
Creating conditions as catalog objects and then using the same condition for action links and their dashboard section formatting ensures that they appear at the same time. Remember, conditions are associated with analysis columns and not the display of query results as associated with selection steps.

The section titled "Customers Ordering More Than $5000 in Cameras!" shown in Figure 8-23 appears only when there are results for the analysis. Note that a background color of yellow has been added to call attention to this important query and action link when it appears.

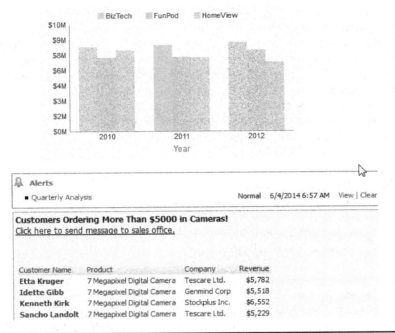

FIGURE 8-23. *Conditionally formatted section placed at the bottom of a dashboard*

It is also possible to place action links embedded within the view of the analysis. The appearance and placement of these action links is dependent on the particulars of the situation. However, you should try to format the cells or columns to differentiate between drilling, zooming, and other interaction effects from embedded action links.

Drill

Drilling is one of the most common actions on BI dashboards and can conceptually be thought of as filtering and asking for more detail in a single click. In general, you should format a cell or column name that can be drilled by changing the color of the font from a pure black or pure white to a font with a slight hue. Cells or column names that act as links are formatted with an underline. Drill actions can either open a new browser window with additional detail in the new view (or in the case of tables, add a new column to the analysis and the table view).

Zoom

Zooming changes the scope of information shown in a browser window to a more detailed view of some information and exclusion of other information, but does not change any data selections or (conceptually) change the browser address. Zooming behavior is covered in Chapter 3, where we talk about graphs, and in Chapter 4 on maps. Zooming is different from drilling in that the data selection is not affected at all. It's only a change in the detail that is shown in the browser window. Zooming in on something shows a section of a window in greater detail and necessarily excludes other information that is no longer visible. Zooming is becoming more predominant as a practice and metaphor in websites and other interfaces and is very common in mobile interfaces.

Open a New Browser Window

Opening a new browser window does not make any changes to the previous session in data selection or view. Navigation links can load a new URL in the current browser window and change the current browser address, or they can launch a new browser session and open a new window. The appropriateness of either choice is entirely dependent on the situation and context. You don't always need a visual presentation difference between opening a new browser window and navigating to a new address (if it seems important, you can communicate this through the use of the link text description itself). The addition of navigational "bread crumbs" at the bottom on the browser page has simplified the issue of sequential navigation and browser window control in OBIEE and lessened the criticality of dealing with some of these issues from a user experience and visual design perspective.

Action Link Menus and Navigation Dashboards

Action link menus are groups of actions where a user can choose which specific one to invoke.

You can include a navigational dashboard whose sole purpose is to provide a large number of links in a minimal space. Figure 8-24 shows an excellent example of this type of "dashboard page of links."

Link or image objects that are embedded directly onto OBIEE dashboard pages have an advantage over action links in that they can be modified through the use of HTML tags. Often, enriching OBIEE dashboard pages with external content can make them more engaging and interactive. For example, you could include a link to a finance website that has live feeds of a client's firm and its more significant competitors on an OBIEE dashboard. You can even include a smallish "window" in a defined pixel space (so that it doesn't dominate the dashboard page) and configure it to act as a link to the full finance website. Do keep in mind that all external links require a certain amount of verification and maintenance. It's a good idea to create

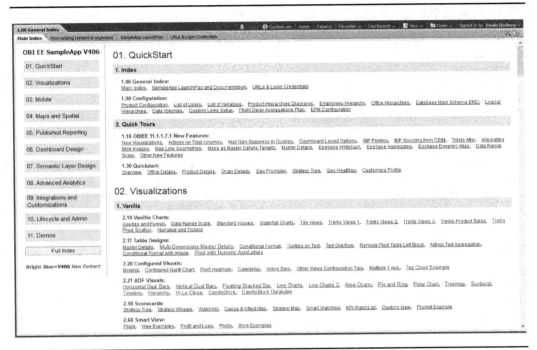

FIGURE 8-24. *SampleApp V406's index dashboard page*

a file with all the external links so that there is only one place to go to verify that these links are current. There are few things more frustrating to users (or damaging to the trustworthiness) of a BI system than a series of old, broken links.

Summary

Enabling and promoting interactions with business intelligence dashboards is one of the very best ways to ensure user engagement, to maximize utility, and to bring value to organizations. However, rather than adding interactions for interaction's sake, you'll find that the visual presentation of the choices available to users and the anticipated effects on subsequent data visualizations are critically important. Choose radio buttons for single selections, check boxes for shorter lists where multiselection capabilities are needed, and list boxes for full sets of interactions. Interaction "signals" work best when they are integrated into the larger pattern of formatting, placement organization, and dashboard styles for the overall system. Make sure that you consciously choose the style of dashboard prompts, understanding the tradeoffs and characteristics of different prompt styles. Place those prompts in a consistent location on the dashboard, and place the analyses and views that they parameterize in close physical proximity. When needed, use border colors and background colors on columns, sections, and analysis containers to visually indicate dependencies and relationships between prompts and the objects they parameterize.

Use only as much color as you need to communicate relationship and exceptions; otherwise, even more important information may be missed because of too much visual clutter and noise. Establish patterns for the formatting of fonts. Try to use underlining for links, colored fonts for drills, large-size fonts for important conditional alerts and threshold events, and bold italicized fonts for Master-Detail linking. Err on the side of including explanatory narrative text views and directional instructions for users. One of the most cited reasons users have for not interacting with dashboards and actively making selections is that they don't know what will happen and they are afraid of making a mistake. Building the confidence of your users is absolutely important to the success of your OBIEE implementation.

Navigational aids are hugely useful, and although action links are easy to add, they should be reserved for in-analysis links, and other methodologies should be used for enabling navigation to external websites, directory structures, and other URLs. Keep a list of links as you develop them so that maintenance and future updates are much easier.

CHAPTER
9

Scorecard and Strategy Management

The Oracle Scorecard and Strategy Management (OSSM) module in OBIEE 11*g* provides a framework and purpose-built visualizations for measuring, evaluating, and managing performance of various key performance indicators (KPIs). Once defined, these KPIs help an organization align corporate strategy and improve the consistency, coordination, and speed of decision making across large enterprises. Scorecards also allow an organization or a department to track KPIs over time.

Scorecard and Strategy Management is founded on the strategy frameworks of "balanced scorecards" and "strategy maps" developed by Robert Kaplan and David Norton. Balanced scorecards provide a methodology for developing, coordinating, and managing organizational strategy initiatives.

Balanced scorecards are one of the most prevalent and influential strategy frameworks. Dozens of books and thousands of web pages are dedicated to the art of designing and implementing balanced scorecard and strategy map programs. By some estimates, more than 50 percent of the Fortune 500 has adopted some form of balanced scorecards.

Fundamentally, balanced scorecard methodology is about the development and management of a hierarchical, integrated set of measures that reflect organizational performance, position, and aspirations viewed from multiple perspectives. These perspectives include both financial and nonfinancial metrics and attempt to integrate both "hard" quantitative metrics and "soft" qualitative metrics. By tracking these measures over time, an organization can ensure that it is "improving," assuming that it uses measures that align with its goals. A key part of the "built-in" functionality is the integration of rolling periods and time-based measures. They provide a continuous framework for comparisons of performance and greatly leverage the work done by and investments made in planning functions. The movement toward continually updated data flows along with an expectation for finer and more immediate adjustments in business strategy heighten the case for implementing OSSM.

OSSM's annotation feature allows people to comment directly on dashboards on why those goals are not met and even comment on other people's comments, adding a unique collaboration feature to OBIEE. With OSSM as an integrated module of OBIEE, it is natural to blend classic BI and OSSM visualizations seamlessly in a series of dashboards. Annotations are particularly important to functions such as risk management, where tradeoffs and alternative courses of action represent strategic choices facing an organization. These are alternative paths that demand a "preference" position be taken and do not respond to a simple optimization function. Comments, questions, and deliberations, presented within the context of KPI reporting, provide tremendous value and aid when complexities are high.

Four different dimensions or "perspectives" provide the "balance" in scorecard and strategy management and ensure that strategy is not completely dominated by a single view. The following is a list of the standard perspectives and some KPIs (not exhaustive!) that relate to these perspectives:

- Financial Perspective (revenue growth, profitability, return metrics, and so on)

- Customer Perspective (customer satisfaction, market share, segmentation, and so on)

- Internal Process Perspective (production efficiency, quality, lean metrics, and so on)

- Learning and Growth Perspective (employee retention, productivity, new product development, and so on)

Oracle Score Card and Strategy Management Objects

The three different kinds of "objects" in OSSM are KPIs (key performance indicators), objectives, and initiatives.

KPIs

KPIs are the building blocks of OSSM. These measurements have associated target values, and they usually vary with time. They include dimensions that allow them to be evaluated in different "slices," and they are often "owned" by an accountable individual or department. You can also build up subjective KPIs such as "improve customer experience" from lower-level objective KPIs such as customer satisfaction survey scores. KPIs simplify the presentation of complex data because goals are tied to the base measures. For example, a SALES measure can be linked to the goal measure TARGET and the variance can be directly measured. OSSM includes several "built-in" derived measures based on the definitional attributes of a KPI, including its current status, trend, difference measures (such as variance value and percent), and comparison values with different time periods. Think of a KPI as a "super measure" from the repository that doesn't require as much conditional formatting in the front end (in essence, the conditional formatting threshold parameters have all been previously established when a KPI is defined and established as an object). KPIs can have any attribute column from the Subject Area set as a dimension (for example, a sales KPI might have a region dimension, a product dimension, and a sales representative dimension). Normal drill paths are maintained for KPIs. You can also set KPIs specifically by "pinning" them to specific dimension values. The OSSM visualizations all make extensive use of KPIs and enable dense visualizations to be built relatively quickly. It's important to note that conditionally formatted measures can be overridden by users with the appropriate privileges and that comments can be added justifying the reassignment of status. This means that not only does OSSM respond to data thresholds and rules, but that it is also responsive to human beings and their judgment in highly complex and volatile situations and is not bound by rules determined in the past.

Objectives

Objectives are the desired summary outcomes that form an organization's strategy and provide a logical, hierarchical structure for KPIs. Whereas an "objective" might be to "reduce operating costs in the current fiscal year by 10 percent," there will be many KPIs that will "roll up" into the overall objective via a hierarchy of objectives. This allows you to build up complex objectives from lower-level, simpler objectives and KPIs. To use an analogy from project management techniques, objectives are like summary objects in a work breakdown structure whereas KPIs are like individual tasks. There are many ways for OBIEE developers to define the contribution of various KPIs to objectives. Think of it like a very flexible "weighting" capability in which different KPIs can contribute to an overall objective score according to complex logical rules.

Initiatives

Initiatives are time-specific tasks or projects that are undertaken to achieve organizational objectives and goals. If you're at all familiar with project management techniques, you'll be familiar with the thinking behind initiatives. Initiatives identify the plan and management efforts to achieve KPI target values and help identify potential causality when significant variances between actual and target values occur. This direct "tie" between actions and measurable results is often missing in traditional business intelligence systems. This also promotes the concept of joining responsible individuals and groups with specific KPIs, planned activities, and progress toward targets. Annotations provide the opportunity to add context and to document important situational factors that should be considered in decision making.

Scorecards Defined

A scorecard is a collection of related objectives, initiatives, and documents in OSSM. The Scorecard editor (shown in Figure 9-1) is where new "documents" (analogous to views in Answers) are created, edited, and added to a scorecard. The score (shown as 56 in Figure 9-1) on a scorecard measures how well the business initiative is doing in a simple summarized statement.

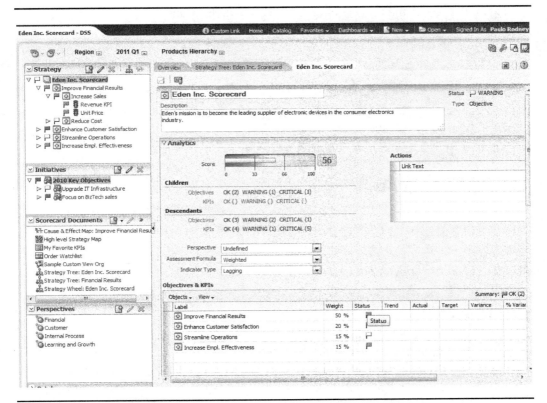

FIGURE 9-1. *Scorecard editor*

OSSM Visualizations

The six major visualization views in OSSM are the best way to show the power of the system. Although many of these capabilities can be leveraged in other ways in OBIEE, we'll focus on the traditional application of the six views in OSSM:

- KPI watch list

- Strategy tree

- Strategy wheel

- Strategy map

- Cause-and-effect map

- Custom views

Figure 9-2 shows the process of creating new visualizations.

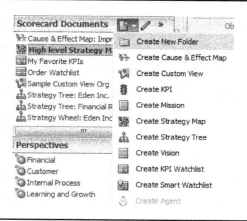

FIGURE 9-2. *Scorecard documents or views*

KPI Watchlist

Figure 9-3 shows a KPI watchlist view. A watchlist is a view with some very special properties. It is, in many ways, similar to a default "table view" in Answers. It shows a grouping of related KPIs in a row-and-column-based view. The columns for KPI show many of the default settings that are established when a new KPI is defined. This view shows measures on rows, and on columns shows derived measures such as variance for each of those measures. The status labels, icons, and thresholds are set for each KPI in the States interface, as shown in Figure 9-4.

KPI Watchlist - Functional Example KPIs

Objects ▾   View ▾   Summary: ⭐⭐⭐⭐⭐ 5 Stars (4) ✓ OK (2) ✗ CRITICAL (1)

Label	Status	Trend	Actual	Target	Variance	% Variance	Change	% Change
Basic 5 State KPI	⭐⭐⭐⭐⭐		$70,000,000	$69,050,000	$950,000	1.38%		
Basic 5 State KPI - Pinned to Biztech	⭐⭐⭐⭐⭐		$25,500,000	$26,727,218	($1,227,218)	-4.59%	No Actions Available...	
Basic 5 State KPI - Pinned to FunPod	⭐⭐⭐⭐⭐		$22,500,000	$19,711,565	$2,788,435	14.15%	📄 Open KPI Definition	
Basic 5 State KPI - Pinned to HomeView	⭐⭐⭐⭐⭐		$22,000,000	$22,611,217	($611,217)	-2.70%	✏️ View Watchlist Entry	
KPI with Self-Sustaining target	✓	⇧	23,973	0	23,973	0.00%	📊 Analyze	
KPI with Self-Sustaining target 2	✓	=	70,000,000	70,000,000	0	0.00%	📇 Contact Owner	
KPI with Self-Sustaining target 3	✗	⬇	5,187,177 USD	28,529,475 USD	(23,342,297 USD)	-81.82%	💬 Add Comment	

FIGURE 9-3. *KPI watchlist view*

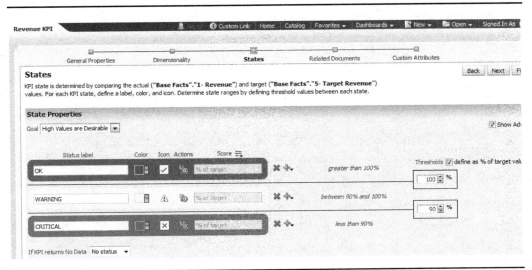

FIGURE 9-4. *The KPI States page configures conditionally formatted display factors*

Smart watchlists go a step further and provide the ability to view a watchlist table view of measure information about objectives, KPIs, and initiatives in a drillable hierarchy similar to a hierarchical column in Answers.

Strategy Tree

Strategy trees show the hierarchical arrangement of objectives and the component KPIs that contribute to them. This parent/child structure is shown in a collapsible tree visualization. The current state of an objective or KPI is revealed through its color. Variance and trend information is shown as well. Each leaf on the tree is highly interactive. Figure 9-5 shows a small portion of a strategy tree. A thumbnail view is also available so that very large trees can be navigated quickly. The cursor has been placed over the Avg Order Size cell, and the drop-down shows the same column values from the watchlist view and provides an interaction menu. One of the most powerful features of OSSM is the ability to annotate views and add comments to them. This collaboration capability in the context of strategy development and management is a powerful feature. The Analyze link creates an analysis in Answers with columns for all of the measures and dimensions associated with the KPI. The Show Chart link creates a mini graph (shown in Figure 9-6) of the relevant measure.

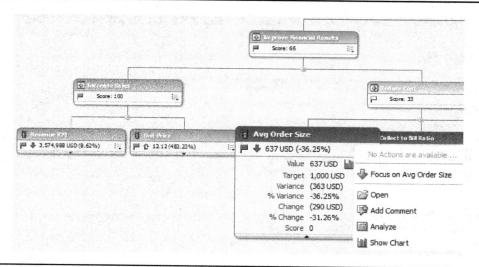

FIGURE 9-5. *Strategy tree with drop-down menu*

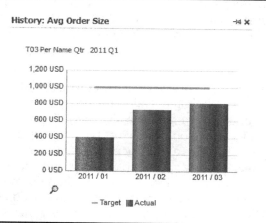

FIGURE 9-6. *Show Chart link for Avg Order Size automatically creates a small bar chart.*

Strategy Wheel

Strategy wheels (shown in Figure 9-7) are a new type of strategy tree that use a "layered" circle to show the hierarchical relationship between different components of the scorecard rather than a traditional "branch and leaf" tree structure. Double-clicking an arc length section moves that component to the center of the circle. Clicking the outer ring of the circle adds new layers and details to the visualization. Strategy wheels can display a dense presentation of the state of an overall organizational scorecard in a small amount of screen real estate as well as add navigational and interaction capabilities with virtually no development effort.

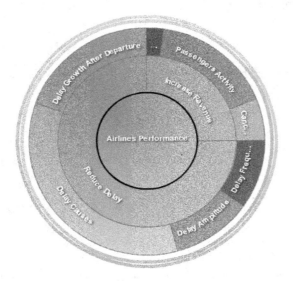

FIGURE 9-7. *Strategy wheels are an alternate view of a strategy tree.*

Strategy Map

Strategy maps (shown in Figure 9-8) show objectives and KPIs organized by their perspectives (shown vertically on the left) and also show cause-and-effect relationships (shown by the directional arrows between the objectives). The arrows are not only directional, but also show the relative contribution of measures to one another through their thickness or weight. This emphasis on causal relationships not only allows executives to understand the relationships between key performance indicators and summary objectives, but also to take action based on the information. A similar menu of action links is available for each cell in the strategy map. Action links can also include navigation to other dashboards, analyses, and strategy objects for additional information and deeper analysis.

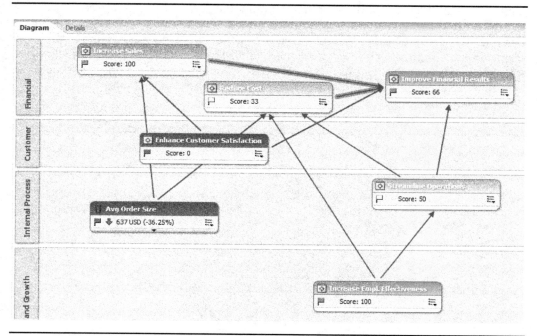

FIGURE 9-8. *Strategy map views show objectives by perspective and causal links.*

Cause-and-Effect Map

Cause-and-effect maps show logical linkages between KPIs and/or objectives in more of a central "spine" layout. Colors of links between objects show the current state, directional relationship, and proportionality or strength of the relationship graphically. Cause-and-effect maps help executives and managers "diagnose" and understand complex interactions and also assist in identifying underlying causes that can be addressed with corrective action. Whereas strategy maps are often excellent for high-level "overviews" focused on differing perspectives, cause-and-effect maps are particularly suited for more detailed presentations of specific objectives and their components. Figure 9-9 shows a close-up view of a portion of a cause-and-effect map. Hovering over a link reveals a dialog regarding the cause-and-effect relationship between the KPI and the objective. Hierarchical levels can also be shown, and action menu options similar to other views are available for objectives in cause-and-effect maps.

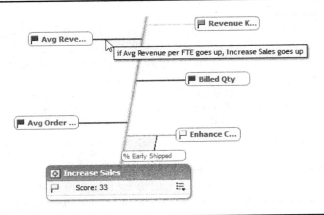

FIGURE 9-9. *Cause-and-effect maps show logical relationships between KPIs and objectives.*

Custom View

Custom views allow developers to attach or overlay KPIs literally on almost any image or graphic, as shown in Figure 9-10. The KPIs can include causal links and relationships, as in many other views. The placement of the KPIs and associations with images allows the developer to communicate a rich set of concepts and associations with the placement of the image. In some ways, the custom view is somewhat similar to an image prompt. Scorecard objects such as KPIs are dragged from the Strategy pane and placed on the diagram. KPIs can be configured to include related strategy nodes as well.

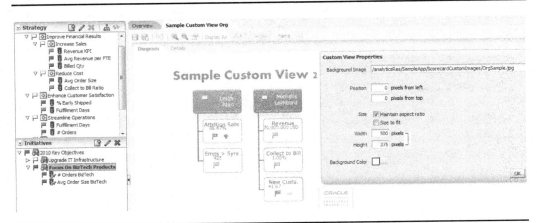

FIGURE 9-10. *Custom view with the Custom View Properties dialog*

Summary

Oracle's Scorecard and Strategy Management extends the power of OBIEE in important ways and adds a tremendous amount of visualization firepower to the OBIEE arsenal. OSSM marries the techniques and frameworks from Kaplan and Norton's balanced scorecard and strategy map methodologies, which have been widely adopted by corporations and organizations around the world, and combine them with the OBIEE's Common Enterprise Information Model (CEIM) in the OBIEE repository and the dashboard capabilities of OBIEE's front end. Unique capabilities are found in all six unique visualizations from OSSM: KPI watch list, strategy tree, strategy wheel, strategy map, cause-and-effect map, and custom views. OSSM excels at showing the cause-and-effect relationships between KPIs and overall corporate strategy objectives. Annotation, action menus, and customization capabilities all contribute to the ability to develop a highly interactive collaboration and decision-making environment. Purposeful-built visualizations make it easy to add appropriate visualizations of KPIs. These can even be used on non-scorecard data to extend the visualizations that OBIEE offers. OSSM enables executive management the ability to see how various aspects of enterprise.

CHAPTER
10

Mobile

The growth in mobile devices as a platform for all kinds of computing has been nothing short of spectacular in the past few years. This includes large enterprise systems based on Oracle Business Intelligence. There have been no fewer than three different major releases and interface changes during the time of authoring this book. We will focus on general principles for designing data visualizations using OBI rather than on specific interface capabilities and processes because the systems and the field in general are evolving so rapidly.

More and more people are using mobile devices to connect to systems and to get information. Because this occurs across every realm of daily life, it is true for enterprise computing, enterprise business intelligence systems, and especially Oracle Business Intelligence Enterprise Edition. This growth/change/evolution will likely continue in the world of mobile BI and spill into the very core of OBIEE. Most users don't just have one computer at their desk that they use; they also have a phone, an iPad or tablet that they carry with them to meetings, another computer at home that they use to log in to their corporate system, and maybe even a Kindle or other device that can connect to the Web via a browser. Although some organizations still control access by issuing standard devices and allowing only "official" organizational equipment to connect, many other organizations are fully embracing the concept of "bring your own device" (BYOD), which makes it critically important that BI content be delivered through a secure channel across all devices, ideally in a consistent fashion without having to redevelop content for each device.

For the past few years, some analysts have loudly predicted the imminent demise of the PC market along with dominance by phones, tablets, and other mobile devices. Although phone use across the world continues to climb, the very latest research by Gartner (as of the writing of this chapter) shows a slowdown in growth of the tablet market in "advanced" economies, combined with a stabilization in the traditional PC market (http://www.gartner.com/newsroom/id/2791017).

The total number of traditional PCs worldwide is still larger than the number of tablets worldwide as well. In many offices, the size and number of screens on desks has never been greater. It isn't unusual to see two or three monitors (many of them large flat screens) on many desks. In the future, many people in business will want to view dashboards on different screens at different resolutions in different situations. A manager who may have a large external monitor at her desk may also grab an iPad on her way to a meeting. Screens of all sizes, running on different systems, and used in different situations are proliferating. However, the user community sometimes expects a "seamless" experience in which every capability and presentation is consistent across platforms. Interestingly, many executives' expectations are far less demanding with respect to how dashboards and reports render on smartphones than on tablets.

These realities place a large set of potential compromises before business intelligence data visualization developers, realities that directly impact how they conceptualize, understand, and establish strategies for the presentation of data visualizations on mobile devices.

Like several other key topics, OBI mobile is a huge topic deserving of hundreds of pages of detailed information. However, the following subjects will not be covered in this chapter: mobile security, third-party tools for OBIEE such as RoamBI and SurfBI, hybrid devices such as Amazon Kindle and other "readers," Google Glass, and the installation and configuration of OBI mobile-related software and plug-ins. As in specialized topics in other areas of the book, we will focus mostly on topics directly related to data visualization for Oracle BI 11*g*.

Three Main Methodologies for Viewing OBIEE Dashboards and Content on Mobile Devices

There are three main ways that users interact with OBIEE via a mobile device:

- A web browser

- The OBI Mobile application (both iOS and Android)

- The OBI Mobile App Designer app (a custom-developed application covered later in chapter)

These three interfaces differ dramatically when it comes to data visualization from development, maintenance, and user experience perspectives. Developers, administrators, and users should all understand the significant differences that exist and the strengths and weaknesses of each method.

Web Browser

Many mobile devices can run a web browser and render an OBI dashboard. If a mobile device contains a web browser, then can't we just start up the web browser and simply connect to the BI dashboard? Of course, the answer is a qualified "yes." Web browser menus often consume enough of the precious screen real estate on a mobile device that they don't leave enough "functional space." Also, controls and gestures may be optimized for web surfing and visiting multiple websites, not for a BI environment. For use cases involving a greater amount of interactivity, lookup, or parameterization, either Oracle BI Mobile or BI Mobile App Designer should be used. Sometimes you'll run into security issues, because mobile devices are often connected to the cloud and BI servers are often behind firewalls. Note that security implications won't be discussed here because they're really not related to visualization. You may also want to check to see if the browser on your mobile device is officially supported by Oracle.

One of the most important factors to consider is that OBI dashboards and analyses often rely on Flash technology, so parts of the interface will not run properly in many browsers. Be aware that parts of dashboards may render on these browsers, but many interaction capabilities such as right-click menus, dashboard animations, embedded content, and alerts may not function properly. As Oracle changes OBIEE to use HTML5 instead of Flash, this situation should get better in later releases.

Developers who want to distribute and use OBI content in widely diverse platforms should use briefing books to publish important reports in PDF format so that they can be viewed and used. Although much of the interactivity may not be available, invariably the most organizationally important use cases involve an executive who simply wants to see the latest results or to receive a message regarding important events or milestones. You can customize agents to send alert messages to different individuals' devices depending on their profiles. You can also make sure that the summary or specific detailed information that they want access to is produced in a briefing book and is available to them offline and on different mobile devices (for example, you could standardize to PDF).

Oracle Business Intelligence Mobile HD and Oracle BI Mobile

Oracle has developed a purpose-built app called Oracle Business Intelligence Mobile HD on the iOS platform and Oracle BI Mobile on the Android platform. (We will simply call the app "BI Mobile" when referring to both platforms.) This application is developed by Oracle and is designed to facilitate the use of OBI dashboards, analyses, BI Publisher reports, scorecards, briefing books, and alerts. This application does not provide a development environment. Instead, you develop Dashboards and reports in the standard OBIEE environment and simply view them on iOS devices such iPhones and iPads and Android smartphones and tablets; no special treatment or configuration is required. There are a number of differences, however, between the desktop interface and the BI Mobile interface, and both versions of the app leverage the unique capabilities of its operating system in subtle but important ways.

BI Mobile is a good tool for consuming dashboards and reports, but not for developing them. BI Mobile allows users to open and view dashboards, analyses, briefing books, BI Publisher reports, scorecards, Oracle BI Mobile apps, and content delivered by agents. Dashboards are rendered (with differences discussed later) and analyses are shown only in their "open" mode and not in their "edit" mode. A shortcut icon (which looks like three progressively larger bars) can be used to gain direct access to dashboards. Similar to how the drop-down

Dashboards menu only shows dashboards in folders titled "Dashboards" in the catalog, this only shows objects placed within dashboard folders. This app also simplifies the user experience, making it easier to find content of interest through search, recently accessed lists, favorites, and other mechanisms familiar to mobile users.

BI Mobile App Designer

BI Mobile App Designer is actually a new application that runs in the OBIEE suite of products. Because it has a different interface, an entire section is devoted to this interface at the end of the chapter; it is simply included here for completeness.

General Principles for Effective Data Visualization on all Mobile Devices

Much of what has been shared in the rest of this book applies equally well to mobile devices. We'll cover a few differences that apply to multiple platforms before we get into the specific differences.

Smaller Screen Resolution

Screen resolution has a tremendous impact on the experience users have with BI dashboards. Here are some of the most common screen resolutions for different mobile devices (as of 2014):

- 2048×1536
- 1024×768
- 1024×600
- 1280×800
- 540×960
- 480×800
- 480×320
- 960×640
- 640×1136
- 320×480

The point here is not who has what screen resolution or even what market share they represent (the truth is that screen resolutions vary widely depending on geographic market, organizational segment, and more), but rather that there is a tremendous variety of popular and common screen sizes, and unless your organization issues a "standard" device for the entire enterprise, you as a developer will not be able to design to a specific screen resolution when developing for a mobile audience. Because of these variations, some of the general advice given earlier in the book will be emphasized. The concept of designing for multiple screen resolutions is discussed in Chapter 7.

Design Dashboards with a Specific Role in Mind

Plenty of organizations simply expect their "standard issue" dashboards to translate to BI Mobile and to be just as effective. Although some dashboards may work well, others invariably suffer when put on a smaller screen or when a user is trying to look up highly specific information quickly. Although this is less of an issue with tablets, organizations should produce some specific dashboards for use with mobile phones for specific roles where the value to the organization is very high. The most obvious example of this is for field sales reps who need to look up information when they are on the road (perhaps at a customer site). A dashboard that focuses on comparisons between customers might be extremely useful in the office, but provide too much information to fit comfortably on a mobile device. However, a dashboard that can be filtered by account and features the most information about an individual account (status of most recent order, unordered popular items, trends, status of accounts receivable, and so on) can produce the kind of actionable intelligence that drives significant returns to the enterprise. Too often developers try to design everything into all dashboards (often at the request of leaders who aren't necessarily thinking through how they will be used) rather than focusing on specific audiences of users and the situations where they will use the dashboard.

Prefer Small Tables

It should be fairly obvious that big tables don't work well on small screens. Large tables with more than five or six columns don't work well on mobile devices. Use smaller tables at a higher level where the users can drill into or navigate to finer-grain presentations, potentially with Master-Detail linking. This "peeling the onion" approach can also work well for situations where the objective is less about exploration or discovery and more about finding specific information that is needed in a particular context or situation. Although many executives are accustomed to scanning large reports, with some gentle encouragement and demonstration they can adapt to navigating to the information they need within the dashboard paradigm.

Prefer Performance Tiles

Performance tiles were made with mobile in mind. An array of performance tiles that serve as navigation aids can be extremely effective for mobile-centric dashboards. Remember, users are typically navigating using their fingers rather than a mouse and therefore need larger targets. Performance tiles also convey information through their conditional formatting and promote the kind of "scanning" behavior that so many executives like. If you have users asking you how to "pinch" visualizations to make them smaller and then "pull" them to zoom, chances are you have too much information on the dashboard and need to focus it. Performance tiles and other "simple statement" visualizations that invite investigation through drilling often make up a big part of the answer.

Prefer Visualizations That Show an Overall Pattern in the Data

Efforts to design for a mobile platform sometimes fall into the "let's do the latest, sexiest visuals" camp rather than "let's present the most important information very cleanly" camp. Although it may seem exciting to splash a lot of color and visual excitement on mobile-destined dashboards, it's actually much more important to edit, refine, and remove noncritical information. Users on mobile devices are less likely to have additional time to decipher visualizations and read explanatory text necessary for consistent comprehension. Certain visualizations can be used to communicate the main message quickly. Highly dimensioned and complex visualizations are best left to exploration-style dashboards, where the screen real estate and the amount of time the audience has to understand complex information is greater. Figure 10-1 shows an example of a BI Mobile app that shows an overall pattern in the data.

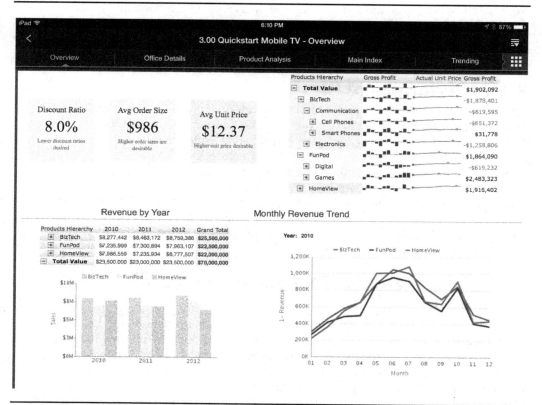

FIGURE 10-1.   *Sample BI Mobile app*

Eliminate Unnecessary Visual Noise

Figure 10-2 shows a mobile dashboard with gridlines in the visuals, and Figure 10-3 shows the same dashboard without them. The extra "visual noise" becomes especially noticeable on a smaller screen, so avoid it.

Include Fewer Prompts and Limit Prompt Selections

Determining a strategy for prompt usage is another issue that becomes even more important in mobile dashboards. Include fewer prompts and limit prompt selections to those that relate directly to the content on a mobile dashboard and are required for parameterization for the envisioned use case on a mobile device. Prompts

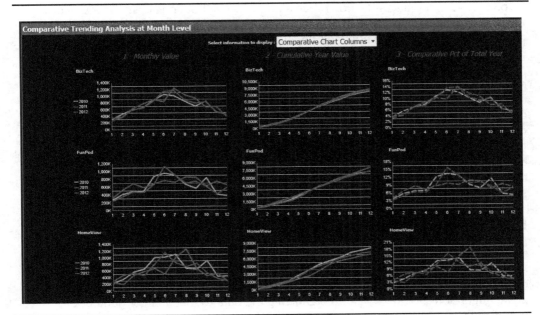

FIGURE 10-2. *Grid lines are extremely strong visually in mobile-themed dashboards.*

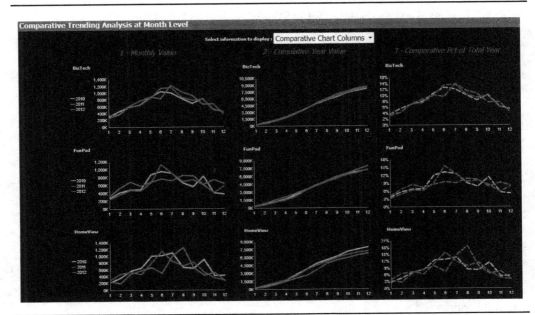

FIGURE 10-3. *Elimination of gridlines makes line charts much easier to read in mobile-themed dashboards.*

involve users in the data selection process and improve both engagement and data transparency. Implementations occur at both ends of the spectrum—those where prompts are severely underutilized as well as those where every dashboard has so many prompts that users are overwhelmed with the amount of work it takes to understand the organization's data. Although many dashboards make sense as data exploration platforms in which the discovery of insights are made, the majority of an organization's dashboards should be geared around communicating a shared understanding of the position and performance of the organization. When the total number of choices climbs into the dozens (if not hundreds) of different versions of dashboard results, you should consider first the primary purpose of the dashboard and its intended audience. If it's not primarily for the purpose of data exploration, reduce the number of prompts and consider including a drill-to-detail paradigm rather than relying exclusively on prompts.

Consciously Organize Catalog Structure and Folders

With greater freedom often comes greater need for structure. Larger numbers of devices and situations in which business intelligence data is consumed mean that greater attention should be paid to organizing the data so that a larger number of optimized versions can be created and used. We the authors often start mobile development projects by adding a new dashboard page to the existing dashboards that focuses on particular information from the dashboards (usually reducing the complexity of the interface). The need to organize, structure, and trim dashboard content is very real in most organizations. Logical structures are learned fairly quickly, whereas poorly considered structures remain confusing. We often go to the business users or find a paradigm close to the functional structure of the business that everyone knows. Structures coming from the IT department are sometimes mysterious and confusing to others in the organization.

Encourage Users to Capitalize on Mobile Navigational Features

Even though you organize your dashboards and folders as intuitively as possible, there will be times when users have trouble finding content. Fortunately, BI Mobile has features to assist with this, using concepts familiar to mobile users. Search can be surprisingly effective, even with a compromised keyboard. Recent dashboards can speed up finding those most frequently accessed dashboards. Thumbnail views also assist in finding content of interest to a user. In addition, frequent mobile dashboard users should be encouraged to tag specific dashboard pages as their "favorites," making them easier to find at a later date. Finally, the ability to save dashboards to the local device makes it possible for users to see a visualization even when disconnected from the server.

Dashboard Layouts and Gestures for Mobile

Good dashboard layouts that are not overcrowded on desktop systems tend to look good on most modern tablets. The general principles of proximity, alignment, and visual signals that indicate interrelationships between dashboard elements apply to mobile-centric dashboard development also.

BI Mobile can automatically adjust and flow dashboard objects when they are rendered. It will also detect the device that is being used and automatically render the content appropriately. The user can select from two "layout options" on the Options menu when viewing a dashboard on a mobile device: Mobile Layout and Original Layout. Figure 10-4 shows the Options menu on an iOS device. The selected layout option persists for the duration of the user's session for each dashboard or analysis.

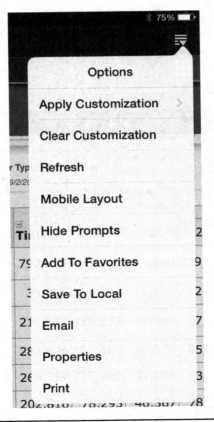

FIGURE 10-4.   *Options menu on iOS devices*

Mobile Layout

The Mobile Layout option places all dashboard objects in a single-column, vertical layout. Objects are placed one below the other, starting with the column in the upper-left corner. All objects within a column are placed together sequentially before either the objects in the next column to the right or below. It's as if the columns were all placed vertically underneath one another, all sections within each column were stacked vertically, and the section layout were set to "vertical." Users scroll down the dashboard to see objects. This layout minimizes the width of the interface and is designed for smaller devices such as an iPhone.

Original Layout

The Original Layout option is similar to the web version, but with some changes. Because Flash is not available, certain visual elements and interactions are rendered differently (using PNG files in version 11.1.1.7). All properties related to the formatting of prompts are ignored in BI Mobile, so any customization of prompt labels will not show. Column prompts (radio buttons, check boxes, choice list, list box, and text field) will automatically display at the top of the dashboard.

Figure 10-5 shows how check box and list box dashboard prompts are displayed. In general, the use of "free text" prompts on dashboards designed primarily for mobile use should be discouraged because typing is often difficult or inconvenient for some

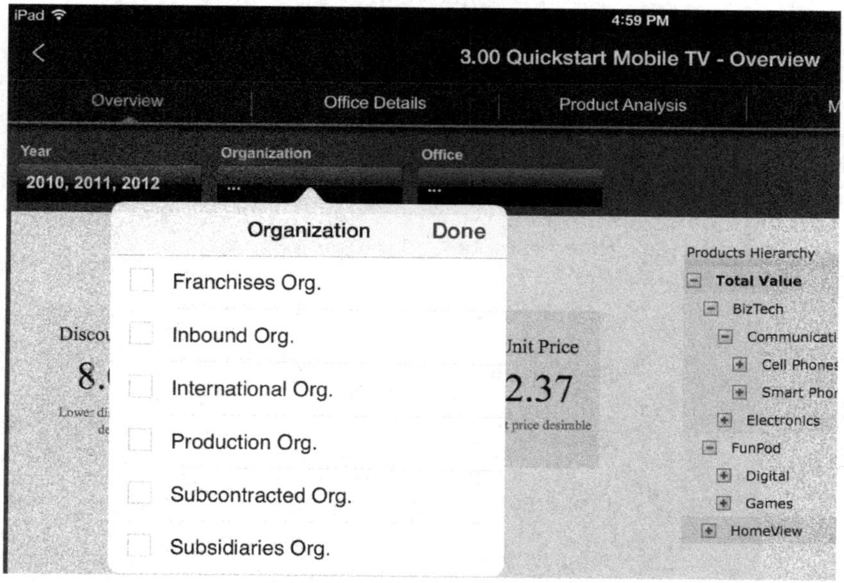

FIGURE 10-5. *Prompts on OBI Mobile dashboard*

(this is changing as people become more accustomed to using tablets and texting on phones). Prompts on mobile also feature a search interface, as shown in Figures 10-6 and 10-7, and advanced search options that are invoked by clicking the "wheel" icon to the right of the search box.

Hierarchical prompts function in BI Mobile, but they take a light and accurate touch to launch (try using a stylus if you're having a hard time with them). Hierarchical prompts and image prompts do not display at the top of the dashboard automatically, but in the order dictated by the column and section in which they are located. The release of OBI 11.1.1.7 fixed the issues with slider prompts and calendar prompts, and while the appearance of these prompts may be slightly different, their functionality is the same.

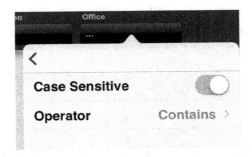

FIGURE 10-6.   *Advanced search options*

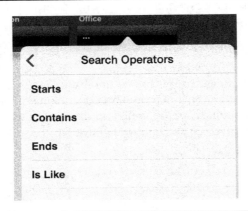

FIGURE 10-7.   *Advanced search operators*

Gestures

A collapsible "mobile gestures" section or text field (see Figures 7-15 and 7-16) can be added to most of the commonly used dashboards to help users learn the differences in interacting with dashboards with directions:

- A single "tap" is the equivalent of a standard left-mouse click.

- "Tap and hold" is the equivalent of a right-mouse click and also is used to show tooltip information.

- A double-tap on a visualization will expand it to fill the entire screen (pinch zoom is not enabled on BI Mobile). Double-tapping is also used to invoke a hierarchical prompt. This is a unique mode allowing for drills and a breadcrumb trail, easing navigation up and down the drill stack.

- A drag with one finger pans within a view or a map and scrolls content in a table, dashboard, or list.

- A pinch with two fingers works on map views and scorecard views, but not on dashboards or other views (double-tap graphs to expand them to full screen size).

White vs. Black Dashboard Backgrounds

One of the most common and important questions that arises is whether mobile-centric dashboards should be designed with a black background or a white background. Black backgrounds have been more common on mobile devices. In general, except for unusual cases where you're trying to lower power consumption or have a conscious purpose for a black background, you should prefer a white background.

Perhaps you're thinking, wait a minute, aren't they just opposites? If we invert everything, shouldn't they just work? It's a bit like saying that you should able to do things just as easily by looking in a mirror and understanding that everything is backward, right? Then try trimming your own hair by looking in the mirror. The reality is that many, many things are different, and different design aesthetics, colors, and techniques are needed to create equally effective dashboards with white or black backgrounds.

Black backgrounds generally need a larger amount of negative space surrounding visualizations, graphics, words, and other forms. That is, black background dashboards need to be less dense than white background dashboards because of the dictates of contrast. Also, whereas black text on a white background provides an ideal reading paradigm, purely white text on a black background can be too strong, requiring a more finely balanced background and text color combination.

Bright colors have even greater visual weight with black backgrounds than with white, making it harder to balance the relative importance of different informational elements. Although bright colors draw the eye against white, they do so even more strongly against black. Black backgrounds also intensify gradients and other visual effects, making them harder to integrate and more distracting to the core message of objective data presentation and interpretation. All of this may make some dashboards appear "sexier" or more visually exciting in black when initially viewed, but it makes it harder to design a functional, effective dashboard for diverse audiences. In short, your users may initially prefer a black background, but then tire of it or simply not use it as much, partly because of the black background.

Can't we just add a cascading style sheet that switches all the colors so that users can choose a black background or a white background? After all, the Dashboard Properties page allows users to set a style for the dashboard. We the authors played with this extensively and found that it's really hard to set style sheets so that dashboards can viewed either in white or black and still have the same amount of functional value. We don't advise that you try to do this. Black background dashboards need to be designed as black background dashboards from the start, and all the visualizations, tables, titles, and other elements need to be designed for use on black background dashboards.

It's possible to have elegant, effective, beautiful business intelligence dashboards with black or very dark backgrounds. It's just harder, and it takes more time to do them well than it does with white backgrounds, at least with version 11.1.1.7 of OBIEE.

Maps on Mobile

One of the most intuitive and exciting visualization paradigms for mobile devices is maps. If possible, you should emphasize maps as visualizations on mobile-destined dashboards even more than you do for traditional desktop dashboards. See Chapter 4 for more on map views. With the new capability of map views functioning both as a "master" view that can control other views and as a "detail" view that can respond to other views, maps and dashboard content can more easily be location and content specific. A feature of OBI Mobile HD 11.1.1.17 is the ability to place a "My Location" pin on a map, as shown in Figure 10-8. This does not require any additional configuration in either the "Administration – Manage Map Data" interface or in the analysis editor (Answers). The feature is enabled as a part of map views on OBI Mobile dashboards. Picture a sales director visiting a city and being shown around to different customer locations. The sales director could pull up key information regarding customer performance and see his or her current location on an OBIEE map view as additional contextual information.

FIGURE 10-8. *Map view on OBI Mobile HD with My Location pin*

Map views in BI Mobile App Designer take advantage of HTML5 capabilities. Figure 10-9 shows a page from a BI Mobile App Designer app featuring a central map view of the United States. The dimensions for analysis are featured on the left side of the page. Additionally, a lasso-style selection tool is enabled as well as a My Location icon, which automatically zooms the map to the current location of the user.

FIGURE 10-9.   *Map view in BI Mobile App Designer app*

BI Mobile App Designer

BI Mobile App Designer is a new addition to the OBIEE suite of products. It is a standalone web-based application that facilitates the development, deployment, and enjoyment of BI dashboards destined for publication, both as mobile applications as well as additions to standard OBI dashboards.

The concept behind BIMAD is to offer users and BI analysts the opportunity to quickly develop insightful presentations and visualizations of business intelligence data that is both easily distributed and fully integrated in existing OBI environments. Apps developed with BIMAD are delivered via a personalized app store within the OBI environment.

Although the *M* in BIMAD is certainly for "Mobile," these apps can run on multiple devices, as shown in Figure 10-10, and can run on browsers as well.

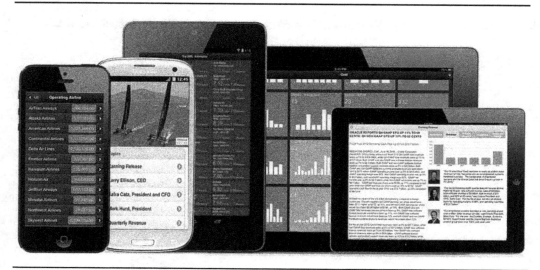

FIGURE 10-10. *BIMAD apps run on many devices.*

Just as OBI dashboards can contain multiple dashboard pages, BIMAD apps typically contain multiple pages. In fact, navigating between pages is enabled through tabs as well as through a carousel visual metaphor common to many mobile environments.

BIMAD requires some (relatively easy) installation and configuration steps that are not addressed in this book. In addition, security, data access, and other administration topics are not addressed. Because BIMAD represents an entirely new interface and design paradigm, we will only briefly look at its capabilities and endless possibilities.

From a data visualization perspective, here are the key aspects of BIMAD:

■ You choose a "layout" (see Figure 10-11) when you create a new app, either in a phone or tablet format. BIMAD uses a responsive web design that adapts these layouts to the device screen resolution and layout. The layout includes a grid for each page.

■ Although you can edit the grid later and modify the number and position of sections, the program essentially performs many of the laborious tasks of alignment and positioning of objectives nearly seamlessly.

■ The page layout features an "editable" interface where you can directly drag and reposition elements.

■ Many of the features of data visualization are designed for fast development and immediate results by presenting the application designer with defined options. For example, data is auto-wired and filters are page specific.

- Apps generated by BIMAD are in HTML5 format and have tremendous flexibility and capabilities within modern browser environments.

- The BIMAD framework is designed to be open and extendable; it provides for both the addition and development of open source and custom JavaScript plug-ins.

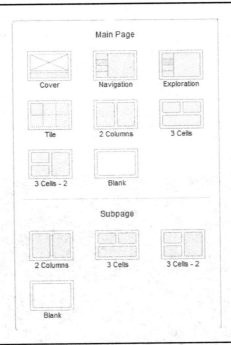

FIGURE 10-11. *Default layouts in BIMAD*

The BIMAD design interface is based on BI Publisher. Many of the default visualizations available in BI Publisher are also available in BIMAD. The power of BIMAD applications will revolutionize the world of OBIEE and will contribute greatly to its maturation and spread as a BI platform. Even though the entire OBIEE semantic layer is available for use, the entire ecosystem, including data models, dashboard distribution, and security protocols, is somewhat different in Mobile App Designer. Make sure you coordinate with your BI Admin group to enable BIMAD capabilities within your organization.

BIMAD is a particularly powerful application related to the development of applications for mobile phones. With smaller screens comes a necessarily tighter focus on specific data sets and perspectives. Many times, users don't have the time to wait for developers to go through the process of documenting and checking requirements, developing and testing new systems and presentations, and finally deployment and verification. BI development will become more like the website editing function in modern organizations. In order for something to appear on an organization's home page, it will have to go through a professional editing and vetting process. This will be similar to what happens for the major BI dashboards that large numbers of executives and managers rely on. They will be produced and vetted by knowledgeable and skilled professionals who gather input from domain experts in the organization. Just as individuals may send their letters and e-mails to customers and don't require approval for every piece of written documentation, they will produce their own analyses and views and, yes, applications and share them within their immediate workgroups. As the audience for these analyses and presentations grows, however, they will require a greater amount of editing and positioning and technical skill in their creation. MAD could be a basic platform and capability much like e-mail and Excel spreadsheets were only a few decades ago.

Figures 10-12 and 10-13 show a typical BIMAD application.

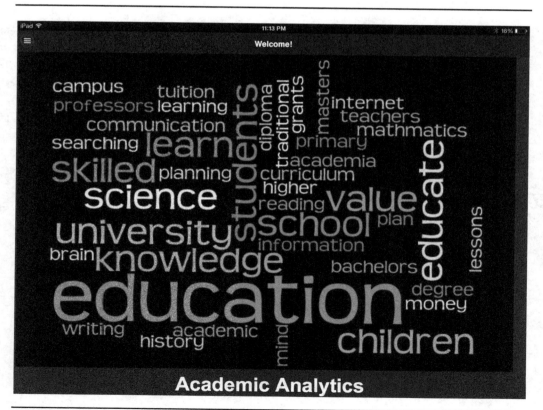

FIGURE 10-12. *Cover page for Academic Analytics BIMAD (a typical BIMAD application)*

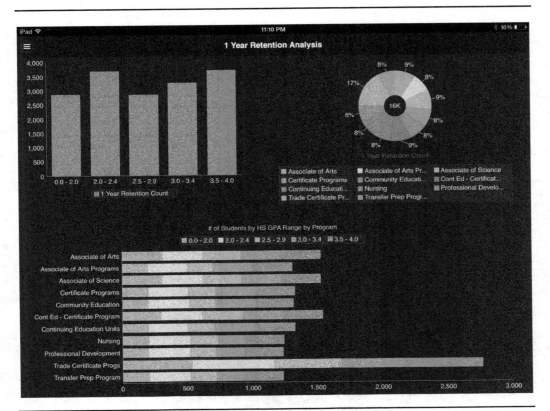

FIGURE 10-13. *Page 1 of Academic Analytics in BIMAD*

Although white backgrounds are generally recommended for all the reasons cited earlier in the chapter, there is no denying that the presentations in the dashboard shown in Figure 10-13 are visually striking. The basic bar graph in the upper-left corner provides summary counts, whereas the stacked horizontal bar graph at the bottom provides similar summary information by program (the totals are the most visually interpretable figures because of the number of the inter-bar ranges). The ring chart provides a comparison for each program to the whole and a total student count in the center. This page does a nice job of providing three different perspectives on highly aggregated data and invites interested users to drill and filter on specific programs or specific student segments for more granular information and insights. The title page shown in Figure 10-12 is a graphic word cloud image (which could be produced easily in D3 or JavaScript). Although visuals can also be included in OBI dashboards, fmap paths and configuration or embedded content (which is not visible on mobile devices) are more involved and complex than in BIMAD.

As shown in Figure 10-14, users manage data selection, transformations such as calculations, and filtering in the far-left panel, and they manage visualization selection and editing in the far-right panel. The layout panel in the middle provides a true WYSIWYG interface. The Properties panel on the left includes only bare-bones editing. Organizations should extend their BIMAD implementations with the use of JavaScript plug-ins (standards should be adopted on which plug-ins will be used). Because BIMAD is HTML5 based, a wide array of animations, transitions, and effects are possible.

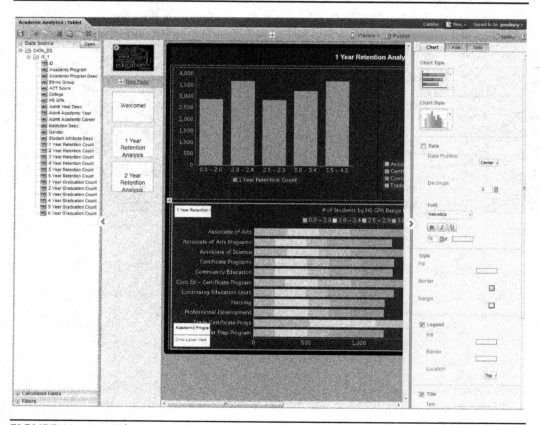

FIGURE 10-14. *Editing interface for BIMAD. Chart types on the right are the same as BI Publisher.*

Summary

The challenge of presenting business intelligence information on mobile devices is not only here, it is growing. We the authors believe that many people will interact with OBI through their mobile devices on a regular basis and that most users will access OBI through more than one interface. Given the tremendous diversity of device screen resolutions and the widely variant situations in which users tend to employ a phone, tablet, or traditional desktop monitor, we recommend that BI dashboards and analyses be designed for specific audiences in specific situations. We do not believe it is possible to design dashboards that function well in every situation. OBI product development has done an excellent job of making some smart default choices for a mobile-style dashboard. Prompts are moved to the top of the dashboard page, and dashboard objects are placed in a single vertical column.

Five Tips for Data Visualization on Mobile Devices

- Simplify content and presentation for quick viewing.
- Prefer white backgrounds over black backgrounds.
- Use fewer prompts.
- Make sure type and data elements are large enough to be selected by touch.
- Develop for specific roles and use cases.

Mobile App Designer is a major game changer for OBIEE and offers many exciting potential opportunities. BIMAD is HTML5 based and utilizes many of the same standard visualizations from BI Publisher. BIMAD can also be easily extended through the use of JavaScript plug-ins.

The mobile environment is evolving and changing very rapidly. We don't know what the future is, but expect it to be more complex with a wide range of platforms, screen resolutions, and capabilities.

CHAPTER
11

Other Visualization Topics

What are "other visualization topics"? This chapter includes a variety of topics—some directly related to one another, some not as much—that did not automatically fit in other chapters in the book. As with many of the concepts we've discussed in other chapters, these topics cross-apply and influence each other in various ways. Some of the sections are a bit more "academic," and some are extremely practical. All, hopefully, will further increase your understanding of and appreciation for the depth of knowledge that is useful when designing data visualizations in OBI 11*g*. You will find information about the principles of design, color strategies, data issues (including filters and selection steps), common data distributions, alerts, and interactions.

Principles of Design

The principles of design are guiding concepts or ideas that help us evaluate the strength of a composition or system. Although the principles of design are shared across all creative, natural, and emergent systems, they apply particularly well to business intelligence and analytics systems and can help guide the evaluation of data visualizations. Words such as *balance, harmony, unity,* and *rhythm* appear again and again, whether the subject is fine wine, economics, physics, basketball, architecture, chemistry, music, mathematics, or a thousand other subjects or disciplines. Accidental? Coincidence? Perhaps not. Superior designs work because they have certain common attributes that we can sometimes measure, often appreciate, but always perceive. No matter the origin of the analysis, the forms, structures, and systems that exhibit certain characteristics are judged to be superior over those that do not.

For each design principle, we will give a definition, a paragraph describing the general concept, and a paragraph describing how the principles of design can be applied directly to BI systems and data visualizations. There are many, many different examples that can be used for each concept. Although we the authors tend not to use these concepts extensively in client meetings, we find that the concepts are useful in diagnosing why a dashboard doesn't look right or when a system isn't as appealing as it could be and user adoption is low.

Unity

A sense of oneness or wholeness.

Unity is achieved when everything in the system comes together to make a single statement. Unity refers to the theme or the idea of the work and occurs through reinforcing or strengthening the central theme or perspective.

Unity is expressed in business intelligence systems when everything "hangs together" and makes sense. It's easy to find a lack in unity in systems where incentives are misaligned with measures. For example, BI systems with a lack of unity may emphasize profitability with sales bonus measures, but emphasize new customer acquisitions in sales strategy dashboards. Strong alignment creates strong unity.

Harmony

A pleasing sense coming from the interaction of the components of the design and the way they complement the other components and coordinate together.

Harmony refers to the physical components of a system. There are many different types of harmony with several different pleasing combinations of components that balance each other and provide interest. All of the elements of design can be involved in harmony, including color harmony, texture harmony, and shape harmony.

Effective dashboards use consistent colors to represent the same elements. If red represents company locations and blue represents competitors in one visualization, the colors and meanings should be consistent and not be different for other visualizations. If they are not consistent, the dashboard will lack harmony. Often, overly bright and garish colors lead to dashboards that lack harmony.

Balance

A sense of stability that comes from having an equal amount of weight on either side of the focal point or central dividing line.

Balance is one of the most universal principles of design and often refers to the inclusion of the proper amounts of different elements in the right proportion so that no one element unevenly dominates or obscures another.

BI systems also require that their computing power be well balanced. It does little good to have an extremely powerful BI server if the presentation server is underpowered and not capable of rendering visualizations for the system. In this situation, the servers would be out of balance. Balance can be applied at a high level to the appearance of dashboards or visualizations, or a low level to specific element such as graph bars and column widths within a table.

Rhythm

A sense of movement created through repetition and line.

Rhythm depends on the intensity and frequency of the components and the number of times an element is repeated. Rhythm typically requires precision in order to create a strong sense of movement.

Alignment and repetition create strong rhythm. An array of pie charts or performance tiles can help lead the eye to a key visualization. When elements are not aligned and lines are broken, it's difficult to quickly scan a page.

Proportion and Scale

Proportion and scale refer to size relationships in a design.

Proportion refers to the size relationship of design components when compared to other design components. Scale refers to the size relationship of the overall design compared to its environment or surroundings.

When the size of x- or y-axis labels is too big or small, they are out of proportion with the visualization. We also often see problems with scale in data. The data elements are "out of scale" with each other and are difficult to represent in a single visualization. They need to be "scaled" to an index. Visualizations should always strive to represent the proper scale of data elements.

Emphasis or Dominance

A central component that dominates the design.

Most successful designs have a component that draws the eye, often called the "focal point." The focal point is the largest or most visually dominate component. In many disciplines, the focal point is also the most expensive component. Lines often lead to and through the focal point, or frame the focal point by establishing its space.

The most important element on a dashboard should occupy the most prominent space, and in many cases it should have additional visual weight achieved through size, color, or background. Having a "central message" for visualizations also means that one insight is necessarily emphasized over others. Systems, dashboards, and visualizations that try to be too many things to too many different audiences usually end up accomplishing very little.

Variation

A pleasing sense of variety.

Variety in a design brings relief, interest, and allows a broader, more diverse statement to be made. Although excessive variety invites chaos, a complete lack of variety communicates stasis. Variety is closely linked with harmony, in that harmonic strategies describe the different types of variation that complement each other and coordinate well together.

Well-designed bar graphs are easy to read and convey information consistently to broad populations, but dashboards that consist of only bar graphs lack variety. Dashboards still need variety to be visually interesting. If too many of one type of visualization are used, the dashboard becomes boring and uninteresting.

Color

Color is one of the most important elements for any presentation of business intelligence information—whether it is a dashboard, table with conditional formatting, graph, mobile application, alert message, or anything else. The best way to use color is to use it sparingly. The less color you use, the more effective it will be when you do use it. Color draws the eye and conveys information extremely quickly and effectively.

The average person can distinguish around a million distinct colors when hue, saturation, and brightness are varied. This capability varies widely from person to person, with the upper range as high as 100 million. In the spectrum, most people can distinguish around 150 distinct hues. Suffice it to say that many people are good at seeing colors. However, about 10 percent of the male population has some form of color perception deficiency, commonly called "color blindness." This doesn't mean that color-blind people can't see colors (more than 99 percent of them can), it's just that their experience in seeing and distinguishing certain colors is somewhat compromised. The most common forms of color blindness are classified as green/ red, meaning that their perception of reds and greens may be somewhat altered (there are several different forms of green/red color blindness). Although not precisely correct, it can be useful to think of reds and/or greens as appearing as different shades of grey for red/green color blind people. Know that there are specific challenges with many implementations of the standard "stoplight" color palette (red, green, and yellow) because of color blindness.

Color perception is highly specific to individual situations. Human beings see colors differently at different times and see colors differently with different surroundings or adjacencies. We the authors often show a handful of optical illusions involving color perception/misperception during our data visualization workshops to drive home the point that we humans don't see color as much as we "experience" it as our brains attempt to construct a color model for a given situation. Figure 11-1 shows a simple black-and-white optical illusion. Although both small squares are exactly the same size and color, the one on the left appears to be smaller and darker than the one on the right (in the middle of the black square). Many color-based optical illusions are even more pronounced.

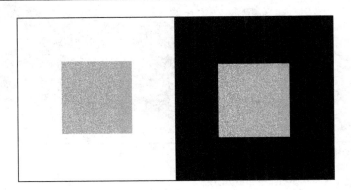

FIGURE 11-1.   *Optical illusion where both inner squares are the same size and color, but appear to be different based on the adjacent color*

Given the importance and the enormous challenges of dealing with color, the last thing we do when working with clients is to leave it up to "taste." We use scientifically based resources to inform our choices for colors and color-usage strategies. Some of our favorite resources include ColorBrewer 2.0 (www .colorbrewer2.org), iWantHue (http://tools.medialab.sciences-po.fr/iwanthue), and the W3Schools HTML Color Picker (www.w3schools.com/tags/ref_colorpicker.asp).

ColorBrewer 2.0

ColorBrewer 2.0 (www.colorbrewer2.org) is one of the most straightforward and helpful sites for determining which colors to use. Developed by Dr. Cynthia Brewer to be used in cartography (map design), ColorBrewer 2.0 is particularly useful for choosing colors for data visualizations. Figure 11-2 shows the interface for ColorBrewer 2.0.

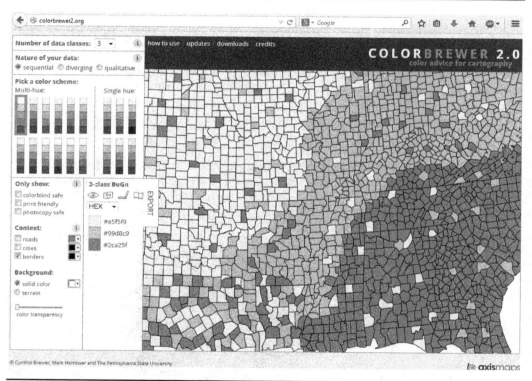

FIGURE 11-2. *ColorBrewer2.org*

Users make the following selections:

- The number of data classes for which they want individual colors
- The nature of the data they are wanting to show
- The format for the individual color information (OBIEE uses hex)
- Any restrictions such as color-blind safe, print friendly, and photocopy friendly (the latter two cases have highly restricted choices)
- Color transparency slider bar (used more frequently for map layers than in graphs)

The user can view a number of scientifically designed color ramps on the sample map to see adjacency and differentiation effects. "Borders" should be deselected to get a true representation.

Color ramps are divided into three different categories depending on the nature of the data that is being represented: sequential, diverging, and qualitative.

Sequential Colors

Sequential colors are used for data that varies in magnitude or size. Different colors represent different threshold levels or "bins." The choice of those levels or bins can greatly affect the perception of the data when you use a sequential or diverging color strategy. Also, as you are assigning the colors to levels, be conscious of the choice you made in creating percentile binning or value binning. See the section later in this chapter on binning strategies for more on percentile and value binning.

In both cases, the idea is to show progression and relative/comparative results. Often, color ramps are misapplied for continuous measures. In all cases, light colors should be associated with low or small values and dark colors should be associated with high or large values. For example, let's say we are using color fill by state on a USA map to show the level of sales. Several color ramps are included by default in OBIEE that would be inappropriate to reflect sequential values because they vary color hue rather than intensity. For example, it is not immediately intuitive if a color range from green to blue-green to blue uses blue or green as its high value. The multi-hue (and single hue) sequential ramps in ColorBrewer 2.0 all are specifically designed to reflect progression through a sequence.

Diverging Colors

Diverging colors are used for data ranges that vary positively and negatively from a central zero point. One color range represents positive values and another color (often a complementary color directly opposite on the color wheel) represents negative values. Divergent color schemes typically have white or very light middle value in the center and then two colors for the end points. Although it may be tempting to use a diverging color ramp to represent sequential data values, the color intensity may afford a differing amount of visual attention to middle values than would be otherwise apparent in a true sequential color ramp. This is particularly troublesome for logistic distributions of data rather than data that is closer to a normal (bell-shaped) distribution. There are times when data is not equally distributed in scale on the positive and negative side (the positive and negative value ranges are significantly different). In such cases, set the total number of colors equal to twice the number of colors needed for the side with the greatest range, but only use some of the colors on the other side. For example, if positive variance ranges from 1 to 50 percent and negative variance ranges from –1 to –15 percent, you might choose a 10-color ramp and use five colors on the positive side and only two colors on the negative.

The best example use case for divergent color schemes is variance against forecast or budget. The forecast value would establish the "zero" line, and variances above or below would be represented in a single divergent color ramp. Divergent color schemes are particularly useful in map views, bubble graphs, and other views where a physical "divergence" from a center may not be the major dimension of the visualization. As such, they are sometimes relegated to more complex visualizations or simply reinforce major insights portrayed through other means. As stated before, they should be used after careful consideration in other circumstances.

Qualitative Colors

Qualitative color ramps are some of the most frequently used in business intelligence dashboards and graphs. In these situations, colors represent separate nominative or nominal data categories. This means that data categories have a name, but that name has no relationship to the data. Chicago comes before New York in an alphabetized list, but it's only because of the way the name is spelled, not because it's bigger or more important or further west. Many graphs and charts are easier to read when data elements are identified by color. Most importantly, however, the color choice should not impart meaning or emphasis that is not represented in the data. Some colors are more visually prominent or attention getting than others. This actively distorts the representation of the data and distorts the insight and meaning that users derive from a visual presentation of the data in the form of a graph or chart. Nominal color schemes should be consciously balanced, maximally separated, and unaltered by gradients and other visual effects. This is especially true when bright, visually strong colors are used. The use of pastel color schemes is recommended for qualitative color schemes because they are easier on the eyes and because they allow for exceptional data elements that are conditionally formatted to use stronger colors and to be more visually prominent on dashboards.

Qualitative color schemes should be used to identify noncontinuous categories of data. Examples include sales region, supervisor, company, product/brand names, and departments. Adjacencies can play a role in the perception of colors. Turn off the "borders" selection on ColorBrewer and look carefully at the boundaries of qualitative colors. When you're using ColorBrewer, the section in the bottom-left corner of the example map helps evaluate overall color discrimination whereas specific boundaries in large areas in the rest of the map help evaluate adjacencies (zoom in to particular spots for a clearer view). Remember that monitors and screens vary widely and data projectors are famous for washing out colors. You don't want colors in your carefully crafted color palette to be indistinguishable in the big presentation in the company board room!

iWantHue

Another popular tool is the "iWantHue: Colors for Data Scientists" website (http:// tools.medialab.sciences-po.fr/iwanthue/). This online tool was developed by some extraordinarily talented people at Sciences Po University in Paris and reflects an extremely insightful approach to color choice in data visualization. Although it is not as immediately approachable and straightforward as ColorBrewer 2.0, iWantHue is extremely interesting and useful. iWantHue automatically generates color palettes of optimally distinct colors by allowing users to refine the Hue (H), Chroma (C), and Lightness (L) of a three-dimensional array of colors that is then "rolled" into a color palette using either a "soft" K-means or a "hard" force vector clustering algorithm. There are also a series of preset HCL settings that assist with choosing colors if you don't have time to learn to "tune" the interface yourself. We the authors often use the Pastel presets. As with ColorBrewer 2.0, you choose the number of colors you want in iWantHue and then you click the Make a Palette button. You can lock down the colors you like and reroll the palette for colors that you don't like.

The strategic approach of the iWantHue tool as shown in Figure 11-3 and Figure 11-4 is to find colors that are distant from one another in a perceptually uniform color space. There is a lot of technical background information on color spaces and the clustering algorithms employed by the tool, including technical papers, tutorials, theory, and examples. There is also an excellent GitHub site with all the source code and extensive documentation.

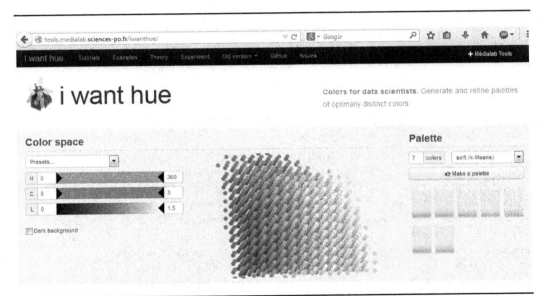

FIGURE 11-3.   *iWantHue online tool*

iWantHue is based on the CIE L*a*b* color space for computation (it fits human perception) and the HCL color space for presentation (it's more user friendly). The three axes interact and affect one another. Essentially, you are applying filter conditions to limit and "slice" a twisted three-dimensional space. Be sure to read the documentation to better understand these interactions. The "Hue" (or H) axis represents the color spectrum of pure hues. You can choose all or any range of the color spectrum. You can leave this set at 360; however, if you wanted a range of blue colors, for example, you could filter the results to show color results for this particular hue. The "Chroma" (or C) axis selects the degree to which the colors are gray or colorful. You can think of this as the "dullness" of the colors. Less intense colors should be used for most dashboard and graph applications, so limit the C axis to the left side or "dull" range. The "Lightness" (or L) axis determines the range from black to white of the colors. If you tend to prefer pastel colors, you will typically restrict this axis to the right, whiter end of the range.

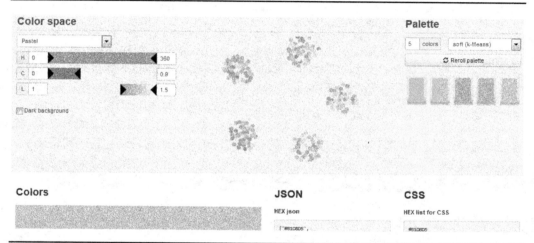

FIGURE 11-4. *iWantHue develops palettes of optimally distinct colors.*

iWantHue includes hex codes for both JSON and CSS applications and even automatically generates JavaScript snippets for use in code (they require the Chroma .js and Palette-Gen libraries). There is also a "dark background" setting that provides a good tool for developing color palettes for dark, mobile-style dashboards and visualizations. Virtually every part of the interface is interactive. The axes all respond to rollovers in the other axes, colors can be refined and locked, and the color space responds as you hover over it and explore it. This is a wonderfully designed tool developed by serious data scientists specifically for use by data visualization practitioners. The more you use iWantHue, the more discerning and educated you'll become about colors, which will drive you to want to use it even more.

NOTE
The GitHub site for iWantHue states the following: "The idea behind iWantHue is to distribute colors evenly, in a perceptively coherent space, constrained by user-friendly settings, to generate high-quality custom palettes."

W3Schools HTML Color Picker

The third highlighted resource is the W3Schools HTML Color Picker (www
.w3schools.com), shown in Figure 11-5. It is extremely easy to use and provides
extensive tutorials on many aspects of web development. An array of 127 colors is
presented in a hexagonal form. The arrangement is a flattened three-dimensional
structure. To understand the hexagon, think of an octahedron or eight-sided die
with its tip extending perpendicular to the page straight at you and its lower half
split and flattened to the outer edges. The most immediately useful part of the page
is the extended shades/tints ramp on the right side of 21 colors (your original color
plus 10 additional colors deepening to black, and 10 additional colors lightening to
white). You can either select a hue from the hexagon or type a hex code in the
field. Figure 11-6 shows pasting in the hex code #99FF99.

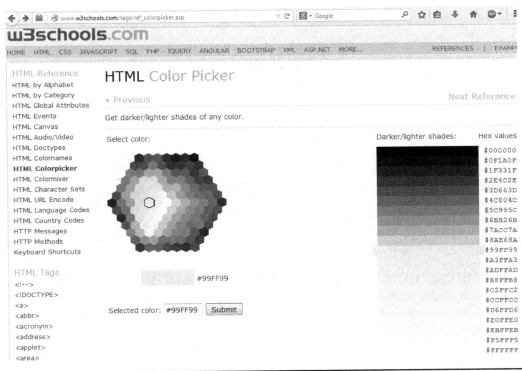

FIGURE 11-5. *The W3Schools HTML Color Picker*

TIP
Although it's possible to "tune" colors on iWantHue, sometimes you'll want to use the same colors on a dashboard, but with different lightness for different purposes. For example, you may want a particularly light tint of a color as a color fill backdrop for text and a darker shade of the color for a bar graph or line graph. The W3Schools Color Picker offers the opportunity to enter your optimally distant colors from iWantHue and then to see a progression of colors with their hex codes available for you to copy and then paste into OBIEE.

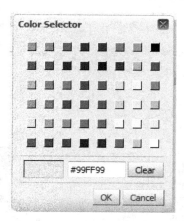

FIGURE 11-6. *Paste your HEX code into the Color Selector field. It must include the # sign.*

Changing the Default Colors for Graphs in OBIEE

Many times you'll want to change the default colors that OBIEE uses for graphs and charts to a more scientifically balanced set of colors, as provided by ColorBrewer or iWantHue. You still have to make modifications on a regular basis, but you're starting from a better place. Unfortunately, there's only one set of default colors. If you tend to use categorical measures most often, you can usually set defaults to a qualitative scheme and then alter colors when you have a sequential or divergent use case. Figure 11-7 shows a revised dvt-graph-skin.xml file (this file lives in different folders in different versions of OBIEE 11*g*). The SeriesItems code has been added to change the default colors to a 10-color ramp from ColorBrewer 2.0. The default chosen here is a pastel scheme that is great for bar charts and other visualizations that have large color blocks. It's not as preferred for line graphs and scatter plots, where individual graph elements are quite small. As stated before, consider the major use cases for your organization and the tradeoffs that exist for different options. There is no "one perfect solution," but rather different solutions that work better in various circumstances.

```xml
[dvt-graph-skin.xml]

<Graph visualEffects="NONE">
        <SliceLabel>
                <!-- decimalDigitUsed is false here so that non-percentage pie slices do not pick up this
value
                        The DVTChartProcessor sets decimalDigitUsed to true if this is a percentage pie
slice -->
                    <ViewFormat decimalDigit="2" decimalDigitUsed="false"/>
        </SliceLabel>
        <Title>
                <!-- attributes supported - fontColor="#0", bold="true", italic="true", underline="true" -->
                <GraphFont fontColor="#0" bold="true"/>
        </Title>

<SeriesItems>
        <Series id="0" color="#80b1d3" borderColor="#80b1d3"/>
        <Series id="1" color="#fdb462" borderColor="#fdb462"/>
        <Series id="2" color="#b3de69" borderColor="#b3de69"/>
        <Series id="3" color="#8dd3c7" borderColor="#8dd3c7"/>
        <Series id="4" color="#fb8072" borderColor="#fb8072"/>
        <Series id="5" color="#bc80bd" borderColor="#bc80bd"/>
        <Series id="6" color="#fccde5" borderColor="#fccde5"/>
        <Series id="7" color="#ffffb3" borderColor="#ffffb3"/>
        <Series id="8" color="#bebada" borderColor="#bebada"/>
        <Series id="9" color="#d9d9d9" borderColor="#d9d9d9"/>
</SeriesItems>

</Graph>
```

FIGURE 11-7. *The dvt-graph-skin.xml file showing changed default graph colors*

Defining OBIEE's User Interface Through Skins, Styles, and Messages

The "look and feel" of OBIEE is controlled and modified through a series of configuration files that function as scripts. Note that before you invest too much time in changing skins, styles, and messages, be sure to research whether future versions of OBIEE support the changes you make to skins and styles and if the changes are still necessary in the next version. This is an active area of development for Oracle, so you may find that your carefully constructed skin is not supported in the next version!

Skins

Skins define the appearance of application-related objects and components such as menus, colors for fields, graphics, images, and more. Skins consist of elements in the interface that cannot be altered or changed. There are no dependencies for skins. Skins are also based on Cascading Style Sheet specifications that are applied to various components. Skins allow you to change the appearance of OBIEE without changing portal pages themselves. If you want to add your corporate logo to the top of all OBIEE pages, ask your BI administrator to create a custom "skin" for OBIEE. Although Oracle has documentation and white papers on doing so, you may also want to encourage your BI administrator to read the blogs and discussion boards for additional pointers.

Styles

Styles define how dashboards and results are formatted for display. Styles control and modify the appearance and layout of OBIEE pages, including such things as fonts (choice, size, and style), borders (thickness and color), padding, background fill colors, and so forth. Most of the elements you are used to editing and modifying in OBIEE's user interface are controlled through the use of "styles." OBIEE employs Cascading Style Sheets (CSS), which define how to display HTML objects in web browsers. CSS files use selectors to treat groups of elements according to their ID, classes, types, and other attributes.

The word *cascading* means that that style sheets are "nested" and are applied in an order of precedence. The exact rules of precedence for OBIEE (and other large systems) can be quite complex. Basically, the more specific modifications overwrite the defaults, and the "closer" you are to the final result, the more likely it is that any applied modifications will overwrite and take precedence over others. In other words, the edits you make on the Criteria tab in Answers will overwrite the defaults set for the system. Edits you make on the Results tab for a specific view will overwrite the analysis setting for the column from the Criteria tab. If you want to understand style sheets further, make yourself a cup of tea, turn off the phone, and stop your mail. There are thousands of web pages and hundreds of books for you to read and plenty of online tutorials to go through.

OBIEE comes with several styles already built in. You can experiment with these styles and use them as the basis for your own custom styles. You can change the style of a dashboard using the Dashboard Properties dialog, as shown in Figure 11-8.

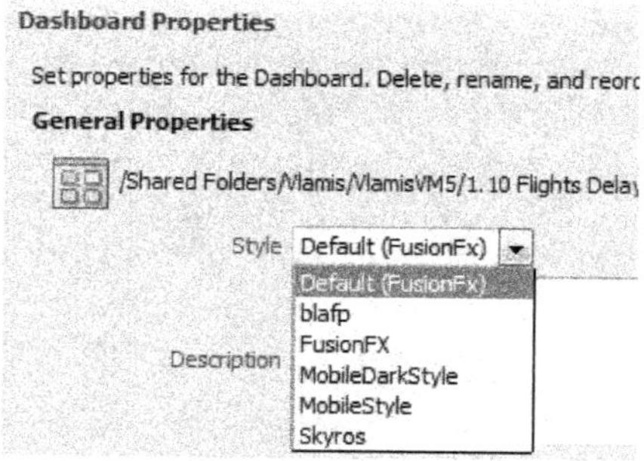

FIGURE 11-8. *Setting the style for a dashboard in the Dashboard Properties dialog*

Figure 11-9 shows the Skyros style on the left side and FusionFX style on the right side. Note the square edges and white background of the Skyros style versus the rounded edges and blue background of the FusionFX style. There is also a slight difference in the alignment and the look of the tabs and the alignment of the views.

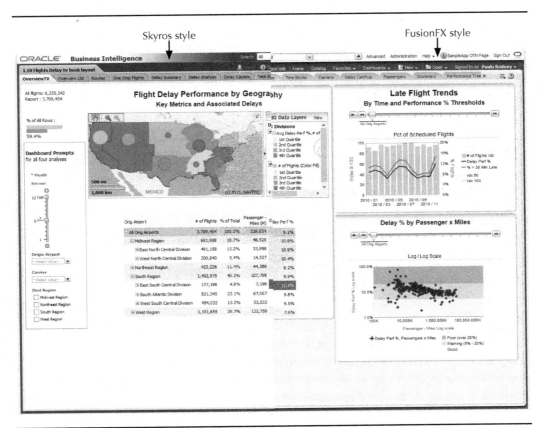

FIGURE 11-9. *Skyros style on left and FusionFX style on right*

Messages

Many of the text elements that are displayed with visualizations in OBIEE dashboards can be customized through the use of XML message files. This includes the text for prompts, the names of links and buttons, and other elements of the interface. Although we the authors are big proponents of the addition of helpful narrative views, informative titles, and other "language-based" communications, we've also found that sometimes the user experience for data visualizations benefits from modification to the user interface. It is also possible for OBIEE to manage multiple languages based on user and other session parameters. These capabilities require the involvement of your system administrator.

As you start to make changes to improve visualizations from the default settings, such as eliminating gridlines, adding padding, removing drop shadows, and changing default colors, you'll want to modify the settings for your system. You do this through the use of style sheets in your system directory. Know that this is very possible, but you'll need to work with your system administrators to ensure that your implementation goes through a proper development/test/production cycle and maintains its ability to be upgraded as well. It's generally a bad idea to start rifling through system folders and modifying config files without a proper backup-and-recovery procedure in place.

Alerts

Think of business intelligence as a business process, not a business project. As business processes, BI systems need to be situationally sensitive to events, thresholds, and time. Key to this then is to begin thinking about logical business rules that help identify the need to communicate data to a particular audience at a particular time via a particular communication method. This "automated BI" capability is an important and continuing trend.

Alerts are often underutilized in OBIEE implementations. An alert is a notification generated by an agent that delivers personalized and actionable content to specified recipients and to subscribers to the agent. Alerts and scheduled reports are some of the most powerful aspects of OBIEE; although they may not be strictly thought of as "visualizations," they are incredibly import in terms of delivering a high amount of value to the users of OBIEE systems. Alerts and scheduled reports are also closely tied with Chapter 8. You may want to review that chapter in conjunction with this section on alerts and scheduled reports because the material on dashboard interactions is related.

Alerts are visual messages that appear on OBIEE dashboards in response to a logical statement that is met (that is, the statement is TRUE, either at a given time or upon the receipt of new data). Alerts appear on the user's home page, in the menu section of the interface, as shown in Figure 11-10, or in an Alerts section on a dashboard page. They can display information that is current at the time or reflect a condition that was met previously. Alerts also show up in BI Mobile and can be very effective in mobile applications where screen real estate is at a premium.

FIGURE 11-10. *Alert on an OBIEE dashboard menu*

The Alerts section can show all alerts for a particular user, user group, or role. The placement of this section has tradeoffs. You want the alerts to be seen, but a long list of alerts can be distracting. You can place alerts beneath prompts in the far-left column, but if the prompts section gets too long, alerts should go somewhere else. You may also place them at the bottom of the page, as shown in Figure 11-11. In the example shown, a red border is placed around this section to help make it more visible and to stand out from the rest of the dashboard. Because alerts are individually dismissed, they disappear from the dashboard section. Once all alerts have been dismissed, the section will not display on the dashboard and the alert notification in the interface menu bar will disappear. Refer to Chapter 7 for further information on how to configure and format dashboard sections.

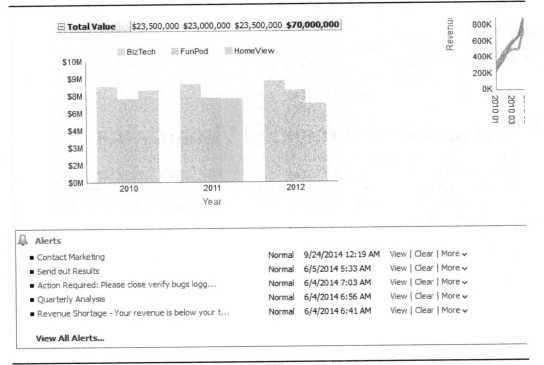

FIGURE 11-11. *Alerts section for an OBIEE dashboard*

Alerts are a very compact way of communicating the specific status of a business situation. As such, they should be considered for the following purposes:

- To alert a user(s) about a change in a business situation

- To alert a user(s) about an important business event

- To alert a user(s) about a threshold that has been met or occurred

Alerts can even serve as a common interface and platform for understanding and sense-making regarding organizational situations and performance. It's also worth pointing out that alerts can be set where conditions have not been met by defining an alert condition that is an exception. For example, the Revenue Shortage alert in Figure 11-11 was triggered because revenue was below the target amount set and a minimum threshold of sales was missed. This kind of exception reporting can prove to be extremely valuable for organizations. An Alerts section should be included on most departmental dashboards and executive dashboards, and organizations should get in the habit of reviewing the business rules governing alerts on a regular basis so that alerts remain useful and provide insight into key business activities and performance metrics. If alerts are allowed to become stale, users will start ignoring all alerts.

NOTE
Alerts act as a rules-based automated communication methodology and should be integrated in most OBIEE implementations.

Best and Recommended Visualizations

With the release of OBIEE 11.1.1.7, a recommendation rules engine for visualizations was added to OBIEE's analysis editor (also known as Answers) interface. When the new visualization icon is clicked, two new options are shown at the top of the list, "Best Visualization" and "Recommended Visualization for…" as shown in Figure 11-12.

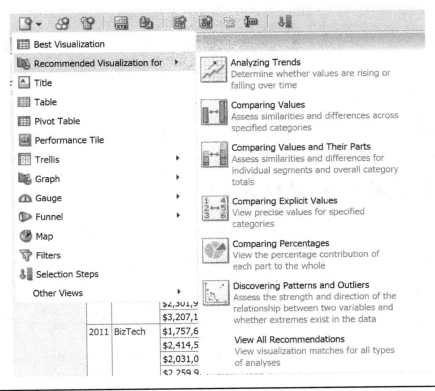

FIGURE 11-12. *OBIEE "Recommended Visualization for" menu*

There are six different analysis situations for which OBIEE will make recommendations:

- Analyzing Trends (determine whether values are rising or falling over time)

- Comparing Values (assess similarities and differences across specified categories)

- Comparing Values and Their Parts (assess similarities and differences for individual segments and overall category totals)

- Comparing Explicit Values (view precise values for specified categories)

- Comparing Percentages (view the percentage contribution for each part to the whole)

- Discovering Patterns and Outliers (assess the strength and direction of the relationship between two variables and whether extremes exist in the data)

Additionally, there is a "View All Recommendations Selection" that returns a default visualization for each category. The usefulness of this recommendation wizard lies largely in the care that has been taken in defining default settings for visualizations in OBIEE. There is no interface or capability for OBIEE administrators or developers to understand or edit the rules that govern the recommendation engine. Observant readers who use the recommended visualization interface will find that the system's recommendation will often conflict with the best practice advice imparted in this book. The visualization recommendation interface can be great for generating ideas and offering fundamental questions for data analysis, but the views it creates should not be blindly accepted as following best practice (just as with all default settings).

Data in the Real World

The entire point of data visualization is to accurately and succinctly present and represent data so that a broad range of people can understand it and its implications in a consistent manner. Working with "demo" data is often very different from working with data in real-world implementations. Real data is messy, full of holes and mistakes, seldom "normally distributed" in a nice bell-shaped curve, and nearly always nonlinear. In short, it's challenging creating "ideal" data visualizations, and the careful, professional data analyst is nearly always balancing tradeoffs and making compromises. In this brief section, we'll discuss some thoughts and recommendations for dealing with data in the real world.

One of the fundamental strategies of OBIEE and one of the most compelling value propositions that it puts forward is to provide large organizations with a common enterprise information model and a single source of the truth. What does the organization mean when the question "What were sales last month?" is asked. Does sales include shipping costs? What about returns? What about samples shipped to good customers? Or backorders that were already invoiced and paid for, but further modified? The fact is, different parts of the organization will likely have different definitions at different times in various circumstances. OBIEE and its repository allows for consistent treatment of data and its elements. In OBIEE (and in data visualization presentations), the definition of the data elements should be emphasized rather than the source or provenance. That is, it's more important that the "what" is clear than the "from where."

Most real-world business data follows the "Pareto principle" or the 80/20 rule. That is, 20 percent of the individual values account for 80 percent of the total amount, whereas 80 percent of the values account for only 20 percent of the total. This leads to visualizations that have a few big bars and many small bars. This isn't wrong or bad, it's simply a reflection of the distribution of the data. In more extreme examples, the data distribution takes the shape of an *L* with a curved corner (an exponential distribution). These distributions tend to follow a "power law" and are excellent candidates for a logarithmic scale (be sure to clearly indicate that a logarithmic scale is being used).

Controlling What Data You Show

Although you may spend a lot of time determining how to show your data, you should also consider very carefully exactly *what* you show. The data is the equivalent of the raw ingredients to your data visualizations. Old data affects the dashboard experience in a similar fashion to stale food. Consider portion size and how you create a focal point in your presentation of the data. Avoid cluttering up your visualizations with extraneous data that distracts users from the central point you are trying to make. All of these techniques help you limit the number of rows you display or help you label them appropriately for the data you are visualizing. Real-world data often looks very busy because visualizations show too many data values.

Filters

Filters are the primary method for selecting data that is shown. Often, dashboards display too much data as well as analyses whose filters are so complicated that users don't really understand how the data is being filtered. If no users are interested in certain data elements, eliminate from the data tables them rather than filtering them. This is definitely an area where less is more. Complex filters require extra processing, which slows response times and degrades the user experience.

Now that we have that out of the way, if you need to filter data in a certain way, consider creating a reusable filter that can be shared among multiple analyses. This provides a central definition so that maintenance is minimized and analyses can be standardized. Figure 11-13 shows a saved filter called "Since July 1 2012." Make sure that filters have explanatory names so that they are easily understood in filter views.

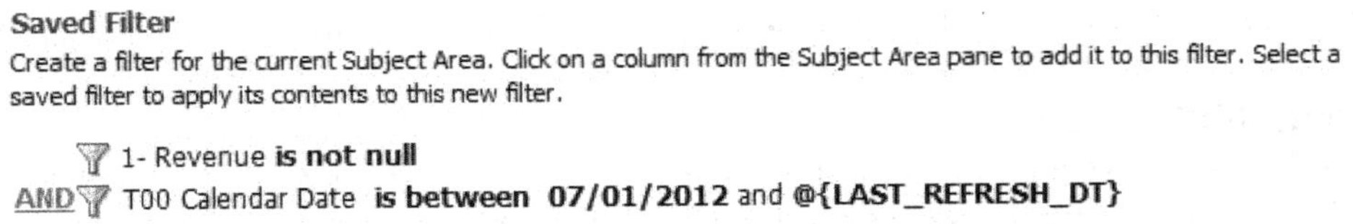

Saved Filter

Create a filter for the current Subject Area. Click on a column from the Subject Area pane to add it to this filter. Select a saved filter to apply its contents to this new filter.

1- Revenue **is not null**
AND T00 Calendar Date **is between 07/01/2012** and **@{LAST_REFRESH_DT}**

FIGURE 11-13. *Saved filter "Since July 1 2012"*

More importantly, consider what data really needs to be shown to make a point. You can often discover what data is truly important by asking users, "What do you look at on this screen?" Often, a report has hundreds of rows, whereas the user only looks at the first few rows of the report. In this case, you can filter the analysis to only include the rows that are of interest. This can speed up the analysis and focus the user's attention to the important data.

The option also exists to trim outliers through the use of filters so that the majority of cases can be viewed more comfortably on a single graph. Outlier treatment is one of the most important issues in data visualization. Oftentimes, the outliers are exactly what you want users to notice. Eliminating outliers distorts the data returned from the query and changes the message. Other times, outliers are a strong indication of "dirty" data and can ruin otherwise important visualizations (a retail store return of $1 million is likely to be an error).

When you do filter the data, ensure that you label the visualization appropriately. If the visualization contains sales for only shipped orders, this should be made clear somehow to avoid confusion and to be transparent about the data selection. This problem often appears in large implementations with complex data models. Complex filters are sometimes applied, but not explained. This can lead to potential confusion and mistrust of the tool.

Of course, filters can also be used to zero in on data that should be viewed. For example, filters can be used to limit down to a certain brand or more complex condition, guiding the user to the intended set of data. Just be sure to label the visualization appropriately.

Filters are generally preferred because they limit the amount of processing work needed on the back end. It makes little sense to process and return extremely large or varied results if only a small portion of the result set needs to be shown.

With that being said, we the authors do run into our fair share of overly assertive DBAs and IT admins who are desperate to limit the work on the server and (in our opinion) demand that filters be used everywhere and are overly suspicious of any front-end use cases where the displayed data is different from the data returned by the query definition. (We're on their side too, after all.) Performance is important; however, analytical insight should drive system design, not the other way around. There are plenty of ways for OBIEE administrators to throttle runaway queries such as row limits and processing time limits without imposing unreasonable requirements on front-end analysts and users. Feel free to tell them we said so.

Selection Steps

Selection steps were introduced in Oracle BI 11*g*. Selection steps are applied after the data is filtered and aggregated and only affect what is displayed. This is especially important for hierarchical columns that often display embedded totals. For example, in Figure 11-14, the Total Value line is the sum of all of the products that meet the filter criteria, regardless of whether it meets the selection steps criteria. Revenue for all of the products that meet the filter criteria totals 70,000,000, but the selection steps refine this list to only those products where sales is greater than 4,000,000. The selection steps do not affect the aggregate values of hierarchical columns that are displayed.

Products With Selection Step
Time run: 9/9/2014 11:27:53 PM

Revenue

	Revenue
7 Megapixel Digital Camera	3,489,231
HomeCoach 2000	5,447,097
Install	4,208,841
LCD HD Television	4,116,134
MP3 Speakers System	3,504,122
MPEG4 Camcorder	3,124,873
Maintenance	4,120,096
Plasma HD Television	3,783,291
PocketFun ES	2,717,556
SoundX Nano 4Gb	3,955,349
Touch-Screen T5	3,826,445
V5x Flip Phone	3,489,226
Grand Total	**45,782,263**

List: ALL ▾

Products - Product

1. Start with all members

2. Then, Keep only members of "Products"."P1 Product" where "A - Sample Sales"."Base Facts"."1-Revenue", *for:* "Time"."T05 Per Name Year": '2010' is greater than 1100000

Edit -Refresh -Export - Copy

FIGURE 11-14. *Pivot table view with selection steps*

As the name implies, selection steps can contain multiple steps, with operators such as Add, Keep Only, and Remove. This provides a powerful capability to determine exactly what should be shown to the user. As with filters, be transparent about what data is being shown. The Selection Step view (shown in Figure 11-14) provides a convenient method for showing the selection steps used for a given analysis. These are automatically updated if the selection steps change. But they also can be confusing if they contain names of OBIEE objects (such as "A-Sample Sales"."Base Facts"."1-Revenue") that are not well known to users.

Be aware that unlike filters, selection steps are applied after the query runs. As such, they can result in asking the server to do a lot more work than required. Do not rely on selection steps alone when a filter will do the same job. If you use selection steps wisely, you're not as likely to arouse the (sometimes unreasonable) wrath of DBAs and admins. They shouldn't mistrust or discourage selection step usage. (Again, you can tell them we said so.)

Grouping Values: Bins and Groups

The best way to group multiple values together (such as New England = Maine + Massachusetts + New Hampshire + Vermont + Rhode Island + Connecticut) is to build this into a hierarchy in your RPD file. And, ideally, you would configure your RPD file to select this data from a summary table or from cubes that are precalculated in a database such as Essbase or Oracle OLAP cubes. This technique provides the best performance because the aggregate values are precalculated on a server and thus avoids having to aggregate the values while the user waits for the results. But what if you cannot predetermine the aggregate values you wish to aggregate?

OBIEE has two handy ways of handling this: bins (found on the Criteria tab | Edit formula | Bins tab) and groups (found on the Results tab | Groups button). Both let you group together multiple values of a column into a single value. Both of these techniques help reduce the number of data values you need to display. For example, rather than displaying all 50 states of the United States, you could group together the states by region to collapse the states into five regions of the United States. Or, you could show the top 10 states and create an "All Other" 11th state. This can help cut down on the number of data values that need to be shown and is a powerful technique for building superior visualizations. These techniques are often used with bar graphs.

Bins are designed to be used when creating the formula for a given column. Essentially, you are creating an on-the-fly expression that replaces the system's expression for a given column. You can override the formula and specify that column values are "binned together" to form a new column value. The original value is not available with this method.

Three Common Binning Strategies

Value binning places results into defined groups bounded by specific values. The number of cases may vary from bin to bin. The aggregated results within each bin have more value when compared to each other than the individual cases possess. Value binning is particularly useful when threshold values have significance to an organization. For example, customer tenure may have significance at three months, one year, and five years. These are unequal term lengths, may have significantly different numbers of customers in each, but otherwise are important for analytical purposes.

Equal-width binning establishes value bins at regular intervals. This allows the natural distribution of the data to be easy to see with a specified number of bins. This is the common type of binning and is relatively easy to graph. For example, if you are graphing customer tenure, you may choose to graph the bins as 0–6 months, 7–12 months, 13–18 months, 19–24 months, and so on. Figure 11-15 shows the distribution of customers by their revenue in SampleApp V406 in 10 equal-width bins.

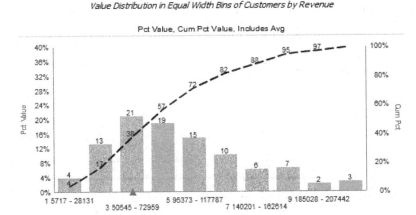

FIGURE 11-15.   *Distribution of customers by revenue in SampleApp V406*

Percentile binning divides results equally into "ntiles." For example, quartile binning divides results into 4 bins, whereas decile binning divides results into 10 bins. Assuming data is skewed with many new customers, this may result in unequal width of the bins, such as 0–2 months, 3–6 months, 7–14 months, and 15–24 months, but each of the bins would have a similar number of customers. As with all data preprocessing techniques used in the front end, these are most efficient when done in the OBIEE repository by the BI server or in the database. Extra columns can be added to represent the percentiles, which is more transparent to users and makes it easier to work with the results.

Using Groups
Groups work hand-in-hand with selection steps to add values that are groups of existing column values. They accomplish a similar goal to bins, but in a more flexible way. You can use these with hierarchical columns and can see the definition of the group. You can even create calculated items that override the normal aggregation rules for a given measure. For more information, see the Fusion Middleware documentation for Oracle BI.

Top/Bottom 10: Exception Analysis
Although users often insist they need to see data for all 10,000 customers, if you probe enough, you will often find that they really only look at the first page of the report (assuming it is sorted properly). If the focus is really only on the first 10 customers, develop your analyses to display only the top (or bottom) 10 customers. This will save

time and make your visualizations much easier to consume. This can be accomplished through selection steps, applying a condition that keeps only the top (or bottom) *n* values. Actually, as shown in Figure 11-16, you will see many types of conditions that can be applied as part of a query to limit the number of values displayed in an analysis. Realize that the formulas and examples give only a single expression and do not fully explain the full range of expressions. For example, the Exception formulas can include less-than-or-equal formulas as well.

New Condition Step - Offices		⑦ ✉
Condition Type Condition Type		▼

Condition Type	Example
⊟ 🖾 **Exception**	
X>=value	Sales >= 10000
X>=Y	Sales >= Costs
X>=Y+10	Sales >= Costs + 10
X>=Y-5%	Sales >= Costs - 5%
X within 10 of Y	Sales within 10 of Costs
X not within 5% of Y	Sales not within 5% of Costs
X between 'min' and 'max' values	5000 <= Sales <= 10000
⊟ 🖾 **Top/Bottom**	
Top 10 based on X	Top 10 based on Sales
Bottom 5% based on X	Bottom 5% based on Sales
Making up to 3% based on X	Making up to 3% based on Sales
⊟ 🖾 **Match**	
Name contains 'abc'	Name contains 'abc'
All X values where Y = values	All Cars where Color = Red

FIGURE 11-16. *Condition steps can collapse the number of rows being displayed.*

Label Visualizations Appropriately

Be sure to label visualizations appropriately, especially if you use filters or selection step techniques to limit the data being displayed. Often, a report developer presumes that everybody knows what is being shown. If a visualization only includes orders that are closed, or only sales from the current year, say so. If only the top 10 customers are being shown, include this in the title. Titles or narrative views should be used to give context to the data being displayed. This is particularly important when using techniques such as bins or groups because the data is purposefully being manipulated (such as collapsing the states). In the preceding example of displaying a total for New England, if your audience may not know exactly which states make up New England, you should somehow indicate which states comprise that total, or at least provide a way to find that information. Otherwise, you are obscuring the data with no way of deciphering it.

Sorting

Sorting of data is often overlooked. We have touched on this topic, especially in regards to tables and the heatmap shown in Figure 2-37 in Chapter 2. Sorting affects how users perceive data, as adjacency and proximity greatly affect how we perceive information. As described in Chapter 2, you can affect the sort order of the data in the Criteria tab of an analysis.

You can also enable end users to sort data in tables when hovering over a column or row label (a triangle pointing up and down appears). This enables the users to sort the data while looking at the data and should be enabled unless you have a good reason to turn it off (it's actually difficult to disable in many versions of OBIEE).

Significant Digits

Often, designers include all of the digits in a number. If the value is a forecast, it's likely that not all of the digits in the data are significant. For example, if we forecast that we're going to produce 11,372 widgets next year, plus or minus 1,000 widgets, should we really display 11,372? Instead, consider showing 11,000 widgets, rounding to the nearest 1,000. Otherwise, we are displaying more significant digits than the data really holds. Another example involves percentage increases. Let's say sales are projected to rise by 5 percent next year. However, when this is applied to a number, there are only three significant figures in the calculation (multiply this year's sales by 1.05). It is actually misleading to show more than three significant figures in this circumstance because it implies more precision than can exist in the number. This becomes especially important if viewers of the data are trying to find patterns and trends. They may see patterns that are not real, because the data is not that accurate. True "significant figures" algorithms should be applied in the repository rather than the front end because of their complexity. A generalized way to express a certain number of significant figures (n) is to round the target number to $n - 1 - floor(log10$ of the target number) digits. For example, rounding 12345 to three significant figures would be 12345 rounded to $3 - 1 - floor(log10(12345))$ digits = 12300, or ROUND(12345, -2).

Null Values

Null value treatment is also important. Sometimes the absence of information is extremely interesting and provides strong insights to users. Other times, it takes valuable screen real estate. Filters, functions (edit formula on Criteria tab), selection steps, and the Analysis Properties Data tab all offer multiple treatment of null values in the front end. Nulls typically also have rules applied to their treatment in the repository file, so you should review their prevalence and relevance for your analysis with your OBI administrator.

Interactions

The ability to interact with data visualization can alter the need to visualize the data. For example, tables are often preferred over graphs because tables offer the ability to display precise values, whereas graphs often provide a visual indicator of magnitude of a value. Graph designers started adding the ability to display a precise value immediately above a bar to indicate that value. But now, the ability to display a precise value when hovering over a bar may eliminate the need to display precise values because the value is readily available, even if only one value at a time. In a similar fashion, other interactions may affect how you need to visualize data and the possibilities for navigating between various visualizations. We do not cover all of the possibilities for interactions in OBIEE; we merely cover a sampling of these as they relate to visualizing the data in OBIEE.

Hover-Over

In many types of views, the hover (or rollover) action can be configured to display additional data label information about the value where the cursor is located. Hover-overs promote user involvement, provide a cleaner interface so that patterns are more visible, and can provide far more information than labels that always appear on the screen. People greatly overestimate their ability to derive patterns from the presentation of labels. It is generally recommend that they not be included at all times, but that they are enabled in hover-over/rollover tooltip views. These can be especially useful in a mobile interface, where people naturally want to "touch" and interact with the data. For example, by default in a bar graph, the rollover action is set to display a data label. This allows a user to see exactly what value is being graphed. This can be configured in the Data Markers section of the Titles and Labels tab of the Graph Properties dialog.

In a similar fashion, you can configure trellis charts to display tooltips that display the Start, Max, Min, and End values for a data range that is graphed in a microchart (or sparkchart). You can also configure maps to display tooltips to display additional information when hovering over areas of a map, as shown in Figure 4-10 and Figure 4-22 in Chapter 4.

Click Events

Many views can be configured to take different actions when the user clicks an area in a view. For example, the default behavior when clicking a drill icon next to a hierarchical column value is to drill that value to include the children of that value (for example, drill United States to include regions in the United States). Drill actions are quite intuitive for most users and provide an excellent navigation and exploration interface. Many times when we're evaluating OBIEE implementations that have an excess of large tables, we will recommend smaller summary tables with drill capabilities. Including these interactions in your dashboards enables users to gain additional functionality with little or no additional effort. OBIEE click behaviors can be changed using action links to many different behaviors, as shown in Figure 11-17.

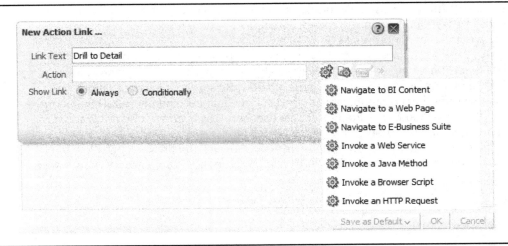

FIGURE 11-17.   *Edit Action Link dialog*

In addition, double-click behaviors and right-click behaviors add flexibility for users. Right-clicks allow for visualizations to be acted upon. For example, Figure 2-38 in Chapter 2 shows many different actions that can be taken on a pivot table. Some visualizations such as scorecards have natural built-in click events. Design your visualizations for maximum flexibility, and your users will be happier.

Summary

When designing data visualizations, you should keep additional topics in mind. Principles of good design should guide your visualizations. Dashboards should have unity as well as a sense of harmony, balance, and rhythm. Keep in mind the proportion of the data and the visualization, but if a certain concept is the dominant concept, grant it the proper space.

Color is extremely important in visualizations. Take care in selecting your colors, using tools such as Colorbrewer 2.0, iWantHue, and the W3Schools HTML color picker, and using sequential, divergent, and qualitative color schemes as appropriate. You can even change the default colors for OBIEE so you don't have to define them in each analysis.

You can configure OBIEE's skins, styles, and messages to suit your organization. Just bear in mind that this can take some additional effort and there is no guarantee that later OBIEE releases will not invalidate your changes.

Alerts can notify users to conditions that exist and can disappear when dismissed. This can help make dashboards more engaging. Just be sure to keep those alerts fresh—nobody wants to spend a great deal of time dismissing obsolete alerts that are no longer appropriate.

Appropriate data visualizations are influenced greatly by the properties of the data that is being represented. Use filters and selection steps to limit the amount of data being displayed and group it appropriately. Be sure to add explanations on visualizations that communicate to viewers how data is being filtered. Think about how the data should be sorted (or let the user sort it as needed), and think about how to handle null values.

Finally, interactions such as hover-overs (rollovers) and click events allow your visualizations to take on multiple roles and increase the engagement of your system with users.

CHAPTER
12

General Advice

The best business intelligence systems are grown, not made. This is particularly true for superior dashboards and data visualizations. We the authors have seen BI systems that created tremendous value for their organizations and provided true competitive advantage. We've also seen expensive BI systems languish and go unused, almost like an abandoned Olympic village that cost millions but was never used on an everyday basis. In this concluding chapter, we'll provide some general advice from our BI consulting practice.

Working with BI Catalog

It's ever so easy to keep the catalog neat and tidy; all that's required is to do little work on data visualizations and always accept the default settings. The reality, however, is that if you plan to use any of the information in this book, you'll have to deal with cleaning up after yourself and others as you develop various analyses, compound views, dashboards, and other catalog objects. It is like creating a beautiful landscape garden. If you work hard the first few years to plant perennials according to a design, and work very hard to weed and prune, in a relatively short time you'll establish the base, and you'll find that the work lessens every year in maintaining the overall lines and structure. If you're overly ambitious and go only with showy annuals and always start from scratch, you'll have loads of weeding that will get progressively worse and you'll have to start over every year from scratch. Also like gardening, it's better to focus on one area at a time and to finish it and get it in shape than it is to try and weed the entire garden in a day and end up doing a poor job that does little else besides encouraging other weeds to grow faster.

Organizing the BI Catalog

If you let users develop and store whatever they want, wherever they want, under the guise of "self-service BI," with no structure and no guidance, you'll end up with a mess. Although we the authors are strong supporters of democratic BI, we also believe that creativity has to be balanced with structure and standards. We suggest establishing a basic pattern for organizing dashboards, analyses, and prompts and then sticking to it. Besides the standard advice of dev/test/prod environments, you should also have a folder for a development environment that is allowed to be a bit "messy." Once objects are determined to be useful and important, they get "promoted" out of the development folder into the overall catalog structure. Try organizing the catalog by major logical divisions and then organizing dashboards and other components underneath those. Here are a couple of alternative strategies from SampleApp.

In the first example, shown in Figure 12-1, all dashboards are placed in their own "dashboard folder" (this is necessary for the dashboards to appear in the Dashboards drop-down menu) while objects such as prompts that are shared commonly among more than one dashboard are organized in a Subject Area Contents folder. Objects such as analyses, prompts, and filters that appear on only one dashboard are organized into their own folder (typically related directly to the dashboard). This is the structure we recommend most often. It allows developers to ask a simple question: Does this object appear on more than one dashboard? If so, it gets organized under the subject area folder. If it appears only on one dashboard, it goes in the folder for that specific dashboard. Use naming conventions that make it obvious which folder goes with which dashboard. When dashboards have a large number of pages and objects, incorporate subfolders for individual pages.

FIGURE 12-1. *Organizing OBIEE's catalog by dashboard*

In the second example, shown in Figure 12-2, objects are organized by their object type rather than by what dashboard they appear on. There are separate folders for actions, agents, conditions, indexes, prompts, and queries. This alternative organizational strategy may make more sense in some cases. For example, we'll sometimes set up a special folder for dashboard prompts, just be sure to keep track of which dashboards use which prompts (there are often subtle differences between prompts, and it can be tricky determining which version should be modified or used on a new dashboard). Many of the techniques and frameworks from Master Data Management apply to the organization of catalogs. It's likely that your organization already has some standards that can be adopted to define a strategy that makes most sense for your OBIEE implementation.

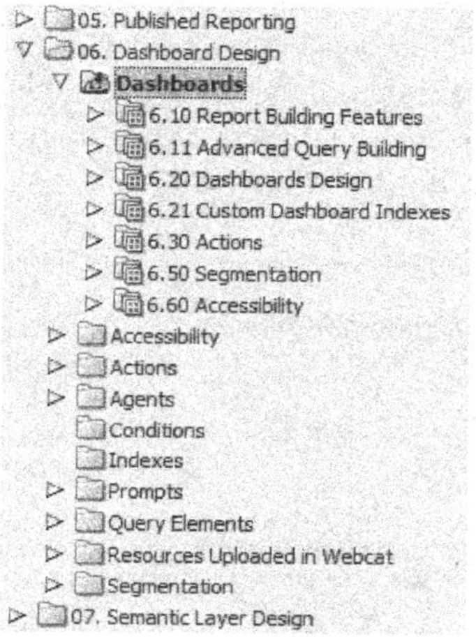

FIGURE 12-2. *Organizing OBIEE's catalog by object type*

Copying Dashboards for Modifying

Developing multiple versions of dashboard pages can be tricky for several reasons. If you edit your dashboard layout in the Dashboard Builder interface, you have to commit your changes or lose them when you navigate to another page (and there's no multilayer "undo" function). This creates the potential of having to re-create an original version and retrace all of your edits. Although the Preview option exists, it's tough to work on a version for a period of time without saving it. Also, the Save As option on the Dashboard Builder creates a new copy of the entire dashboard, not just the page you're working on.

When making minor changes to dashboard pages or when creating multiple versions for review, here's a tip for faster and more flexible development. Start in the catalog view. Copy and then paste individual dashboard pages into the same dashboard from the catalog view. Figure 12-3 shows how to highlight an individual dashboard page and click Copy. A new dashboard page titled "copy of …" will be inserted onto the dashboard when you choose the Paste button (next to the Copy button). This preserves the original dashboard page and places an identical page in the same dashboard. Analyses, prompts, and other objects can be reused or modified and copied into the same folder structure with this method. Be aware that any changes to the analyses or other objects are shared between the old dashboards and the new dashboard, so be careful with changes.

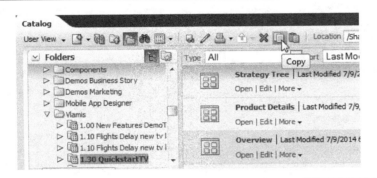

FIGURE 12-3. *Copy and paste dashboard pages in catalog view for fast development.*

Using Save As

Beginning with OBIEE version 11.1.1.7, there is a Replace Analysis option in the Save As menu (shown in lower left corner of Figure 12-4) when the Edit or Analyze link is clicked for an analysis that is embedded in a dashboard page. This greatly speeds the development process. Be sure to enable the Edit and Analyze links in the dashboard development process for access. This enables a developer to be looking at a dashboard and simply click the Edit button to make a quick change. You can also make a few different versions of views in the analysis itself, create a few different compound views, and then select the view you want to show on different dashboard pages. If you find yourself constantly going back and forth between Answers and the dashboard layout editor, consider whether there are some methods that might speed your development process and keep the "mess" in the catalog to a minimum. You can also open multiple browser windows so you can be in multiple places at once.

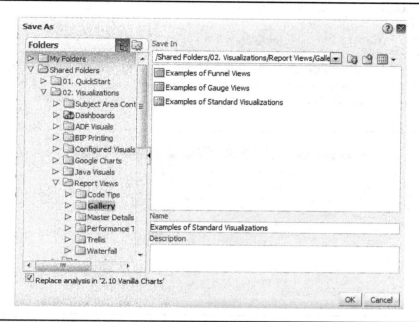

FIGURE 12-4. *The Replace Analysis option is enabled when using Edit and Analyze Report links for analyses embedded in dashboards.*

For more involved development processes, copy the entire dashboard into a development folder. Be sure to rename and replace any modified catalog objects to avoid modifying original versions. Make sure you regularly archive your catalog so that if you want to revert to an earlier point in time (say, before you made a major change to a dashboard and its analyses), you can restore your system.

Keeping the Catalog Clean

Neat and organized catalogs with a minimum of redundancy and clutter are important. However, the development process often requires the evaluation of multiple copies of otherwise complete analyses. Just as work on the job site often involves stopping before quitting time so that the worksite and tools can be cleaned and put away, make sure you allocate sufficient time in your work plan to straighten, organize, and standardize your catalog during data visualization development. Recognize that development best practices are sometimes at odds with production best practices.

Search to the Rescue

You should use the techniques outlined in this chapter to organize the BI catalog properly, but there are tools you can use to navigate through the catalog to find objects more easily. For example, the search bar at the top of the screen can find specific types of objects that contain certain words. Expect that this feature will only become more powerful and easier to use with the integration of Endeca technology in Oracle BI. You can also use the Catalog screen for sorting by last-modified date to find a catalog object you modified the day before.

Development Standards

As stated earlier in the book, we borrow heavily from the web development community when determining best practices for BI system development generally and dashboard development specifically. Ask if there is a web standards guide or manual. Standards manuals are common in the world of big brands, licensing, and, increasingly, large web implementations. These manuals typically specify guidelines for font usage, color palette, screen resolution, and layout grid, to mention only a few items. These documents are immensely useful for the following reasons:

- They have already typically gone through some type of corporate vetting process.

- They are typically user focused and possess a strong sense of community identity (particularly when compared with documents originating in the IT department).

- They outline the style that many in the organization associate with website interfaces.

- They are often put together by professional designers who have an appreciation for presentation.

- They offer a context in which alternatives and options can be presented. It's much easier to start with something than with a completely blank canvas.

- They contain highly valuable specific information about corporate preferences. There's nothing worse than getting halfway through a project and discovering that the corporate "red" is more a "brick red" with a specific hex code and then having to spend hours changing several dozen analyses and dashboards.

Why Have Development Standards

Organizations should establish a BI standards manual that guides all interested stakeholders in the organization's preferences and establishes a common foundation for development. There are many, many benefits for this approach (and, as always, some need for deviation in specific cases), and the costs of establishing these kinds of standards always have an extremely high return on investment. Here are just a few of the reasons it makes so much sense to establish a BI standards manual:

- Development is faster and more efficient because many "design" choices such as color ramp, font, prompt placement, and layout choice have already been made.

- Battles over "look and feel" with executives who are highly experienced in their particular discipline, but maybe not so much in data visualization, are minimized.

- Dashboards and analyses have a consistent interface, thus minimizing the amount of explanatory text, legends, and guiding visualizations needed to make common dashboards function well for a majority in the organization.

- Dashboards and analyses are more functional and meaningful because patterns and associations are established and reinforced.

- Users are better able to develop their own individual dashboards and analyses because they have established and effective patterns to follow.

The power and importance of easing user development efforts should not be underestimated. The best BI systems with the highest organizational returns always have a vibrant, active user development community. These communities are much more likely to grow and flourish when they have standards to follow.

What to Include in Development Standards

Here is a short list of some of the topics you may want to address in your BI standards manual:

- Consistent placement of certain prompts. Users become accustomed to finding options for parameterizing and customizing dashboards in a common location.

- Consistent use of navigation links and options. Navigation difficulty is one of the most consistent complaints in large BI systems.

- Common meaning attached to formatting options such as bold, colored font, underlining, and italics. These minor formatting options can help users understand and leverage BI interfaces.

- Common symbols in table views, maps, trellis charts, and scorecards. People learn to scan dashboards very quickly for meaningful messages. Consistent usage patterns lead directly to speed and completeness in scanning.

- Elimination of gridlines, green bar styling, and other unnecessary visual noise. Old preferences sometimes die hard. Having a visual standards manual paves the way for eliminating legacy views that hinder consistent interpretation. People adapt to new presentations much, much faster than they think they will.

- Common meanings for certain colors. For example, the Midwest division should not be blue in one dashboard and green in another.

- Reinforcement of a "best practice" approach to business intelligence rather than a personal "taste" or opinion-based approach.

Working the Project

Working in a BI project inevitably involves multiple communities and often—shockingly!—the interests of those communities do not align perfectly. Still, it is definitely worth involving multiple communities in design sessions, sign-off sessions, and user-acceptance testing.

We the authors often hear that users are accustomed to seeing their information in a particular format and that we should replicate the existing system as a "first step." This typically means replicating hundreds or even thousands of static reports (many which have had extensive modification in Microsoft Excel). This often means that BI projects "embalm" old structures, old habits, old processes, and old perspectives. We often tell clients to think of it this way: We are building a new house together. Sure, you want people to know where things are, have a sense of continuity and comfort, but do you really want to lay out the rooms exactly like they were in the old house and to put the same old furniture exactly where it was? Sure, keep your favorite comfortable chair (especially if it's a classic leather club chair) and the rosewood dining table, but doesn't it make sense to take full advantage of the power of the software and to deliver maximum value to the organization? Of course, we need a strong foundation and we also want to make the house comfortably large, but we shouldn't we finish it and furnish it appropriately so that people will want to use it?

This analogy of getting the physical systems right (electrical, plumbing, heating and air, and so on) and of finishing rooms professionally often helps break through the tyranny of either replicating the existing system or just focusing on the "back end" and doing the absolute bare minimum on the front end. After all, who wants to work in a cold concrete room sitting on a broken-down hard metal folding chair that is 20 years old? Most IT professionals are understandably enthusiastic about the systems they work on. (The plumbing is all copper! It will last for generations, and it's easy to work on.) However, truth be told, most users simply want decent water pressure and to not run out of hot water while taking a shower. What we're talking about here is extending the overall style, concept, and function of the building to the design and finish of the interior.

Working with Executives

One of the most challenging aspects of working in business intelligence in general and data visualization specifically is the need to guide powerful, opinionated, self-confident executives toward "best practice" visualizations that may look different from their legacy reports. Just as everyone who eats thinks they are an expert on food and "what tastes good," everyone who has ever looked at a report thinks they know how information should be presented. Part of the secret of making progress in improving data visualization in BI systems is to understand how to work effectively with successful people who are used to being in positions of influence and power.

There is no substitute for having a strong technical understanding of data visualization best practices in terms of human cognition and being able to explain *how* different visualizations differ from a cognition/interpretation perspective and *why* a particular version of a table, graph, or dashboard might be more effective than another version.

When working with executives, consider using mobile technology. Many executives develop a personal relationship with a mobile device that can help you "sell" the rest of the technology to the organization. If it can run on their favorite mobile device, you may gain an ally in the organization!

Working with IT and DBAs

Although working with executives and convincing them of the importance of data visualization best practices can be challenging, it can be equally challenging working with the "other side of the fence" in the IT organization. IT administrators and DBAs are often so focused on data management and processing issues that it may be dangerous to assume that they will be supportive of data visualization investments and initiatives. It's important to garner their favor by addressing the advantages of superior data visualizations on their terms and from their particular perspectives. Most DBAs care about the data—its accuracy, its completeness, its timeliness, and so on. Always emphasize that data visualization is all about the data and representing it accurately.

Whole Organization

Different managers and executives will always have different perspectives and preferences on the same issues. The key to delivering value to the organization is not finding out what individual preferences are; instead, it's understanding what common positions are most powerful in driving attention and influencing decisions between alternatives. Therefore, the better question to ask an executive is not "Do you like this?" or even "What do you want see?" but rather "What do you want other people in your organization to pay attention to?" Again, don't ask executives "What are you hungry for?" or "What do you want to eat?" It's better to ask them, "What should we put on the menu for others in the organization to have for dinner?" It's like they're ordering for the table.

We advise against just letting users choose whatever they want. Typically, that involves building a huge buffet with lots of waste and poor quality as the food sits around. Because there are always cost constraints, the preparation and presentation quality also get somewhat compromised. Of course, it's important to offer some choices and to have an array of dishes, but if you end up trying to do a little of this and a little of that, it's likely to not be very good. If everything is a "made-from-scratch dish," where the diner gets to choose whatever they want, it will be hard to make it quickly, to have efficient processes, and to do it at scale. In short, you need a balanced menu with plenty of choices for different audiences, but it's probably better to focus on a certain style of food rather than trying to cook anything and everything.

Developing Trust in BI Systems

Trust is perhaps the most important issue. You want everyone to trust that the data is good quality and that it is correctly prepared. Listening carefully, responding to reasonable requests for customization, and confirming confusing orders before they are prepared all work hand-in-hand to build trust.

Here are some simple recommendations:

- *Ask executives to choose between two or three recommended solutions.* It's always a good idea to offer a choice, but make sure that the choices offered are in keeping with what can be delivered and make sense. If you are designing a dashboard, prepare a couple of versions, make a recommendation (along with why), but also offer an alternative or two. Give them time to actually try it out using an interface that makes sense to the group. Don't prepare only one and ask, "Do you like this?" Even if they do like it, they may offer suggestions for changes that are not helpful or, even worse, they may come up with their own ideas that are impractical or misguided.

- *Always find out what perspectives or comparisons are of most interest to executives.* This is of paramount importance, not only in "selling" BI dashboards, but also in designing them for organizational effectiveness. Although executives are not always anxious to schedule time in the design phase, they are usually more than willing to share their insights once a version is designed and presented. It's best to present an initial design and get some feedback early (even if it's only one dashboard) than it is to present an entire system and ask them, "Do you like it?" Work hard to hear their first-time input from a business perspective and strive to integrate what they are saying on future designs and iterations.

■ *Know that executives are your client and that the client is always right.* You won't win if you try to convince someone that they are wrong (especially about their own preferences). Try to understand the root cause of their preferences, but also try to stay away from conversations that are dominated by various people's impressions of "style" and "look" regarding data visualizations. There's more to be gained by understanding their motivations than there is their surface opinions. Pivot feedback to be about understanding data, finding evidence to support decisions, and focusing organizational attention on specific issues and perspectives.

■ *Use legacy reports to understand what information carries value, but not as a template for development.* If you can get actual usage data, all the better (existence doesn't equate to usage). Reassure users that they will get the same quality data and the same information, but the format and presentation may be modified (assure them that they will have the opportunity to state preferences and offer feedback). We the authors have often started BI projects with a "replicate the reports that already exist first" mandate. Replicating 2,000 legacy reports with 2,000 dashboards doesn't make a great deal of sense. When we encounter this situation, we try hard to focus on data and data integrity first (they understandably don't want to "go backward"). We try to understand the comparisons and thresholds that have business significance and develop those reports/dashboards first, and then we get feedback on them rather than replicating everything that is 20 years old. In other words, you should use the past as a guide to shape (not constrain) the future.

■ *Keep legacy views, reports, and dashboards, but put new visualizations at the top and push the old to the bottom and the back.* Executives are sometimes terrified of having their legacy reports and views "taken away." They may be intrigued with new visualizations, but they don't want to lose anything. For example, let's say that an organization has been using a complex table view for many years (legacy Excel view with lots of columns that someone designed 20 years ago). In this case, you can keep the old view, but place it at the bottom of the dashboard. You want to put newer visualizations (such as a graph and a smaller table designed for quick scanning and drilling) on top. Invariably, the old table will be used less and less, and it may even be able to be demoted to a different dashboard page in the future. The point is this: understand that taking views away from people is threatening and that it is much easier to add new views than it is to replace old ones with new. As stated before, people adjust very quickly to new presentations that are well designed, but they sometimes need reassurance that they will not lose their old, familiar visualization.

- *Continually revise, edit, and improve the most critically important dashboards and analyses.* Business is not static, and deriving insight from data that is constantly changing and finding evidence for business decisions that must evolve with changing times means that BI systems must evolve and not be static. Although we encourage a "development/test/production" progression for important new system elements, visualizations are somewhat different from pure data accuracy and verification. The "dev/test/prod" mindset should not present an obstacle to incremental improvements. Obviously, care must be taken in promoting any changes. Although we often work on "projects," we encourage our clients to adopt a "process" mentality over a "project" mentality for business intelligence and analytics. Although plenty of ink has been spilt in praise of "agile" development and in critique of "waterfall projects," we work in both environments. Despite the metaphor, we try to get whatever directional feedback we can get from users whenever possible. You might say we believe in the spirit of agile but live in the reality of waterfall. We don't believe, however, that superior BI systems are ever "finished." We also believe in revising the most important elements and pieces and not just in building new extensions. The system is strong when the core is strong. It takes pruning and training as well as weeding and feeding to make it so.

Getting Started

At our data visualization workshops and seminars, we consistently get asked one question afterward: "How should we get started?" Most OBIEE implementations are large, complex, and represent significant investment in time, money, and effort. There are few "greenfield" situations where everything can be designed from scratch and data visualization best practices can be entrenched as the incumbent. We typically encourage firms to consider a few different options.

Workshops

The first option is to identify a core group of stakeholders from the OBIEE community and to conduct an internal data visualization workshop, typically either a half-day or full-day session. Although we are used to leading such sessions, this book would provide a good outline for topics and issues that an interested reader could use to put together their own workshop. You don't necessarily need to hire experts; just get it done sooner rather than later. The goal of the workshop is to expose users to best practices and to get them to consider what portions of their implementation are strong from a data visualization perspective and what areas need improvement.

You will have a more engaging and productive time if you have wide representation from as many different departments and functional areas as possible and a safe environment where people can ask questions and challenge assumptions. Often, the simple act of bringing together different people with different perspectives enables design priorities to emerge. Assign someone to take notes to capture the feedback. This is particularly productive with users who create their own queries in Answers. Most everyone wants to do things "correctly" and not to make mistakes. People who design queries and analyses are understandably proud of their work and do not want to be criticized for it. It's often easier for them to hear about data visualization best practices for the first time in a "safe" group environment such as a workshop than it is to have their work corrected by a supposed expert. After the workshop, it's easier to approach people and find out if they want help improving their dashboards and visualizations (many will). It's easier to help people improve their work than it is to fix their mistakes.

Assessments

The second recommendation is to seek an independent assessment of your OBIEE implementation from an outside party. This typically includes an evaluation of the strengths and weaknesses of an OBIEE implementation and ranges from dashboard design, to query and analysis work to the repository. The central aim is to develop a growth and improvement plan for the system. Some systems have strong data modeling and need only minor tweaks to dashboards and visualizations. We sometimes find that work on data visualizations uncovers weaknesses elsewhere in the system. A "health check" assessment before engaging in extensive catalog reorganizations or dashboard development projects will often enable a faster and smoother development path. As mentioned earlier, envisioning a BI system as a living environment helps identify which areas can be weeded and which need to be replanted.

Training

We find that very few OBIEE implementations include sufficient budget for training. Because they are often treated as "waterfall projects" with defined deliverables (typically enumerated as a given number of reports and/or dashboards) and not as ongoing systems that grow in size and capability over time, developing skills for both users and developers is often overlooked. There is only so much information that people can absorb at any moment in time. Our experience is that training without a follow-up mentoring and assessment program only goes so far toward developing the full potential of a group and of a system.

Imagine starting a sports team where one week of training is deemed sufficient to teach a group of players the rules to the game and their basic positions. The team can just learn the rest "while playing the game." In contrast, our typical guideline is to set aside 10 to 20 percent of the total project budget for training. We also recommend that the training budget be allocated over an extended period of time (six months on average) and include not only standard classroom or online training sessions, but also follow-up assessments and advanced sessions.

It's a mistake to try and cover all techniques in one session. Instead, it's best to get people started using the software and completing tasks and then to come back and refine, redirect, and extend their skills and capabilities. This is particularly true when training programs are designed for report and dashboard development in OBIEE. Because OBIEE is such a large system with such broad capabilities, most organizations are using only a fraction of what it can do and are seriously underdelivering on the total value that it can deliver to the organization.

Metadata Communication and Documentation

Organizations should invest in metadata communication, not just documentation. Although most IT professionals understand and appreciate the need to document new systems and processes, they overestimate the knowledge of their users. Users will seldom read full documentation sets, but they will often take advantage of hover-over and mouse-over tips, collapsible narrative views, and information. Training and, metadata communication (considered to be a part of data visualization) are typically underutilized. Many of the problems with the consistent interpretation of data visualizations such as tables and graphs can be avoided by using well-considered and edited titles, field descriptions, viewing and interpretation tips, and data transparency such as filter and selection step views. Although a picture is sometimes worth a thousand words, the addition of a few well-chosen words can clarify a message in a smaller amount of space.

The Long Road

Once one starts on the journey of improving the quality of data visualizations and dashboards, one must accept that there is a long road ahead. There will always be those who choose not to understand, or those who cling to legacy presentations. The good news is that effectiveness and quality generally win the longer races because their value shows over time.

There are two mutually exclusive and yet compelling views on developing superior systems of any kind (including data visualization in OBIEE): "If it's worth doing, it's worth doing right" and "The perfect is the enemy of the good." The first warns us of the dangers of incomplete, sloppy, or poor quality work that will likely impose ongoing costs for rework or inefficiency. The second advises us of the laws of diminishing returns and that opportunity costs exist for over-engineering and not putting systems into production.

In most situations, we strive to balance competing interests, priorities, and strengths. We take inspiration from Goldilocks, who "called 'em as she saw 'em" and found that steering away from extremes toward a middle solution is usually a sound approach. We often describe a particular solution as "Goldilocks," not too big or too small, not too cheap or too expensive. We also take inspiration from Steve Jobs of Apple who famously said, "In most people's vocabularies, design means veneer. It's interior decorating. It's the fabric of the curtains and the sofa. But to me, nothing could be further from the meaning of design. Design is the fundamental soul of a human-made creation that ends up expressing itself in successive outer layers of the product or service."

Make things simpler and cleaner and strive to tell clear, concise stories. Data visualization is ultimately about communicating data stories and guiding both individual users and organizations.

Summary

Creating effective data visualizations in Oracle BI is not only about the visualizations—it's also about how you keep track of changes, run the project, and more. The BI catalog is the heart of your system. If you keep it clean and organized, other developers will be able to find your visualizations and work more effectively on content. Also, think about what you might modify before you edit a dashboard or visualization. Saving and keeping track of intermediary copies encourages experimentation—you won't be able to create effective visualizations without experimenting! Just be sure to clean up after you are done experimenting.

You will save time and have improved dashboards if you set standards. This also helps encourage buy-in from your users. Speaking of users, make sure you take into account all of your stakeholders' needs, including executives, IT personnel, and the rest of the user community. Instead of asking these people what they want, ask them what they think the organization would benefit from. That will encourage each stakeholder to think of the system from others' perspectives.

Learn from past systems, but don't necessarily replicate them. You will encounter some resistance to change, but if you can get people focused on the future and the benefits of the changes, they should agree to the changes. This is helped if you emphasize that the system will continue to evolve. BI is about making better decisions. Business conditions change and organizations learn, so BI systems need to change as well. BI is a mindset, not an end goal.

Good ways to start focusing on data visualization are with workshops, assessments, and training. This helps stakeholders recognize the value of proper visualizations. Focusing on standards and best practices takes the subjective topic of competing "tastes" off the table and allows people to discuss what benefits the organization the most. Effective visualizations help organizations create cohesion and make better decisions.

Index

B

Join the Largest Tech Community in the World

 Download the latest software, tools, and developer templates

 Get exclusive access to hands-on trainings and workshops

 Grow your professional network through the Oracle ACE Program

 Publish your technical articles – and get paid to share your expertise

Join the Oracle Technology Network
Membership is free. Visit oracle.com/technetwork

🐦 @OracleOTN 📘 facebook.com/OracleTechnologyNetwork

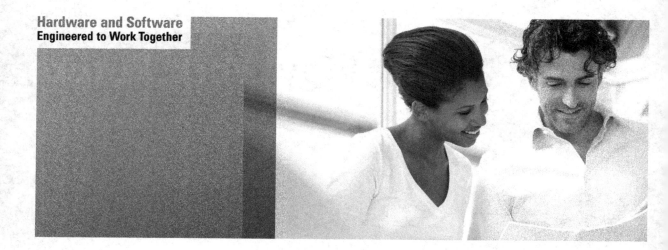

Hardware and Software Engineered to Work Together

ORACLE®
ACE PROGRAM

Need help? Need consultation? Need an informed opinion?

You Need an Oracle ACE

Oracle partners, developers, and customers look to Oracle ACEs and Oracle ACE Directors for focused product expertise, systems and solutions discussion, and informed opinions on a wide range of data center implementations.

Their credentials are strong as Oracle product and technology experts, community enthusiasts, and solutions advocates.

And now is a great time to learn more about this elite group—or nominate a worthy colleague.

For more information about the Oracle ACE program, go to:
oracle.com/technetwork/oracleace

Stay Connected

oracle.com/technetwork/oracleace

 oracleaces

 @oracleace

B blogs.oracle.com/oracleace

ORACLE®

Reach More than 700,000 Oracle Customers with Oracle Publishing Group

Connect with the Audience that Matters Most to Your Business

Oracle Magazine
The Largest IT Publication in the World
Circulation: 550,000
Audience: IT Managers, DBAs, Programmers, and Developers

Profit
Business Insight for Enterprise-Class Business Leaders to Help Them Build a Better Business Using Oracle Technology
Circulation: 100,000
Audience: Top Executives and Line of Business Managers

Java Magazine
The Essential Source on Java Technology, the Java Programming Language, and Java-Based Applications
Circulation: 125,000 and Growing Steady
Audience: Corporate and Independent Java Developers, Programmers, and Architects

For more information or to sign up for a FREE subscription: Scan the QR code to visit Oracle Publishing online.

Beta Test Oracle Software

Get a first look at our newest products—and help perfect them. You must meet the following criteria:

- ✓ Licensed Oracle customer or Oracle PartnerNetwork member

- ✓ Oracle software expert

- ✓ Early adopter of Oracle products

Please apply at: pdpm.oracle.com/BPO/userprofile

Join the Oracle Press Community at
OraclePressBooks.com

Find the latest information on Oracle products and technologies. Get exclusive discounts on Oracle Press books. Interact with expert Oracle Press authors and other Oracle Press Community members. Read blog posts, download content and multimedia, and so much more. Join today!

Join the Oracle Press Community today and get these benefits:

- Exclusive members-only discounts and offers

- Full access to all the features on the site: sample chapters, free code and downloads, author blogs, podcasts, videos, and more

- Interact with authors and Oracle enthusiasts

- Follow your favorite authors and topics and receive updates

- Newsletter packed with exclusive offers and discounts, sneak previews, and author podcasts and interviews

@OraclePress

CPSIA information can be obtained
at www.ICGtesting.com
Printed in the USA
FSHW04n1732130418
46835FS

9 780071 837262